Date Due

MAR 23			
APR 23			
APR 20			
MAY 4			
NOV 23			
DEC 6			
NOV 27			
DEC 11			
JAN 21			
FEB 18			

No. 293   DEMCO-MADISON-WIS

THE TRUE LIFE

OTHER WORKS

BY LUIGI STURZO

include

Organizzazione di Classe e Unioni Professionali, Cultura Sociale, Rome, 1901

Sintesi Socali, Cultura Sociale, Rome, 1906

Dall'Idea al Fatto, Francesco Ferrari, Rome, 1919

Riforma Statale e Indirizzi Politici, Vallechi, Florence, 1923

Popolarismo e Fascismo, P. Gobetti, Turin, 1924

Pensiero Antifascista, P. Gobetti, Turin, 1925

*La Liberta in Italia, P. Gobetti, Turin, 1925

*Italy and Fascism, Harcourt Brace, New York, 1927

*The International Community and the Right of War, Richard R. Smith, New York, 1930

*Il Ciclo della Creazione, Bloud et Gay, Paris, 1932

Essai de Sociologie, Bloud et Gay, Paris, 1935

*Politics and Morality, Burns, Oates and Washbourne, London, 1938

*Church and State, Longmans, Green and Co., Inc., New York, 1939

Les Guerres Modernes et la Pensée Catholique, L'Arbre, Montreal, 1942

The books marked with an asterisk have been published in London, Paris, Cologne, Madrid and Buenos Aires.

THE
TRUE LIFE

SOCIOLOGY OF THE SUPERNATURAL

by LUIGI STURZO

THE CATHOLIC UNIVERSITY OF AMERICA PRESS
WASHINGTON, D. C.
ST. ANTHONY GUILD PRESS
PATERSON, N. J.
1943

Translated from the original Italian by
Barbara Barclay Carter (Lic. ès L., Paris)

CONTENTS

Page

Introduction 1

PART ONE
SOCIETY IN GOD

Chapter

I. The Supernatural 25

II. Vocation 44

III. Predestination 62

IV. Communion 81

V. Mystical Union 100

VI. The Glory of God 137

PART TWO
FROM EARTH TO HEAVEN

VII. Evil 161

VIII. The World 182

IX. History 198

X. The Incarnation in History 224

XI. Christianity in History 245

XII. New Heavens and a New Earth 269

Index 301

v

The author wishes to express his gratitude to Miss Barbara Barclay Carter for the English translation so intelligently made; to Monsignor F. Lardone of the Catholic University of America; to Father John Forest Loviner, O. F. M., Director of St. Anthony's Guild, and to its Editorial Department for their very friendly help in publishing THE TRUE LIFE in a fine and accurate edition.

He must also mention here his brother Mario, the late Bishop of Piazza Armerina (Sicily), who, maintaining constant contact with the author through writings and letters on philosophical and mystical subjects, gave him inspiration and help in composing this book.

Jacksonville, Florida
January 5, 1943

THE TRUE LIFE

" ...ad vitam quae vera vita est...."

(ST. AUGUSTINE, TRACT. 120 IN JOANNEM)

INTRODUCTION

THE true life is life complete on every side, corresponding to all our deepest aspirations and forming the highest synthesis of our potentialities and activities. The true life is that of the spirit at its highest level, where alone inner discords and contradictions may find appeasement and every want and pain be satisfied, comforted, transcended.

This life is the supernatural life, to which we have been predestined and called by God, not through the exigency of nature but by a gift of His goodness, a gift that raises and ennobles us, calling us to fellowship with God and plunging us in the abyss of His mystery.

The supernatural life is not something accidental added to or superimposed on man's life of nature; it is a real transformation of human existence and activity. While on the surface man's life as a reasonable animal remains what it is, with all its wretchedness, it acquires another, inner principle to which its own forces could never attain and which, unifying it, gives it the supernatural imprint.

In the face of this transforming reality, the conception of an exclusively natural life becomes quite a mental or methodological abstraction; just as it is possible to make abstraction of man's intellectual life, analyzing only his animal element. Yet such analysis will not be complete, for not a few phenomena of our sense-life can be explained only by the influence of thought and of consciousness; and in the same way a great part of natural life must remain dark with-

1

out a supernatural explanation. It is possible also for man, subconsciously or deliberately, to attempt a renunciation of the higher life, striving to limit his activity to what he regards as natural. In both cases, that of intellectual abstraction and that of practical renunciation, he runs away from reality.

As will be seen throughout the present work, it is not metaphor nor hyperbole to call the supernatural life the true life; for while the supernatural life implies no denial, but indeed the perfecting, of the natural life, since without it there cannot even be wholesome enjoyment of all that nature offers, neither can we without it develop all our spiritual forces, or hold ourselves intellectually immune from errors, or win moral victory over faults, or attain the destination that gives meaning to the immortality of the spirit, or reach that communion with God which makes us sharers in His very nature. This is why I have affixed to my book the title *The True Life.*

* * * * *

The subtitle, *Sociology of the Supernatural,* must sound strange to the general run of readers, and calls for a preliminary explanation of how sociology may venture to the threshold of the divine. There is such confusion of ideas on sociology, held as it has been within the boundaries of nature, that the need of carrying it into the supernatural field has not been clearly recognized. I intend to face here a problem of capital importance, and, in venturing to present a solution, I hope that my endeavor will inspire others of riper preparation than myself to renew the trial.

Sociology, as a neologism formed by combining two words, Latin and Greek, means literally "discourse (*science*) of society." Such a science is not a study of society in the abstract as a metaphysical entity, nor a study from the moral standpoint of what society should be in political and economic or other fields, but it is a study of society as it is in the concrete — its origins, structure, form, character, process — with the aim of discovering the inner laws that are bound up with its very nature. This is the way in which sociology is a science. Its study can be divided up into branches, it can be carried on by particular analyses of this or that question, but there will be no true sociology if the branches are not united to the tree, if analysis is not brought back to synthesis the better to understand society in its concrete and living complexity. To fulfil its scientific purpose sociology should carry the study of society in the concrete into the fourth dimension, that of time, considering the formation of society from its most rudimentary beginnings down to the most advanced stage of present reality, seeking to divine the purposive tendencies that it reveals and to understand its orientation towards the future.

With this in view, society must be taken in its living nature and not reduced to a conceptual hypostasis, or, worse, considered as a mysterious being outside and above the individuals of whom it is composed, a kind of divinity informing the personality of the separate individuals and endowing them, by means of collective coercion, with a potentiality foreign to their nature. Society is nothing other than the operative coexistence of individuals in an inexhaustible process. There cannot be either individuals without society or society without individuals. Society is not a *tertium quid,* presupposing the single individual and coexisting individuals, or else forming individuality by means of association. Society exists and coexists only through individuals.

The second chapter of Genesis touches on this social fact in the divine dictum: *"It is not good for man to be alone; let*

Us make him a help like unto himself. . . . " Society is born
with Eve, the woman, intimate formation of the very body
of man: *"This now is bone of my bones, and flesh of my
flesh; she shall be called woman, because she was taken out
of a man."* It is impossible to imagine a greater intimacy or a
more effectual fellowship. The whole of society is the projection of individuals in their relationship and inter-activity; the
more living and continuous this projection is, the broader
the relationships involved, the more intense and constant the
activity of each single member, then the wider, more effective
and more deeply rooted is the society they form.

We now ask: Why should not the study of sociology be
extended to that supernatural life which forms a special synthesis, indeed the ultimate and pacifying synthesis, of society
as a whole? Sociology belongs to the group which we call,
to distinguish them from the physical and natural sciences,
the moral sciences. There has been an endeavor, it is true,
to reduce sociology to a biophysical or psychological science,
but in so doing analogy is made to change places with scientific
postulate in an attempt to confuse the data of man's free
activity with his material environment; or else the psychological experiences of the individual or of associated individuals
are transferred to the social entity as to a special kind of
psychophysical being. True sociology is the science of society
in its concrete existence and in its historical development. If
the supernatural is a historical and social fact, it must fall
within the field of sociological investigation.

Even positivist sociologists have felt the need of studying
the phenomena of morals and of religion as proper objects
of their science. Yet there are two errors to be imputed to
their system — that of eliminating or minimizing the freedom
of the individual and that of abandoning any idea of the
supernatural. Hence they reduce religion, as a social fact,

to pure naturalism or to a political moralism fostered by the dominant classes for their own interest. Such errors spring from considering sociology an experimental science of external facts, and eliminating both philosophy, as a metaphysical construction, and history, as the inner process of society.

What is strange is that these sociologists believe that their study of the facts, their experimentalism, is a truly critical study which will enable them, by comparison and statistics, to discover the sociological laws. Criticism is valid only insofar as it rests on principles that guide investigation and appraisal, and insofar, moreover, as these are founded on the certitude of truth. It would be a mistake, of course, to think that positivist sociologists wholly lack principles to guide their research; even in pure experimentalism there must be general criteria. But these sociologists are not aware of this, and hence, for want of that philosophy which they despise, they do not subject their principles and methods to critical examination.

Here, at bottom, is the cause of their failure to perceive the inner character of history. For the true sociologist, history is simply society itself viewed in its temporal activity, that is, in the process of its existence. Is there any other way of learning to know a living being? Society is not a museum piece, set in a glass case, petrified into the immobility of death, the witness to a past already extinct. Society, while obeying the basic laws of human life, has always its historical novelty, its aspects of revelation, its inward dynamism. It is precisely history — not the outer history of the material facts but their inner reason, their logical connection, the metaphysic to which they give birth — that enables us to learn the laws of our social nature.

With a deepening of sociologico-historical research we see clearly how false is the conception of society as the blindly determined product of natural forces, without realization that the freedom and responsibility of individuals play an essential part. And it is history too that attests the supernatural fact as existing and inscribed in the human process, thus opening to us a window on the invisible world.

A certain type of sociology has confined itself to studying the various social institutions in what are taken for primitive peoples, with the idea — a purely literary one — that there we shall find nature unsophisticated and almost in a pure state; or else with the idea — this time pseudo-scientific — that there we shall find the initial germ of social evolution. The very men who proclaim that experimentation must proceed without the interference of any general principle, assume on their own account such arbitrary principles as the innate naturalism of savage tribes and a social evolutionism from the savage to the civilized: principles that cannot be verified without philosophy and without history.

Unfortunately, sociology was sired by positivism. Up till now it has been almost a positivist monopoly. The positivist method, applied to the special branches of sociology or to the classification of determined social data, has produced interesting studies and penetrating analyses, and has advanced the knowledge of social structure; but all this material lacks a soul, it does not rise to human value, it cannot find a scientific synthesis.

* * * * *

One of the reasons why sociology has been kept in a closed compartment is that historians, philosophers and theologians — who should be concerned with it — not only do not recognize its scientific character but question whether sociology may be described as special branch of study, with its own proper object.

In another book, *Essai de Sociologie,*[1] the present writer sought to place sociology on such a plane that no one wishing to study it could deny it the character of a special science. As has been said, its object is the study of society in the concrete. If in analysis it is possible to study one side rather than another and to stress this rather than that, for synthesis it is necessary to embrace all human manifestations and all the social forms in their concrete outcome, which is society in act and in process. If one of the various social manifestations is omitted from the synthesis through arbitrary preconceptions or irrational methods, the result is an anti-scientific mutilation; and if the temporal measure is omitted from sociology, it is deprived of the means of studying the social rhythm and its inward life.

A fossil exists in space but no longer in time, save as a witness to the past. Yet the fossil participates in time because, as its antiquity grows, it renders an ever more interesting testimony to the past by the fact that it has survived when time has swept away so many others. Thus the fossil becomes historicized, it becomes alive again in human thought. But the society seen by certain sociologists as an unmoving morphology or structure is worse than the fossil — which as such has still its reality; for such a society, taken out of time, is never experienced as living, and does not bear witness to its past because it remains an inexistent abstraction. We must and should study the morphology of society; but if we wish to hold fast to the concrete, we shall take society at a given point of the globe and at a given historical date and shall examine it in the concrete, seeking the constant elements it has in common with other societies in other places and at other times. And we shall always inquire into the title-deeds of its formation, that

---

1. *Essai de Sociologie,* Bloud & Gay, Paris, 1935.

is, its origin and history, the value of its institutions, their
rational and moral, political and economic, natural and supernatural significance, and the trends of action and social finali-
ties that mean its historical projection into the future. In
doing this we are systematizing the constant data of society
in the concrete into principles of value. It is then that histori-
ography, philosophy, theology — which in the course of our
studies we shall encounter as conspicuous manifestations of
associated life — will bring the light of their laws and deduc-
tions to verify the sociological data of value.

What is important to fix as a point of departure is that
human life, whether individual or social, is one; thought and
speculation are one, though distinguished according to matters
of study and groups of matters; society is one in the multiplicity
of peoples and social characteristics and forms. How, then,
can sociology be presented as a self-sufficient construction isolated from human thought, rejecting any intervention from
history, philosophy, theology, and arrogating to itself the
position of true and sole interpreter of society? Only by
making sociology take upon itself the functions of history,
philosophy and theology. This absurdity has been attempted
by those who have established a *primum sociologicum,* like
Durkheim with his "sociologism." Indeed, this theory of
society as the whole (we might call it the theory of "creative
society") is precisely a theology, and his society is a divinity.

On the other hand, the endeavors of the sociologists who
profess a spiritualist philosophy have either failed through
making sociology a slight variant of political economy on the
one hand and of moral philosophy on the other, or else have
been inadequate, seeking to introduce into sociology the principle of free will in combination with a limited determinism
either psychological or mechanical.

Sociology needs to be revised from top to bottom, utilizing all the scientific and historical gains made in the past hundred years through many new and most useful studies, in order to give it the integral character it deserves as the study of society in the concrete. It is time to stop restricting the whole of sociology to analytic research, classifying material facts which as such are barely comprehensible, and framing them in provisional and incomplete schemes without real significance — it is time to abandon the abstractionism based on deterministic interpretations of collective activity and social fact as though these were removed from the action of individual men.

The reader may think that the charge of abstractionism is aimed at theoretical philosophy rather than at scientific sociology; this has been the current and unchallenged opinion. Here, however, abstractionism does not mean the legitimate derivation of a theory from facts, but an interpretation of concrete reality which makes abstraction of its essential factors and their concrete syntheses. Let us take an example that will bring us back to the theme of the present work. Philosophers and theologians study natural man as related to or opposed to supernatural man. When they analyze the factors that make up human nature they are engaged on a useful, indeed a necessary study, enabling us to understand in what that nature truly consists; theirs is therefore a scientific work. But if some among them were to claim to have thereby discovered natural man in the concrete with no shadow of the supernatural about him, or else supernaturalized man stripped of all natural characteristics, they would be guilty of abstractionism: that is, of presenting as concrete what is a mental abstraction of their own, of presenting as a synthesis what has been only their philosophical or theological analysis.

As we shall see, the mistake of conceiving of natural man as actually existing is not confined to sociologists but is shared by philosophers and theologians. However, the latter are capable of self-criticism and have the instruments for it, which sociologists lack. Yet sociologists too have at hand many data that might well lead them to question their naturalistic conception; for a mass of religious phenomena, considered in their nature and in their historical process, cannot be reconciled with the naturalistic thesis or the deterministic theories of environment put forward by so-called scientific sociology. That is why I accuse it of abstractionism: it presents a society in the abstract above or below the concrete of actual facts and their intrinsic value and significance.

Can it be denied that those who reject individual freedom and reduce the social fact to a mechanism of coercion are abstracting from reality? In sociology we must always clearly distinguish what is free individual initiative entering into the life of the social nucleus, from its conditioning social environment. This environment is formed through free human activities, which create a social structure or scaffolding necessary to the further action of individual men. But the social environment itself can and must be surpassed and transcended by the same free human activity. The study of this individual-social cycle presupposes an initial recognition of individual liberty and of its influence in social life, which sociology partly borrows from philosophy and partly verifies by its own means.

There is no lack of sociologists who frankly admit free individual initiative, or at least presuppose it in their works, but I know of no sociologist who as such admits that there can be a free supernatural initiative through divine action entering into mankind and being freely received and reactivated by men. I do not say there are no Christian sociologists who believe by faith in the divine revelation; what I do say is that even their sociology remains on the purely natural plane — as if a natural society really existed free from any influence of the supernatural, when, on the contrary, all that does exist is a society making a real synthesis with the supernatural. This is the subject of the present study: the supernatural life in human society as integrating, synthesizing and transcending nature — the supernatural life viewed both as the divine initiative towards man and as man's response to the divine summons.

*   *   *   *   *

Those who do not understand what the supernatural in man and in society is, may perhaps mock at the idea of a sociology of the supernatural. But not the theologians, although to their ears the phrase may sound novel and perhaps almost profane. St. John speaks of a society with God and with His Son as a single "fellowship with us," the followers of Christ: *"that you also may have fellowship with us and that our fellowship may be with the Father and with His Son Jesus Christ"* (1 John 1:3). The present book will bring out what type of society this fellowship represents — its nature, its value, its reflections. Both the inward relationship of the soul to God and the relationship of each man to others (his neighbors) form, from the supernatural viewpoint, a single society, for the bond that unites them is one: Christ, faith in Him, the grace He has won for us, His function as Head of the faithful and Head of mankind. The social bond is one: love. If this love has two objects, God and man's neighbor, this does not mean that the love itself is or can be divided, as if a man could love God without loving his neighbor, or love his neighbor without loving God. Hence our gratitude to God, not only personal and inward but social and public, is involved at the same time as our whole life of relationship with other men, without exception, as the actuation of a love conceived as an outpouring of God in us, in a single society.

Can there be a more radical transformation of the character of a society than when at the center of our relationships there is a disinterested, purifying and transforming love? and when this love has the inner force to oppose the hatreds, jealousies and pride which perturb and dissolve human fellowship? The sociologist cannot deny the transformation effected by Christianity, whether he regards it from the historical point of view, or compares Christian societies with non-Christian, or truly Christian societies with those which are Christian in name only or which have degenerated in faith and morals. All the naturalistic explanations cannot suffice to elucidate the reason for such a transformation. How, for example, is the general adoption of monogamic marriage to be explained? It is true that monogamy is to be found outside Christianity, but without the moral features, or the scope or the same beneficent results. Christianity alone has been able to render this immense service to mankind, thus providing a most important means of civilization.

It will be said that the sociologist cannot look upon these and analogous facts — the missionary apostolate, to give one instance — as supernatural facts. This I feel I have the right to challenge. The natural and the supernatural are so intertwined in all social life that in the concrete of history it is hard to discern where one is at work without the intervention of the other. The facts themselves, in their complexity, show the imprint of a higher value as soon as we discern the motives of faith and love that have shaped them.

It will be said that I start from a ready-made thesis and am seeking to introduce an extraneous dogmatic element into sociology, thus falsifying a science grounded on experiment and induction. Here I must be fully understood, to avoid unfounded charges or worse, confusion of ideas. I am not unaware of the experimental and inductive method, nor do I evade the study of society on the natural plane. In the *Essai de Sociologie,* I faced the problem of society on the twofold plane of its inward formation and its historical development, analyzing the various social forms, primary and secondary, as projections of individual activity in community life, and throwing into relief the concrete syntheses of human relations in their groupings and their dynamism. But although I wished to establish the natural data of society and keep to historical experience, I could not but bring into light what history itself teaches us about Christianity in its special characteristics, not to be confounded with those of any other religion. In doing this I started from no dogmatic preconception, but from historical elements, elements which I interpreted from a strictly sociological viewpoint, as every author has the right to do. My theory of historicist sociology obliged me to study the thesis of supernaturalism in history, given that this is accepted and professed by the Christian peoples, whose number, geographical extent and continuity in time surpass those of any other human experience historically known.

This theoretical premise led me to consider, still from the sociological standpoint, the relations between Church and State in Christian society from its beginnings up to today. The result was a second work, also of a sociologico-historicist character.[2] Here too the attempt was made to analyze the historical facts and the theories connected with them, their reciprocal influence, the activity of those who believe in the supernatural, those who, while not believing, yet treat it as such, those who, not believing, do not deny that there may be

---

2. *Church and State,* Geoffrey Bles, London, 1939; Longmans Green, New York, 1939.

relationships between creation and God, and finally, those who reject anything supernatural. All this world which history brings back to life, as well as the world in which we are living today, was studied from the angle of the relationships between Church and State; relationships which concern not only the theologian and the jurist but the sociologist too, for they reveal a notable part of the social structure of our civilized world.

How could a sociologist do otherwise? If he is not a believer and starts from another point of view in his study of the forms of religious life, he will assuredly have to lean on some theory to appraise their bearings, if only to justify his method of research. One who denies the supernatural root and branch will place all the data of his experience on the natural plane and will seek to explain in his own fashion how so many millions of human beings and so many thousands of studious men, men of genius and worth, have been able not only to accept the supernatural thesis but to live by it and even to give their lives for it. His will thus be a sociology of the supernatural in the negative sense. Between his and our sociology there will be this difference: he, presupposing as proven the naturalistic thesis, will exclude any theory of the supernatural, while we, interpreting the historical datum in its twofold aspect of natural and supernatural, will accept the existence of the latter and seek to explain it in its effects. But this difference is big with consequences from the scientific standpoint. If sociology studies society in the concrete of existence and in its temporal process, and this is a mixture of natural and supernatural, any naturalistic study is either simply analytical (presupposing the synthesis with the supernatural), or is falsified by the omission of essential data on the social reality.

This consequence will surprise not a few readers, even if they are believers; it will seem hazardous to affirm that for true sociology the sociologist must be a believer. I answer without hesitation: for integral sociology, that is for sociology as the science of the concrete — yes, it is needful to believe in the supernatural. For the other sociology, abstractionist, analytical, morphological, particular, there may be, as there have been, many interesting studies worthy of the name of science, but only as contributions to sociology.

A few examples will make this point of view clear. A student of society before the coming of Christ, if he faced the problem of slavery, would accept the idea that the slaves were an inferior race, without parity of nature with other men, even as philosophers supposed. The principle of human equality escaped them in both the juridical and the sociological field, and even as a moral idea it did not rest on a real and vivifying religious universality. Since the advent of Christianity, any theory that ignores the principle of the equality of human nature rings false and is never accepted in its practical consequences. The humanitarian sociologist, even if an evolutionist or accepting the struggle for life in theory, does not in practice recognize the legitimacy of slavery, which is one aspect of that struggle. The sociologist who sympathizes with the theories of the superior race would have to renounce many generally accepted sociological postulates in order to be able to maintain that other peoples, believed of inferior race, might be reduced to slavery, like the Poles and Czechs under Nazi Germany.

It will be said that sociology notes facts and does not approve or disapprove. That is true, but it cannot avoid noting the historical cases of the degeneration of social institutions when there has been an earlier form of regeneration. It is the case of the Christian and monogamic family, in the face of the polygamic family of the time before Christianity or of countries not completely civilized. The sociologist, in studying the nature, development and decadence of a natural institution, must arrive at a knowledge of their causes, or better, of the factors that, as it were, go to make them up. When he attains to a complexus of higher social life, he has reached a point from which to survey human institutions and their vicissitudes, and through this very fact he has a wider knowledge and can develop a deeper intuitive sense of truth. A student of social matters coming from a primitive people, who has no knowledge of our civilization save the little he has been able to glean from a missionary or traveler who speaks his language with difficulty, will not be able to grasp the reality of our society and will strive by the aid of certain similarities to reduce it to the level of the tribe in which he lives. We should say that he is mistaken, but that his horizon is bounded and his experience does not allow him to get to know another society, of which he glimpses only certain shadowy and meaningless outlines or else something exceptional that may seem to him wholly unreal.

Why should we wonder, therefore, if a believer is in a position to introduce us to the world of the supernatural, which for a non-believer is unexplored and unexplorable? And, if he is a sociologist and wants to build up an integral sociology, he will try to study the laws of the social structure in the light of the contribution of the supernatural with its transforming influx. This does not mean that his sociology will cease to be a pure and true science; it means only that he will be able to penetrate more deeply into the syntheses of that concrete reality which is the supernatural life in the world.

Sociology has been too much materialized by those who have made it a science of outward relationships or of merely psychological reactions, without including the thoughts and affections of individual men, that is, the original and fundamental centers of social living. These sociologists have lost sight of that process of rationality and liberation towards which social man is impelled in order to break through the bondage of evil, oppression and pain, a process which must be set at the basis of sociological laws. The conflict between the mystical and organizational currents in the course of history has never been sufficiently appreciated, or has been reduced to a fact governed by the deterministic law of social coercion and its contrary reaction. Thus we find many of the sociological laws transported to the supernatural plane, not as an escape from nature, but as the living reality of a society which has lost nothing of its natural character, evolving novelty of action in a higher sphere for sublimer ends. On this plane new syntheses of all human energies are formed. The sociological law of the trend to unification — which in its deeper aspect corresponds to the vital rhythm of the cosmos — has its characteristic and unique realization in the supernatural life, which moves beyond the limits of creation towards the Uncreated.

It is not a case of theology but of true sociology when the supernatural is studied in its sociological values. Theological knowledge will be necessary, just as philosophy is necessary for anyone studying natural society in its reflexes of rationality, or psychology in order to find its psychic reflexes, or biophysics for its vital laws. To interpret society in the light of one of these sciences alone would be to reduce it to philosophy or psychology or biophysics, and thus to fall into the very abstractionism that has been so roundly criticized in these pages. And since the supernatural surpasses and crowns the natural,

yet in the close coexistence of the two, the sociological study of
the first presupposes that of the second, only thus is it possible
that sociology comes to interpret the synthesis of such coexistence in human society, a synthesis which is, or might be,
conclusive.

*   *   *   *   *

To prevent misunderstanding, the reader is warned that this
Sociology of the Supernatural does not duplicate either the
study of the Church as the visible society of the faithful or
the study of the mystical body of Christ, but it does take into
account the theological and mystical elements of such studies
in order to gain a deeper understanding of the supernatural in
society. The supernatural is not made a separate section of
social life, something juxtaposed to the natural, which individuals may accept or reject at will. In studying society in its
complex wholeness, in the concrete, it is found to exist within
the atmosphere of the supernatural, and to act and react to it
according to the sociological laws which are at its natural basis.

It should be clear from these preliminary outlines that this
work has no kinship with certain recent studies on the contribution of Christianity and on the action of the Church in
what is known as the "social question." By common acceptance
the adjective "social" is taken to indicate economic, juridical
and moral work and activity for the welfare of the working and
proletarian classes. Sociology does not overlook certain aspects
of "social" problems; they are matter for its scientific research
insofar as they help to characterize the laws and structure
of society.

To indicate more narrowly the type of my work, I used in
the *Essai de Sociologie* the term "historicist," explaining in the

Introduction what was meant by this "historicism,"[3] and distinguishing it from that which in the philosophical and juridical fields has had a vogue in Germany and Italy. Here there is no need to return to the argument, since the present work, like its predecessors, is imbued with this historicism.

Later, for a better understanding of the terms, use was made of the title "Integral Sociology," to indicate that — the object of sociology being society in the concrete and not in the abstract — the study of sociology must reach its complex reality through all its constituent factors and from every point of view, as a living being that contains its past and presses forward towards its future. *Integralism* in sociology means at once a deeper scientific penetration and a reaction against that *sectionalism* which either stops short at social morphology as conclusive, or, while accepting the historical dimension, reduces everything to a mechanical and psychological determinism.

It will be said that thus we shall have as many sociologies as there are philosophic systems: Hegelian or Bergsonian or Blondelian; or religions which pretend to be supernatural: Christian, Jewish, Mohammedan, Hindu; — whereas up to now only the scientific limits of sociology had been fixed.

This too is a mistaken outlook. Just as in philosophy and theology, in law and ethics, there are many systems, so it is in sociology; no science indeed can escape a multiplicity of systems. A sociologist who accepts individual liberty writes differently from one who accepts social determinism; willy-

---

3. Certain books by the present author — *The International Community and the Right of War* (Allen & Unwin, London, 1929, R. R. Smith, New York, 1929), *Politics and Morality* (Burns, Oates & Washbourne, London, 1938), *Church and State* (already referred to) — have been an application of this type of historicism to sociology.

nilly, they appeal to different philosophical systems. A sociologist who accepts the existence of God writes differently from one who is an atheist; both are concerned with theology without knowing it. A Mohammedan or Hindu sociologist has the experience of his own religion and of the environment in which he lives; hence he will present problems otherwise than a Christian and western sociologist, even if he does not go into religious and supernatural questions.

Sociology cannot draw away its skirts before the complex reality of society and of history, and at the same time claim to be the sole true science of social facts. That is why I ask for an integral sociology, for true experimental science studies its proper material in its full concreteness. The concrete remains at the basis of all my sociological research. I want to give the interpretation that fits it as closely as possible; to scrutinize its inward structure, its laws, its process, its finalism, its fulfilment. It is a lofty ambition; it is also one which I hope will not remain isolated but will find others better able to venture along this new road.

I may be reproached with having left my integralism incomplete, since in my books I have dwelt little on the investigations of the biological or psychological sciences as applied to society, or on ethnographical studies or even on economics. This does not come from any unawareness of the contribution which these branches of study have given and may give. Apart from the special character of my books, I wished above all to bring out the contribution to be made to sociology in other fields, especially that of history, to widen its horizon and to achieve a certain integration insofar as I was able to do so. I wished, moreover, to impel sociology on to the plane of our western civilization, of our own history, and the prevailing political and religious conceptions. That is why, I believe, the critics who have been concerned with my books have said that my sociological studies were now too historical (as in *Church and State*), now too juridical (as in *International Community*), now wholly political (as *Politics and Morality*), and at the same time works of philosophy. *L'Essai de Sociologie* has been called a philosophy of sociology. In the same way it will very likely be said of the present work that it is wholly theological and Scriptural. The sociological character of the foregoing studies escapes those critics whose ideas on sociology are ready-made, forged by the positivist school and current tradition. It needs an effort to throw off these blinkers and to give to sociology the integral character it requires.

The True Life — Sociology of the Supernatural is divided into two parts. The First Part, *Society in God,* examines and interprets the supernatural life in each one of us and in the social formations, according to revelation and historical and mystical experience. The reader, be he sociologist or no, must not be alarmed if the chapters of this First Part are headed as though it were a spiritual work. I am trying to seize the essence of the Christian life, and therefore must enter a field essentially theological and mystical.

Such studies as those contained in the chapters on "Pre-destination," "Communion or Mystical Union," have their value in the domain of sociology, for all that passes into the spirit of man either naturally or supernaturally affects his asso-ciative life, which, as I have said, is nothing other than the projection and prolongation of individual life.

The Second Part, *From Earth to Heaven,* considers the ethico-historical problem in the reflection of the supernatural, always so as to elucidate the sociological elements inherent in it. The last chapter too, "New Heavens and a New Earth," illuminates that road on which mankind is journeying, not blindly or purposelessly, but towards a historical and revealing term.

Need I repeat that I am studying the society of this world as it is in concrete fact? The reader will judge.

Part One

SOCIETY IN GOD

CHAPTER I

THE SUPERNATURAL

WHEN we wish to analyze human life, we speak of vegetative, sensitive, intellective life. If we seek its social character, we speak of family, professional, political, moral life. And we can distinguish it by the manner in which it is lived as worldly or spiritual, earthly or religious. When we deal with our own personal life we do not analyze it, but look upon it as a concrete synthesis in which all our faculties blend and all relationships converge.

Such life is specifically human, synthesized and expressed by the higher faculties of mind and will. It is characteristically personal, the resultant of all the special features of each one of us, his development, his qualities, his needs and desires, his relationships, his environment, his activity, his particular ends. Life is not the sum of all this but a continuous blending, selection, grading of all the elements of which it is woven, up to the center of life: the light of the mind which guides and warms the heart and moves to action through the work of the will.

It is true that in the strict sense life means for us existence as biopsychic individuals. But who would say that a life without understanding, or with understanding but without will, is human? The synthesis of the lower faculties with the higher is what we call our natural life, providing for it as such in its material needs and in its cultural, moral and social needs.

From an abstract and analytical point of view, we might consider natural life as complete. As such it does not demand a higher life but tends to its own development and the fulfilment of all its potentialities, and seeks to perpetuate itself indefinitely. Yet there is another life which we call supernatural, which is, as it were, grafted on to the natural life and has its own characters, development and finality. There are not two lives juxtaposed within us, natural and supernatural; but the latter raises the former to itself, coördinates its values and ends, and synthesizes it in its own form.

The distinction which we draw between the two lives is a notional or practical analysis. It does not — unless it springs from superficial appraisements which fail to penetrate the intimacy of personal life — mean either separation or opposition. In the concrete of experience, just as the vegetative or animal life within us, although distinct from rational life, is not autonomous, so there is not a purely autonomous natural life implying no relationship with the supernatural.

The notion that we speak of supernatural life simply by analogy, that it is not life in the real sense of the word but only a special way of conceiving the relationship of man with the Deity, is the product of strictly naturalistic thinking. At bottom, it comes either from a denial of the supernatural and vital character of our relations with God (and hence with ourselves, with others and with the subhuman world), or else from an overabstract way of considering such relations, not in the synthesis of the living human person but only on the ethical or metaphysical plane (moralism or theologism).

From another aspect, it may seem that to speak of the supernatural life as a fact attributes to divine grace (by which that life is actualized) a quasi-physical character, a "worldly or sublunar" quality of existence, modifying, albeit qualitatively, the human soul and personality. Apart from any theological opinion on the physical character of grace (into which we need not enter), such an objection may indicate only a false conception of what is implied by the supernatural state, in-asmuch as it is looked upon as modifying or changing the nat-ural characters of man.

In concrete reality, the supernatural life cannot be granted save to a living person; hence it presupposes natural life as its necessary basis. And though in pure nature we do not find a true exigency of supernatural life, which is a wholly free gift of God, yet in the concrete existence of man as he is we equally do not find a state of pure nature sufficient unto itself and developing in spontaneous process towards its own perfection.

This statement, which is grounded in the psychological and historical experience of mankind, is explainable only by reve-lation. The first man, and in him all mankind, was raised by grace to the supernatural state. He fell from it through a sin which affected all men. There remained in him no right, there was left in his nature no exigency of a return to the super-natural state. This was merited for us by the Son of God made man, who by His sacrifice redeemed us and made us sharers in the divine life.

But neither did Adam by his fall return to the purely natural state, nor does any man who does not attain to re-deeming grace or who loses it by his own fault, so return. The fall, in addition to causing the loss of original grace, shattered the equilibrium of human faculties. There is a kind of nemesis that follows sin and cannot fail to bear its fruits of devastation. Whether the sin be personal or collective, it shows its effects not only in perturbation of conscience and the spoiling of relations with others who have been injured, antagonized, scandalized, but by penetrating as a stigma to the very heart of life.

This does not explain the mystery of original sin, but the natural indelible effects of personal sin give us an image of it.

Collective sins too have their effects, and these too give us an image of original sin. Historical sins are easily forgotten, but their effects remain, to weaken individual liberty though they cannot destroy it.

The state of sin, individual and social, original and actual, psychological and historical, is not a natural state but a *subnatural* one; the cumulative negative effects of sin lead to a progressive deterioration which makes it virtually impossible to rise again under the power of nature. Therefore in the consciousness of mankind there arose the need for expiation, for prayer, for divine invocation, as a means, indeed *the* means, to reactivate human faculties themselves, to cancel the effects of sin and to wipe out, if possible, the sin itself, in a beginning of psychological, social and mystical catharsis which aimed at a new purity, an elevation towards the divine.

In the midst of a thousand deviations, confusions, perversions, there emerges the consciousness that a supernatural life has circulated in us from the day of the first divine revelation given by God to man, with its summons to grace and mystical communion. Ever since then human nature, without ceasing to be such, has been assumed into a higher life with new potentialities and the aptitude for a new destiny.

* * * * *

The Incarnation of the Divine Word is the center of human reality and existence, of its life and its finality. His redeeming grace was operative from the beginning. God communicated Himself to man from the first moment; He wished to restore and maintain this communication in its most bountiful form at the very moment that He announced to our first parents the tragic effects of their disobedience. And thus the whole of mankind, from beginning to end, is in the sphere of grace; all are not only called to the supernatural life and potentially sharers in the merits of the Redemption, but under such conditions that those who do not actually share in it fail to do so through their own fault, inexcusably.

The facts seem to contradict this truth, in regard both to the universal opportunity of attaining to the supernatural life, and to the fatality of sin, which drags us down below the normal conditions of nature. But this is an appearance only. The original revelation of God and the moral law imprinted in our hearts persist among all peoples. And if through errors and sins the knowledge of the moral law has faded and become mixed with superstitious ideas and practices, in spite of this it emerges sufficiently to shed its glimmering light on the practical life of each man.

All those who, being outside Israel in pre-Christian times and outside Christianity since then, have not shared in the successive divine revelations and do not directly know their fulfilment in the Incarnation of the Word and the outpouring of the Holy Spirit, are not on this account to be regarded as outside the rhythm of supernatural life. They are within it in the measure that it has reached them, taking concrete form for them in submission to God as the Supreme Being and in the keeping of the moral law as they understand it.

This acceptance presents itself to such peoples as natural because they have lost the historical consciousness of a primal revelation; they have only the consciousness of a tradition, which may be confused with the more or less religious traditions of ancestors, pious men inspired by God, or else symbolized by myths in which the religious and the profane, the fantastic and the realistic, intermingle. The description "natural" is also applied because man by his reason can arrive at the conception of a Supreme Being upon whom all creatures depend and of a moral law to be observed; from this angle of vision the mystery does not yet present itself in its intimate incomprehensibility. But this does not mean that a given man conceives of a Supreme Being and a moral law, and keeps its precepts, by his purely natural forces, without an impulse that is the gracious intervention of God. Of ourselves we are not able to perform a single act drawing us near to God; neither reason nor tradition nor the example of others can be effectual without grace.

All St. Paul's controversies with the Jews and his relevant allusions to pagan society are founded on this principle: reason of itself could not avail for the Gentiles nor the Mosaic Law of itself for the Jews without the grace given by God through Jesus Christ. But when this grace is given, reason with its pretensions and vanities fails, the Law falls to the ground, whether regarded in its special function as preparation for the Messias, or as the investiture of Israel; all are called by faith to the grace of God, as children of Abraham. Neither reason nor the Law can wipe out sin, raise us to supernatural life, give us grace, make us sharers in the Kingdom. Those who live the so-called natural life with honesty and rectitude are, even without knowing it, sons of Abraham.

"This is everlasting life, that they may know Thee, the only true God, and Him whom Thou hast sent, Jesus Christ." Thus St. John (17:3). All those who lived before the coming of Christ did not know the historic Christ, but in varying degrees they had a glimmer of the promise of salvation coming from God, of the need for a forgiveness they could not achieve for themselves, of the hope of a Redeemer who might win it for all.

Those populations which after the advent of Christ remained and still remain remote from the Gospel because they have not known it, likewise in varying degrees come to a consciousness of the personal impossibility of drawing near to God, of a fundamental impurity that must be cleansed, of a mysterious need for expiation. This is not yet the revelation of the Gospels, but it may be the beginning of spiritual life. If, with the little light they have, they conform to it in their customs and seek in a positive manner in their inmost hearts to offer up a sacrifice for sin — that is, to recognize their own impurity, to call upon the Supreme Being for purification and help, to obey the precepts of the law of nature — then they will be implicit partakers in the grace won for us by Jesus Christ.

St. Thomas holds that such will not be denied a divine revelation and baptismal grace, even by means of an angel if there is no apostle or missionary. Apart from this comforting miraculous hypothesis, it is today the common theological opinion that the faithful observance of the moral law is a sign of participation in redeeming grace. May it not be said that those who are thus faithful receive the grace of Baptism of desire? Baptism is necessary for all. Those of the time of the patriarchs and the people of Israel who remained faithful shared in the desire for the Baptism of Jesus Christ, without having any idea of it save that of purification from guilt. Those likewise since the coming of Christ who have never heard of ritual Baptism, or while knowing of it have not understood its mystical value, if they worship God and keep the moral law can be considered as implicitly partakers in Baptism of desire. In this way they do not live merely by natural life, but they too are already within the rhythm of the supernatural life.

*   *   *   *   *

It will be asked, what need then for the Gospel, the Church, the Sacraments, if in what seems to be purely natural worship and in the observance of the moral law men may partake of supernatural grace? Because, without the Gospel, the Church and the Sacraments, neither would these reach grace. Grace has been given to the world through the merits of Jesus Christ; the Incarnation is at the center of the life of mankind, the Church is its prolongation in time, its continuous application, its radiating focus.

The light of the sun, the center of the solar system, shines more or less brightly according to distance, orientation and interposed obstacles; but even in those regions where its direct influx is not felt its action is necessary, for the sun is the hierarchy-creating, unifying and quickening force. In the same way Jesus Christ, inasmuch as He has been or was to be, is at the center of the world. He has merited redeeming grace for all, and has made all potential partakers in the supernatural life.

Could those who lived with Him, Mary, Joseph, John the Baptist, the apostles, the disciples, the holy women, have gone back as if they had never known Him, and confined themselves to keeping the natural law? Could those who heard the Sermon on the Mount be as if they had not heard it, as if it had not been a light enlightening their eyes and a fire warming their hearts? A man who is born blind does not know light and color and learns only by hearing and touch. If by a miracle or by an operation, as the case may be, he gains sight, he will acquire a wider and specifically different perception of objects. Could he ever again conceive of them as he did when he was blind?

Thus for him who has once reached the Christian life, whether the converted pagan or the child baptized as soon as he is born, there can be no going back to a life founded solely on natural morality; just as a man who has gained a certain culture cannot voluntarily return to ignorance, or one

who has had experience of life revert of himself to the childish feelings of a baby just learning to talk.

This does not mean that there cannot be in practice a
renouncing of faith, a separation from the Church through
schism or heresy, a loss of grace through mortal sin. But the
choice offered is never between supernatural and natural life,
between two perfections of diverse order and with diverse
ends. The choice is between the supernatural and the subnatural, between perfection and decadence.

We have not always a precise understanding of this choice,
for we are not always capable of objective appraisement of the
good and evil put before us, so that we may even invert the
terms and their relationships. Good and evil are mingled and
confounded both in the complexus of our outward personal
and social life and in the synthesis which we create in ourselves, in our judgment and consciousness.

It is here useful to recall the teaching of St. Thomas,
which is that of the theologians in general: "For not only
indifferent matters can receive the character of goodness or
malice accidentally; but also that which is good can receive
the character of evil, or that which is evil can receive the
character of goodness, on account of the reason apprehending
it as such. For instance, to refrain from fornication is good;
yet the will does not tend to this good except insofar as it is
proposed by the reason. If, therefore, the erring reason pro-
pose it as evil, the will tends to it as to something evil.
Consequently the will is evil, because it wills evil, not indeed
that which is evil in itself, but that which is evil accidentally,
through being apprehended as such by the reason. In like
manner, to believe in Christ is good in itself and necessary to
salvation; but the will does not tend thereto, except inasmuch
as it is proposed by the reason. Consequently if it be proposed

by the reason as something evil, the will tends to it as to
something evil: not as if it were evil in itself, but because
it is evil accidentally, through the apprehension of the reason. . . . We must therefore conclude that, absolutely speaking,
every will at variance with reason, whether right or erring, is
always evil."[1] St. Thomas takes the two examples, one from
the law of nature, the other from revealed faith, so as to show
that an erroneous conscience may come under either order,
natural or supernatural. In such a case the material choice
would be for evil, but given the erroneous conscience (in what
the moralists call invincible error), the formal choice would
be for the good, inasmuch as that evil is believed to be a good.

Under this aspect let us consider the problem of Christians
cut off from the Church. Only through good faith can heretics
and schismatics really partake of the life of grace, so long as
their good faith is full and not undermined by doubts, and
they fulfil the duties of the moral law and of the worship due
to God. From the historical point of view this good faith may
be diminished as we go back through the years or centuries
towards the origin of the separation from the Church, the
moment of passions, conflicts, struggles, blindness, at least for
those who are more directly and consciously implicated. The
same happens when a man personally acquires such knowledge,
or has such opportunities offered to him, or experiences such
inward impulses, as make him realize that his spiritual position
is neither integral nor secure. In such a moment, either historically initial or psychologically terminal, arises the responsibility for the attainment of a fuller truth; and then is born

---

1. S. Th. I-II, Q. XIX, art. V. Translated by the Fathers of the
English Dominican Province, London, 1911. Where St. Thomas uses
the word *ratio* or *conscientia* in this context, we should generally use
"conscience," which is not only theoretical but also practical reason,
utilizing both deductive reasoning and direct intuition.

the sense of the duty of the quest or the guilt of refusal, good faith having been dissipated by doubt, or doubt having become an element of bad faith. The grace that nourished the conscience of the heretic or schismatic, making him live in the rhythm of the supernatural, ceases if he refuses, as he may through inertia or passion, the greater grace offered him, that of a fuller integrity.

The same criterion applies to those who fall into grave sins and remain attached to them. Insofar as they are conscious of their guilt, they draw away from the supernatural life. Any grave and conscious sin means the loss of habitual participation in grace, but it does not wholly quench the supernatural life if faith is still alive and if there remains a certain sensitiveness to the impulses of conscience, impulses which are true graces, crucial moments of the rhythm of a life seeking to be reborn.

There are indeed those who not only have cast away faith through culpable error, but who refuse even the observance of any moral law, through a conscious perversion. No one will attribute to such any grade in the ladder of human perfection. Apart from the degrees of human decadence, down to the most abominable depravity, it is plain that those who consciously and habitually cling to sin, whether they be Christians or no, not only place themselves outside the supernatural order but must be considered as outside any natural order ideally conceived. Their clinging to sin is in itself a disorder which has its repercussions psychologically in themselves, socially in others, mystically in the whole of creation in its subordination to the Creator.

Insofar as a certain good faith or spiritual insensibility shapes their lives through invincible errors, collective contagion or the blindness of passion, thus far may their responsibility for successive sins be attenuated. On the other hand, all the good or pious or merciful actions which they may perform, even in the midst of their sins, may render them receptive to certain impulses of grace, opening a road of return. Physical and moral pain may set them on the way to a mysterious catharsis; even in mistaken ideals they may find motives of abnegation and self-sacrifice. The ways of grace are God's mystery. The potential state of the supernatural life, even in the degradation of sin and the moral or religious crises of conscience, may become actual through higher impulses and secret responses when, to human eyes, it could least be expected or hoped.

*   *   *   *

In what does the supernatural life consist? Jesus said to Nicodemus: *"Amen, amen, I say to thee, unless a man be born again, he cannot see the Kingdom of God."* And to Nicodemus' question, *"How can a man be born when he is old?"*, Jesus replied: *"Amen, amen, I say to thee, unless a man be born again of water and the Spirit, he cannot enter into the Kingdom of God. That which is born of the flesh is flesh; and that which is born of the Spirit is spirit. Do not wonder that I said to thee, 'You must be born again.' The wind blows where it will, and thou hearest its sound but dost not know where it comes from or where it goes. So is everyone who is born of the Spirit"* (John 3:3-8).

St. Paul speaks of the supernatural life in sublime words where he writes: *"Do you not know that all we who have been baptized into Christ Jesus have been baptized into His death? For we were buried with Him by means of Baptism into death, in order that, just as Christ has arisen from the dead through the glory of the Father, so we also may walk*

*in newness of life. For if we have been united with Him in
the likeness of His death, we shall be so in the likeness of
His Resurrection also. For we know that our old self has been
crucified with Him, in order that the body of sin may be destroyed, that we may no longer be slaves to sin; for he who is
dead is acquitted of sin. But if we have died with Christ, we
believe that we shall also live together with Christ; for we
know that Christ, having risen from the dead, dies now no
more, death shall no longer have dominion over Him. For
the death that He died, He died to sin once for all, but the
life that He lives, He lives unto God. Thus do you consider
yourselves also as dead to sin, but alive to God, in Christ
Jesus"* (Rom. 6:3-11).

In describing the process of our death, burial and resurrection in the dead, buried and risen Christ, St. Paul is not
simply using an imaginative symbolism to give us a vivid idea
of a liturgy of outward purification. He is speaking of a full
and transforming reality. It is a true rebirth, regenerating and
transporting us to a new and higher life, in which and by
which our whole being begins to breathe.

Just as within us the vegetative life is integrated with the
sense life, making not two lives but one, the higher affecting
the rhythm of the lower, and just as the sense life is integrated with the intellective life, making again a single life,
the higher affecting the rhythm of the lower, so the supernatural life integrates the whole of natural human life, making
of it a single life inasmuch as it affects the rhythm of all
human faculties. *"It is now no longer I that live, but Christ
lives in me"* (Gal. 2:20). Thus St. Paul in sublime fervor,
with an imaged phrase that is yet real and mysterious. No
one will think that grace personally communicated becomes
our substantial form, absorbing into itself the intellectual soul

in the same way as the intellectual soul, according to St. Thomas, absorbs into itself the sensitive and vegetative soul in unity and simplicity of form. Yet that very soul, which is the substantial form of the body, is itself sanctified by grace. And if by mortal sin it is deprived of grace, it retains the potentiality of receiving it anew. Positive privation of grace in the soul calls, by the will and gift of God, for reintegration.

The parable of the vine and the branches, which Jesus gave before His death, makes this clear: *"As the branch cannot bear fruit of itself, unless it remain on the vine, so neither can you unless you abide in Me. I am the vine, you the branches. He who abides in Me, and I in him, he bears much fruit; for without Me you can do nothing"* (John 15:4-8). This does not mean that we are reduced to automata, no longer able to think and will, but that a life has been set in us which renews our thoughts and our will.

The idea of life as initiation, participation, development, ripening, fruition, carries us into the mystery of grace and of union with God. This union cannot be other than of mind and will, but the other faculties, sensitive and vital, will be affected not only because they are affected by any orientation of mind and any natural tendency of will, but through a higher finalism to which, mediately, they are ordered. At the summit and as the specific quality of the new supernatural life stands the union through grace: God known as truth, the One Supreme Truth, God loved as good, the One Supreme Good.

If man had remained in the purely natural order, if he had never been raised above it, never fallen, never been redeemed, through the forces of reason and will he would have come to the idea of God as Creator, providential Disposer, Supreme Good, Center of spiritual and cosmic unification, to whom he would have paid religious worship and observance of the moral law. God would have communicated Himself to man through external nature and the inner depths of the soul; man would have honored Him by respecting the order of rational knowledge and morality. This hypothesis has never been realized and remains a pure abstraction. God revealed Himself to the first man and gave him knowledge of His mysteries and made him His friend. After the fall He wished to redeem him, uniting him to Himself in a still more intimate manner, in abundance of supernatural life: truth and love, no longer of a rational character but transformed, in a supra-rational order, partaking through grace of the divine nature itself. Thus it can really be said that Jesus Christ, God and Man, is for us the vine and that, united to Him by grace, we are the branches.

To win for us this participation in the life of truth and love, Jesus Christ really suffered death and burial for us and really rose again for us, so that we might undergo mystically the same process of death, burial and resurrection, that is, might be born of water and the Spirit, and so be able to know the supernatural truth and love the supernatural good. Death to sin (both symbolized and made real by Baptism) makes us capable of this, for it brings rebirth to the newness of the life of grace, so that it may inform all our activities and we may bear its fruits. There is no question but that here is a true life, not an imaginative symbol nor a ritual and outward purification: a life that coördinates and quickens all other natural life, sensible and intellectual, lower and higher, intimately uniting us to God.

*   *   *   *   *

A life on this earth is never wholly and completely lived: how many occurrences, varying and complex needs, weaknesses, limitations, in our contingent life! We cannot always feed our hunger to know and our thirst to love; the body has need now of rest, now of movement, now of nourishment, now of restorative and healing care. It is the same with the spiritual life, whether considered from the natural side as ascetic striving or from the supernatural side as a renewal in Christ. In the same way that the life of mind and will is developed by training, exercise, activity, the various tendencies becoming habits, special aptitudes, scientific, artistic, professional, developing and growing more acute till the maturity and fulness of all the faculties and of their inner connection is reached, so the supernatural life has its educative formation, its inner and outer adaptation, its maturity and fulness.

By illness we may lose important organs, eyes, ears, hands, or become paralyzed, or waste away to death. The will can become vacillating, the character weak, the mind lose its understanding. And the social life, too, of a family or nation may suffer from disorder in its relationships, upheavals of passion, the oppression of tyranny. In the same way in the supernatural life there may be the negative experiences of daily disturbances and sins, the loss of sanctifying grace and of faith, habitual slavery to sin, and at the same time recoveries, improvements, healing treatments, revival, return, rebirth, the rewinning of health up to the fulness of sanctity.

The supernatural life influences the natural life and vice versa. There is an important interchange between the two, not only in the activities of mind and will but also in the sensible reality of the body. Supernatural experiences take place in our natural being and the functioning of the two lives interweaves with a continuous reciprocal efficacy. It is a common experience that professional habit affects the senses, that a naturally sober life has happy effects on our physical make-

up, that intellectual speculation refines our sensibilities, and
that, on the other hand, a body trained to discipline is obedient to the demands of the mind and will. Thus the practice
of a supernatural life truly lived has great efficacy in disciplining and raising all the natural faculties, in the soul and in the
body, to the point of achieving wonderful and unexpected
results in the obedience of the lower faculties, their docility, their adaptability, their decisive subjection to spiritual
impulses.

The ideal of a complete harmony between the lower and
higher faculties, between the claims of body and soul, between
the natural and supernatural life, has been cherished by exceptional men or divined as an ideal of perfection at which to
aim. All feel its beauty, even when they do not clearly understand in what the supernatural life consists, but not all are
able to overcome the difficulties of the arduous path. Yet we
are told: "Be ye perfect." By this intimation Christ expressed
both the possibility for every man of reaching such fulness of
life, and God's offer to men of the means of perfection.

Every effort we make on this earth should be in response
to this intimation and this divinely generous offer. Perfection
may be looked upon as the synthesis of the life truly worthy
of being lived. Nature finds there that higher unification that
comprehends, pacifies and transcends it. The tendency towards
unification is a law of life. We seek it all the more in that,
formed of sense and spirit, we have within us two laws that
are often in conflict, disturbing even natural activities. A principle that pacifies the finite with the infinite is in itself vital
and unifying; it is the new order, penetrating the spirit and
reverberating through the whole of human activity.

Mankind taken as a whole, the several human groups
taken as societies, neither demand the supernatural nor can

clothe themselves with the supernatural character given by grace. Yet they too are affected by the tendency towards unification in the supernatural life. It might be thought that for each society to seek its particular end would be enough to harmonize it and fulfil it in its earthly reasons of existence. In concrete fact, the perfection of the supernatural life of each individual becomes such that the various social forms are either affected by it, becoming subordinate to it, or else are perturbed and, ceasing to fulfil their functions, decay, and with them the life of the individuals.

Is not the family, which holds the noblest human affections and may be infected by the most ignoble passions, differently conceived and realized by Christians who know the ways of perfection and by men indifferent to good and evil? Therefore the family in the supernatural order is confirmed by a Sacrament, and in the natural order is placed under the ægis of law. In an analogical sense, the same applies to any other natural form of society, even those voluntarily formed, whether political, economic or cultural. Everything comes within the atmosphere of the supernatural, individual life as social life.

We shall frequently, in the course of the present work, have to distinguish between individual life and social life, or take them together to define their full range and content. But it is well to remember — let me write it once for all — that the real life is that of individuals, whether separate or associated, that it is one life and not two, and that it is ever unifying for the whole activity of such individuals. We often speak of the individual and the social as though of inner and outer, but in reality the inner, too, is social. Or they are taken as the subjective and objective, but nothing is objective that is not subjective also. Or at other times they serve to distinguish the idea from its realization, but every realization contains the idea and is the fruit of individual activity. The analytical forms of speech are always incomplete; they elucidate only insofar as they presuppose or prepare the synthesis.

Once this is grasped, it will not cause surprise to declare that both mankind as the abstract expression of the totality of men, and society, as the projection and realization of associated activity, partake in a certain manner in the supernatural life granted us by God, and that their natural ends are unified in the supernatural, through which they too live by the true life. It is a real and concrete synthesis, as newness of life for all men and in each one of us and in the world (as the world is the necessary condition of our earthly life for a supernatural end), a synthesis of the whole of life, physical and spiritual, individual and social, natural and supernatural, journeying towards an ideal of perfection.

CHAPTER II

VOCATION

THE idea of vocation is intrinsic to our personality. Each one of us has an inherent finality. Our development, our welfare, the full realization of our ego and of its modes of expansion, constitute this inward finality. Since each has his own particular way of knowing himself, loving himself and seeking the fulfilment of his being, he may well be said to have a particular vocation, a goal towards which an inner voice urges him in the midst of the difficulties in which he finds himself, of his surroundings, of the position he has attained.

The particular end of each man cannot exist outside the orbit of the ends connatural to man, which can be summed up as the quest for the good. The more the particular end of each is conformable to nature, the more it contributes to his good. Under this aspect, a man's personal vocation would be his mode of achieving the good, according to his inclinations, qualities and possibilities. Among the myriad particular ways, each man finds those best fitted to him and makes a choice conditioned by circumstances in varying degrees. He who is best able to overcome cramping or adverse circumstances (which have their uses in promoting the growth of conquering energies), will be best able to decide his own destiny. Others, on the contrary, will submit with more or less resignation to the course of events.

More usually the word vocation is applied to the choice of a state of life, matrimonial, professional or religious, on the part of those who, having reached a certain age, are in a position to decide according to inclination and possibility. In the religious order it is God who chooses His own for the ministry of divine worship and the apostolate, as He chose Moses and Aaron, as Jesus chose the apostles, summoning them to a higher vocation. I am not speaking here of those chosen thus; I am considering every vocation, including those of a special character, under the general law of vocation whereby every man must follow the inner voice and realize his own personality, both in the natural order and in the supernatural.

Some conceive of personality — and the idea is not new — as an individual reality to be achieved by degrees as we become conscious of ourselves, of our own destiny, of ends and means; as each one of us gradually frees himself from the bondage of outward dependence, developing inward autonomy, gaining a character which becomes the physiognomy of the soul, markedly distinct from the featureless physiognomies of the many who are perhaps ignorant of their own destiny.

Without entering into the question whether personality thus dynamically conceived does not presuppose a personal reality already differentiated — that it does is evident to us who admit the separate creation of each human soul — we may say that this conception undoubtedly stresses the idea of a finalism intrinsic to personality, which we call by the pregnant and significant word of vocation.

If man were an illimitable and self-creating being, whose "I" was immersed in the universal spirit, the vocation of each man would be only the apparent phenomenon of a single reality. There would indeed not be vocations but determinations, even if these were called, as they are by idealist philosophers, auto-determinations. Man is, on the contrary, a finite, bounded, temporal creature, and he is at the same time an indestructible spiritual entity. On the one hand he realizes himself and is self-realizing; on the other, he is helped to realize himself, to overcome his limitations, to create his own happiness. He is called to this by the creative voice of God; following this voice he achieves his own perfection.

As in the concrete of history man has not a purely natural life but a natural life raised to the supernatural state, so there is not a natural vocation as an end in itself, which is not ordered to a supernatural vocation.

We are too accustomed to think in terms of our earthly life, reserving for religion a compartment just sufficient to maintain a certain harmony between ordinary existence and our relations with God. We are so preoccupied in fulfilling our natural activities that worldly interests engage us from waking to sleeping and outward life absorbs nearly all our time and our energies. A certain naturalistic conception prevails, which through general culture and a practical and unconscious materialism that is very widespread, has become habitual even for religious men. Others, brought up to consider the two domains from the point of view of abstract speculation and not in concrete reality, end by unreflectingly transforming the distinction between natural and supernatural into a kind of intellectual separatism. The non-existence of pure nature, the close interweaving of nature with the supernatural, through a mysterious and absorbing fact, is not made the basis of a thoroughgoing scrutiny of reality. Nevertheless there is a voice that recalls us to this reality, an inner though not a subjective voice, which has the value of a vocation.

This cannot be purely natural. I do not deny that there is a natural vocation, an intermediate end that may become the means for a further end. What I do deny is that this natural vocation is definitive and conclusive. The quest for individual welfare, in the purely natural field, is either subordinated to the ethico-religious conception or else it is an illusion; actually, the way leads from diversion to perversion. Nature itself reveals its deficiencies, which spring not only from the contingency inherent in us and in the world in which we live, but from an inner disorder disturbing the spiritual equilibrium of mind and will, alike in each person and in society as a whole. An integral natural vocation for the achievement of the perfection towards which we feel ourselves impelled, cannot exist either as subjective conquest or as social order.

The natural vocation is a call to life, which cannot be ignored, and which impels us to work and to make conquest of ourselves and of the surrounding world. Our personality is formed and characterized by a vocation (the inner voice), which becomes a finality (the good to be attained). It is a necessary premise for the fulfilment in us of the supernatural life to which we are raised. Just as the supernatural life is not realized in the concrete save in man as a living individual, so the supernatural vocation in the concrete renews and subordinates to itself the natural vocation.

The supernatural vocation is as universal as the natural one. We can view the two, under a certain aspect, as a single vocation to the good to be attained by man in the twofold order, natural and supernatural. For the true, sole good, that which can satisfy us, is God alone; all other goods are good only insofar as they partake of the Sovereign Goodness. Yet, in the natural order, God is reached in a rational and mediate manner; in the supernatural order we come to union with God by means of grace. In the natural order, through the original decadence, the possibility of the full achievement of rational welfare is wanting; in the supernatural order we break through the boundary set by sin, and come to participate in the divine nature.

The universality of the Redemption, extended to the whole human race, is the foundation of the universal vocation of all men to partake of it.[1] This universal vocation has to be realized in the concrete. The supernatural has to unite with nature. That which is outside time comes into time and history to reach each man in the singular, as the voice of God.

*   *   *   *   *

The Church may be consided as the central realization of the supernatural vocation in its historical aspect. It is the union of believers in a society, under the guidance of a magistery of faith, partaking of the Sacraments instituted by Christ. Those who are part of it are so because they have been called; it is a vocation from God, not a human choice, in order that in each of those called the universal vocation of all men "to the knowledge of the truth" shall be fulfilled.

The visible Church forms a social and historical unity from the descent of the Holy Spirit upon the apostles to our own times, and will last, by the promise of Christ, till the end of time. It is a living reality, which has its specific end — to continue the mission of Jesus Christ and of the apostles, to be the light-house of the world, the sheep-fold of safety and the chosen means of salvation, and to keep the divine revelation and the sacramental means of sanctification in their purity and perennial life.

All the faithful are called to coöperate according to the measure of graces they receive, in the place that is assigned to them, partaking, each in his degree, in the gifts of the Holy Spirit, in the hierarchic position in which they are placed. "We are God's helpers," writes St. Paul to the Corinthians

---

1. "God . . . who wishes all men to be saved and to come to the knowledge of the truth" (1 Tim. 2:3, 4).

(1 Cor. 3:9). And he adds: *"Let everyone take care how he builds* [God's building].... *If anyone builds upon this foundation* [which is Christ Jesus] *gold, silver, precious stones, wood, hay, straw — the work of each will be made manifest..."* (ibid. 10-13). In the same Epistle he goes on to speak of the gifts of the Spirit, saying: *"the manifestation of the Spirit is given to everyone for profit"* (ibid. 12:7). With the simile of the members of the body, St. Paul speaks of the special function of each one of us — not all are apostles, not all prophets, not all doctors....

There is thus a twofold vocation, to come to the knowledge of the truth and to be the coadjutors of God. This vocation is fulfilled for the faithful in the Church and through the Church. Just as in the concrete we do not find a purely natural life untouched by the supernatural, so we do not find a purely natural religion untouched by the supernatural. Primitive revelation, the Mosaic and prophetic revelation to Israel, the Christian revelation, make up an indissoluble whole and form the positive religious complexus which cannot find concrete actualization save in a church. Those who are called to the knowledge of the truth and to be coadjutors of God, are by that very fact called to build the Church. Each of the faithful under a certain aspect partakes of the priesthood, which is a special vocation, culminating in the apostolate and in the unique vocation of Peter to be the rock on which the Church would be built.

Therefore the concrete synthesis of the whole of revelation as actuated in the world is the historical Church, the visible society of the faithful, called to be partakers in the "one, holy, Catholic and apostolic Church." The vocation of each of the faithful is in the Church and through the Church, because it is not a singular vocation though personal to each man. It is a universal vocation, which is fulfilled in society, in mutual help, in mutual edification, in coöperation, personal and collective, with God.

The case of the dissident Christian Churches is mysterious, but not for this devoid of a vocational finality. The words of the Scriptures that may be applied are grave and perturbing: " ... *it must needs be that scandals come ...* " (Matt. 18:7) ; *"I hear that when you meet in church there are divisions among you, and in part I believe it. For there must be factions, so that those who are approved may be made manifest among you"* (1 Cor. 11:18-19). The parable of the weeds (Matt. 13:24-30) may be applied. The history of the visible Church is a continuous skein of scandals, schisms and heresies. From the clash of passions, from the debates of opinions, from the friction between members of the priesthood and between the priesthood and the faithful, amid the conflict between spiritual and worldly interests, the dogmatic formulas become clearly defined, the hierarchy is organized, the churches are unified, the mystical currents develop, and the sanctuary is purified. In the natural-supernatural history in which we live, evil always exists, but a higher will makes of it a motive for good; splits end by consolidating the living body, making it compact; the separated members end by readjusting themselves in fulfilment of a providential function of which often they are unaware.

This does not justify the scandals: *"Woe to him through whom they come"* (Luke 17:1). If the personal responsibility persists and will be judged, the divine utilization of evil for the purposes of good leads to a special vocation for those who, cut off from the center, still carry the name of Christ as their own, preserving the Hierarchy and the Sacraments, like the Greek and Eastern Orthodox Churches, or even only Baptism, like some of the Protestant and reformed Churches. Insofar as such Churches preserve something of revealed truth and of the spiritual gifts (given good faith among their members and the practical impossibility of their knowing the whole truth), they participate in the social end of the true Church, in the manifestation and testimony of truth, that is in building the Kingdom of God. Insofar as they are in opposition, they stimulate the study of the truth, lead to its elucidation through controversy, to its realization through emulation of good, the apostolate of the true faith, and if need be, martyrdom. This is a negative way (mysterious for us as the evil that creates a motive for good) of coöperating in the vocation of the Church of Christ.

*   *   *   *   *

Outside the Church and beyond the dissident Christian communities, we may find peoples and social groups with vocations for historico-supernatural ends, or bound up with such ends. More than any other people, Israel had a manifest vocation. To preserve the faith in the one God, Creator and Lord of everything and of all, to maintain and foster the Messianic tradition of a Redeemer to come, was a supernatural vocation. From age to age it had its particular form of actuation. It created great actions and collective responsibilities, it had its prophets, its martyrs, its betrayers and its vindicators. The whole existence of the Hebrew people, its vicissitudes, its wars, its defeats and deportations, were subordinated to this vocation. Tobias sang: " . . . *He [God] hath therefore scattered you among the Gentiles, who know not Him, that you may declare His wonderful works: and make them know that there is no other almighty God besides Him"* (Tob. 13:4). And further on: *"Nations from afar shall come to thee: and shall bring gifts: and shall adore the Lord in thee"* (ibid. 14). This is repeated again and again in the

Psalms and prophetic books. After the advent of Christianity, Judaism did not cease to have a special function, that of bearing witness to the holy books in all the reaches of the earth. We see here a permanent vocation with the longest tradition of any in the world, from Moses to today, in a living reality and a mysterious solidarity.

The Fathers of the Church also noted the vocation of republican and imperial Rome to prepare for the spread of Christianity by the unification of the known world under the central power of a city which was to become the seat of the See of Peter. Under a similar aspect we may speak of the twofold vocation of the Greek world before Christ: in the formation of the Macedonian Empire, stretching as far as India, a means of communication for the Good News to the furthest and least known regions, and in the philosophical and literary culture which served the human elucidation of Christian thought.

The prophets of Israel, in stressing the vocation of the different oriental empires in their relations with the Chosen People, gave the idea of similar particular vocations. In the course of history, God calls upon this or that people, this or that personage, king or prophet, pagan or otherwise, to serve as the minister of His will, to fulfil a function in the economy of divine manifestations, to render a service in the building of the Kingdom of God.

With the small compass of our minds, we may attribute a given function to peoples or historical events, near or far, in Christian or infidel countries, but we can never pass beyond the bounds of supposition. Where a Scriptural and prophetic word is lacking, or a clear tradition of Christian thought, we can only grope our way and give credence to our opinions. It is better to refrain. In a general way, it can be stated that insofar as a social group, family, people, nation, kingdom, brings truth and goodness to realization in accordance with its specific historical character, thus far it partakes, perhaps indirectly and on the plane of earthly life, in the vocation to coöperate in the Kingdom of God.

St. Paul said to the Athenians that *"from one man He [God] has created the whole human race and made them live all over the face of the earth, determining their appointed times and the boundaries of their lands; that they should seek God, and perhaps grope after Him and find Him, though He is not far from any one of us. For in Him we live and move and have our being, as indeed some of your own poets have said: 'For we are also His offspring' "* (Acts 17:26-28). Societies, States, empires, seek their own vital developments. They have natural and specific ends, they should not go beyond their own ends, nor arrogate to themselves higher ends. Providence can give them vocations extrinsic to their worldly nature, vocations which may remain unperceived and which will be evolved from the circumstances of their existence, from chance happenings, through human virtues or faults, through the qualities or the defects of their people. "Men move but it is God who moves them" is an adage of traditional wisdom which corresponds to a profound feeling. It is the mysterious contact with God not only of individual men but of whole communities.

In the religious conception of the Christian family, the supernatural finality flowers from the natural one of bearing and rearing children and of exchanging mutual help in a human love ennobled by religion. The Christian vocation of all families is to coöperate in saving their children. The parents in giving them being coöperate with God, who in that instant creates the new souls which He sends into the world. The non-Christian family, too, has the same vocation of saving its children and bringing them up in natural morality and religious worship. What is said of the family, in regard to its specific end, can be extended to every natural society, including States, federations of States and international societies. The pursuit of the ends of each society, insofar as these are moral in themselves or founded on morality, leads to a coöperation for good rendering each in varying degrees a docile instrument in the hands of God.

What is to be said of the States of Christian countries? In the traditional conception, they should coöperate with the Church for supernatural ends. But, apart from the historical and practical mode of conceiving such coöperation (with which we are not concerned here,[2] we cannot ignore that a special vocation has been given to the States of the Christian countries, a vocation made plain in so many historical circumstances, as in the spread of Christian civilization and culture, in missionary action throughout the world, in the defense of Christendom against the Mohammedans, Tartars and barbarians. It is true that often, instead of serving as a help to Christianity, the Christian powers have been grave impediments and, becoming persecutors of the Church, have prevented its spread. These facts prove nothing against the special vocation of the social groups concerned; they merely indicate the measure in which these groups respond or fail to respond to the divine vocation. Even in the diverse conditions of the various societies and races, in the differences between civilized and uncivilized peoples, higher or lower, dominant or subject, at their zenith or in decline, we may see the signs of special vocation or the utilization by God of the variety of human conditions for the building of His Kingdom.

St. Paul in the Epistle to the Romans sheds a beam of light on the mystery of the vocation of peoples, in their or-

---

2. See Luigi Sturzo, *Church and State*, pages 44-52 and *passim*.

ganization on earth and in their worldly activity as destined
to higher ends. Jacob and Esau, born at one birth, were destined the one to dominion, the other to subjection: " 'The
elder shall serve the younger'; as it is written: 'Jacob I have
loved, but Esau I have hated' " (Rom. 9:12-13). Here it is a
case not only of the subjection of Esau through the rights
of the firstborn, which were conferred on Jacob, but also of
the subjection of the people that descended from Esau (Edom)
and were subject to the descendants of Jacob (Israel). In the
same context St. Paul, quoting Exodus (9:18), writes: "For
the Scripture says to Pharaoh: 'For this very purpose I have
raised thee up that I may show in thee My power, and that
My name may be proclaimed in all the earth' " (ibid. 17).
These references serve St. Paul to affirm the unfathomable
will of God over the destiny of peoples, all of them, each in
its place, called to a higher vocation, whether they present
themselves as "vessels of honor" or as "vessels of wrath":
"Or is not the potter master of his clay, to make from the
same mass one vessel for honorable, another for ignoble
use?" (ibid. 21).

It is not the people, as a collectivity, that is the resolvent
term of the divine action; this reaches each man in the singular. Yet society as such and the men who work on the social
plane and are responsible for it, assume an important position
in the mystery of the vocation "that My name may be proclaimed in all the earth." Society, as an earthly element of
human activity, becomes the matrix of men destined each to a
particular mission.

St. Paul, dwelling upon the theme of the election or
reprobation of peoples, quotes Isaias: "Though the number
of the children of Israel are as the sand of the sea, the remnant shall be saved" (ibid. 27). Isaias was here speaking of
the expedition of Tiglath-Pileser and of the remnant that will

escape because *"they ... shall lean no more upon him that striketh them: but they shall lean upon the Lord, the Holy One of Israel, in truth"* (Is. 10:20). Continuing, St. Paul, again quoting Isaias, insists, *"Unless the Lord of Hosts had left us a posterity* [a seed],[3] *we should have become as Sodom, should have been like Gomorrah"* (Rom. 9:29). This remnant, this seed, for Paul are the Jews converted to Christianity; for *"God has not cast off His people whom He foreknew"* (ibid. 11:2). And recalling the invocation of Elias, when he believed that he alone in Israel remained faithful, St. Paul applies the answer which the prophet received from the divine voice: *"I have left for Myself seven thousand men who have not bowed their knees to Baal"* (ibid. 4). The special vocation to which Israel was called was understood by few, continuously selected from among the many who forgot it. So has it been in every time, even the Christian, and so will it be till the end of time.

The function of the "faithful remnant," of the "seed of the just," of the "few chosen," has a capital importance in the history of peoples and of the Church. The "many called" do not answer the call, either because they do not understand their vocation or because they are too deeply engaged in worldly life. The few who remain faithful, "who have not bowed their knees to Baal," the "seven thousand" (a symbolic number, for seven stands for fulness of virtue), are set apart by God to realize His Kingdom; they respond to a supernatural vocation which may remain unknown to them, being identified for them with fidelity to the law of God, naturally apprehended but Christianly lived. This seed is reproduced through the ages *"until the full number of the Gentiles should enter, and thus all Israel should be saved"* (ibid. 25-26).

---

3. Vulgate: *"Nisi Dominus Sabaoth reliquisset nobis semen."*

This final prophecy is bound up with that other in the Gospel foretelling that *"there shall be one fold and one shepherd"* (John 10:16). Through diverse paths will come the Christian unification of the peoples in the knowledge of the truth. The patriarchal tradition, with its deviations, misunderstandings, forgetfulnesses; the fatherhood of Abraham in faith and faithfulness to God; the mission of Israel; the prophecies; the glimmering light of reason and of tradition combined among the Gentiles — all prepare the way. Then the fulness of time and the coming of Jesus Christ, the foundation of His Church, the persecutions and triumphs, the heresies and schisms, the periods of decadence and recovery, the deviations and the missionary action of the religious orders, the laicizing negations and the vocation of the laity to Catholic and social action — what a road has been traveled in the actuation of the supernatural in history!

When it seems that the spiritual unification of mankind (one fold, one shepherd), is further off and more compromised than ever, then the seed of the elect sprouts anew, and we find again "the seven thousand who have not bowed their knees to Baal." Elias is no longer alone; a step has been taken towards the future, because there are those who have responded to their vocation.

Mankind is still young. The two thousand years of Christianity are "as yesterday which is past." Who knows how many thousand more will have to pass before "the new heavens and the new earth"? But God does not count the centuries, He looks on those who answer His call.

* * * * *

Any historical vocation of social groups is inconceivable save as something destined to condition, develop and perfect the vocation of each individual. For the supernatural life, too, society is a means and not an end; the end is man. Even in the order of charity, when it may seem as if the individual becomes a means and society an end — *"Greater love than this no one has, that one lay down his life for his friends"* (John 15:13) — the inversion is only apparent, for *"he who loses his life for My sake, will find it"* (Matt. 10:39). Such a man in sacrificing himself has fulfilled his vocation; he has realized all the good that had accumulated in his personality so that he should be able to offer it for the benefit of his brothers.

The supernatural life consists in supernatural love of God and of our neighbor through grace, just as the natural life consists in love of God and of our neighbor through simply natural forces. What is mysterious and comforting to us (and so heavy with responsibility), is that we cannot live a complete natural life, having been called to the supernatural life and raised to it either potentially or actually. The only alternatives are — either to unify our natural love with the supernatural love, carrying all natural values into that higher life and there giving them a deeper truth, or else to fall below nature itself, denying even natural love, which turns into selfishness, hatred and death.

Therefore every social form is considered under a twofold aspect, as a means for the development of the spiritual personality of each member, and as a communion of good through mutual love. For those who live the supernatural life, society itself becomes a kind of end which, unable to exhaust itself in itself, calls for God, in whom alone both the spiritual life of the individual and the communion of social goods find their perfection.

The problem of our salvation, which is basic for each one of us, cannot be set and solved save in society with God and with men. *"That you also may have fellowship with us, and that our fellowship may be with the Father, and with His Son Jesus Christ"* (1 John 1:3) — here is all that needs to be said of the social value of our personal vocation to the supernatural life.

Let us imagine a man alone on a desert island, to whom an angel or God Himself should directly reveal the mysteries of salvation; who receives Baptism of desire and remains faithful to God till death, without ever seeing or meeting any other man. That man would be accounted in fellowship with the faithful through Baptism of desire, in fellowship with God through grace received and faithfully kept. He is within the visible Church, though only God knows it. In God he lives a life associated with men. He prays, merits and sacrifices himself for the brothers he does not know and will never meet. He can give more to society than some of those who live and work within it, for the benefit of their parents and friends, for their native town, their country, the Church.

Each has his task to fulfil in his earthly, social life; each gives his own activity to the common benefit, also for natural ends. But *"for those who love God all things work together unto good, for those who, according to His purpose, are saints through His call"* (Rom. 8:28). Earthly values are transformed into supernatural values through the call to a unification of life. In the Christian conception there is no denial of human life; it is perfected. Partial denial, when it comes (as with those who embrace virginity by vocation), is for a more intense life of love of God and of men. Society under its twofold aspect, natural and supernatural, is lived by the Christian through love, in all the stages of his activity, in all the forms of his vocation, through the same act by which he seeks his spiritual salvation.

A selfish conception of personal salvation as a withdrawal into self, a denial of social relationships, is not a Christian conception. There does not and cannot exist love of God without love of our neighbor, nor fellowship with God without fellowship with our brothers. An egoistic sense has been falsely attributed to those who prefer the hermit's solitude or the monk's cloister, or in general give themselves up more to contemplative than to active life. But this, when it is not the result of prejudice and incomprehension, comes from an error in perspective. There is no supernatural life that does not combine contemplation with activity; the classification as one or the other comes only through the general orientation and the practical ends that are sought. There is no lack of activity, in the famous Benedictine synthesis *"Ora et labora,"* in those who seek in silence and contemplation the best way to live with God. The practical ways of goodness are numberless and in their variety fit the needs, inclinations and vocations of every man.

The two vocations interweave: the natural serves and is subordinate to the supernatural, the supernatural gives full meaning to the natural and consolidates it. The individual influences society, creates the social environment, gives it his imprint, mars it with his faults, shapes it by his virtues. Society in turn pours back upon the individual the complex values formed within it through associated and collective activity. With a mysterious vitality the spiritual sap of grace circulates, permeating all human organisms, moulding the tissues, expelling malign humors, releasing benign forces; it transforms children into heroes, old men into militants, sharpening the sense of the divine, raising men up to sublime contemplation of the truth, the light of the world.

All, individuals and societies, in mutual action and reaction, on the natural plane and on the supernatural, respond or coöperate, directly or indirectly, in the universal vocation to be fulfilled by means of the social forms in each one of us, the vocation to good and to the knowledge of God. All thus become, in a mysterious way, coadjutors of God for the building of His Kingdom.

CHAPTER III

PREDESTINATION

THE raising of the human nature to the supernatural state, the historical mission of every human group, the special finality of the Church, are all directed to the realization of the individual vocation of each one of us, which cannot be achieved save in the spirit of the universal vocation of all men and in the historical environment of social life. Now since the vocation of each is a beginning of eternal life, the whole complexus of our individual destiny resolves itself into our predestination.

An unfathomable mystery here opens before us, of which we have only the analytical data supplied by revelation. We are not able to assemble them in a single synthesis, for the mystery outstrips our power of comprehension. And yet we are drawn, like moths to the light, to live by this mystery, which is the mystery of the justice and mercy of God, the mystery of our freedom, of the existence of moral evil, of our relation to God, in the synthesis of nature with what is above nature.

Predestination was defined by St. Augustine, in a formula accepted throughout the ages, as "the foreknowledge and preparation of the good things of God, through which those who are saved are most certainly saved." This implies first of all that without grace we cannot have the seed of salvation within us, nor obtain merit by good works, nor persevere in good to the end. Grace is freely given, it is not a due; thus the distribution of grace depends wholly on God's free will.

He chooses His own, to whom He gives the necessary grace, and more, for them to reach salvation.

On the other hand, it is also of faith that "God our Saviour wishes all men to be saved and to come to the knowledge of the truth"; that to those who respond to His call He does not deny the graces necessary for salvation (which none the less remain always His freely given gift; and that to those who do not so respond, or who after having responded return to sin, He applies His justice in condemnation. St. Prosper of Aquitaine says that if some are saved, it is by the gift of Him who saves, and if others perish, it is their own doing: "Quod quidam salvantur salvantis est donum; quod quidam pereunt, pereuntium est meritum." The synthesis reconciling these two terms — God's love of predilection for the elect and His justice towards the lost — is for us a mystery. Such reconcilement comes about in the will of God, which we are able to know only in its effects, but these present themselves to us analytically, in apparently irreconcilable conflict.

If the saving will of God, in order to be efficacious in each one of us, had to be conditioned by our good works, it would not be sovereign and free. But if it does not depend on our works, for what reason was it not efficacious in the reprobate? Theologians tell us that the elect have responded to grace and in the continuity of their response have disposed themselves to receive the grace of final perseverance, whereas the reprobate have wilfully failed to respond to it. All this is incontestable, but we might question further why the reprobate should not have received grace to overcome their failure so to respond as to prepare themselves to receive the gift of final grace. Could not God have done this? Could He not have dealt with Judas Iscariot as with Peter and Paul?

No one can claim to know the mystery of the distribution of graces, and how these can be so efficacious as to overcome

our will without taking away its freedom, or else barely sufficient to make us feel the existence of good, without moving
our will to cleave to it. It is certain that whether we do good
or whether we choose evil, we are freely responsible for our
actions; God counts the good as merit for reward, the evil as
motive and measure of chastisement. It is certain, too, that
without grace the good we do avails us nothing, being devoid
of the character of supernatural good; that only through grace
is the evil done wiped out, giving a motive (through contri-
tion and repentance) for new and perhaps greater merits.

There is thus a mystery within us, wherein unknown to us
grace is reconciled with freedom, evil is overcome in supernatural good, personal merits coexist with gratuity of grace.
And there is another mystery in God, wherein the will to save
all men is reconciled with the condemnation of the reprobate,
divine foreknowledge with our freedom, the objective efficacy
of the grace given with the possibility of its rejection by the
obstinate sinner.

Theologians, in order to throw some clarity on the terms
of this mystery in ourselves and in God, or at least to present
them to our minds freed from contradictions, have followed
various schools, while remaining within the terms of dogmatic
teaching. According to the Thomists: "It is impossible that
the whole effect of predestination in general should have any
cause as coming from us; because whatsoever is in man dispos-
ing him towards salvation, it is all included under the effect
of predestination; even the preparation for grace."[1] The
Molinists, on the other hand, opine: a) that prevenient grace
is given by God to him who, in virtue of his free will and
with his natural forces, seeks to do his best in the moral life;
b) that the grace of perseverance is efficacious in accordance

---

1. S. Th., I Q. XXIII, art. V.

with God's foreknowledge of our consent to it; c) that if pre-destination, taken in its complexity, is always free and inde-pendent of our merits, yet God has foreknowledge of the use that we shall make of our free will.

The Thomist theory, in its rigidity, corresponds to a total conception of the mystery of God's predilection and justice as free and sovereign Arbiter. It calls for a blind and total trust from His creatures, stressing their subjection and adherence to the divine will. The Molinist theory throws into relief our freedom, our personality, and stimulates us to an active re-sponse to grace.

In the concrete experience of the supernatural, it may be noted that for beginners in the spiritual life or those who still live between the world and God (divided, as St. Paul has it), the Molinist theory is more satisfactory psychologically, lessen-ing the anxiety that may come from lack of understanding or from a too great desire to understand, and stimulating them to abound in good works. For souls on the road to perfection, for the contemplatives, for the perfect, the Thomist theory is very helpful in detaching them still more from themselves and drawing them closer to God in His inaccessible light and the dazzle of His infinity. Between the two theories there are intermediate positions in which the attempt is made to recon-cile more than the terms of the mystery, the states of mind created by its study or contemplation.

* * * * *

Insofar as it serves the purpose of our study, we must here make clear what our free will consists in, and how it can coöperate in our eternal salvation without becoming even partial cause of our predestination.

No one today goes so far as to deny (as was once the fashion) at least a modicum of inner freedom in our action; the idea of a fatal human determinism can be considered as belonging to the past. Still there are many who argue that free will cannot consist in the possibility of a choice between two different goods, or else between good and evil, the latter being apprehended as good. In actual fact, they say, the choice, if there is a choice, may be said to be made as by an act of judgment prior to any intervention of the will; any comparison between goods to be chosen is submerged by the intervention of sensitive or intellective appetites, instinctive or reflective, which while stimulating the will lessen its responsibility; the physical, economic and social conditioning of every human activity lessens the possibilities for a true choice, placing us under a kind of negative necessity.

This heap of objections can easily be overturned if we recognize that the nature of free will is not affected by the multiplicity or fewness of the possibilities of choice and activity. The conditioning factors of our existence, whether physical or psychological, economic or social, may end by stimulating our activity to an exceptional intensity, just as they may reduce it to a kind of automatic habit.

What shows free will is the attainment of self-mastery, in whatever circumstances we may find ourselves. First, the beginnings of a liberation of our higher being from the bonds of sense life, a greater ease in willing against our own desires, even the keenest and most lively ones, a dominion over our passions and a readiness to hold them in check. Again, the expanding liberation of our mind from the presumptuous arrogance of judging everything, and hence the acquisition of a better understanding of the environment in which we live. Again, a more loving trust, made up of kindness and compassion for neighbor and enemy alike, which becomes a deeper

understanding of history. Thus we come to a progressive
liberation of ourselves, an achievement of freedom of will, an
assimilation of ourselves with others through a kind of voluntary self-identification with them which resolves itself into an
inner purification and an intense love of truth.

Truth brings freedom from error, and from evil deviations.
Love raises us above ourselves in the understanding of others.
Truth and love are, at one and the same time, the life of our
personal spirit and the life of society. These lives are not two
but one, a single individual-social life. How, without inner
freedom, could our spirit live by truth and love? How could
it pour forth the treasure of truth and love upon society?

It is said that we are forced to give our intellectual assent
in the face of the evidence of truth, whether it be the evidence
of a fact or the evidence of a first principle. This is true —
there is a kind of intellectual determinism. Not to wish to
yield to the evidence of truth is to wish to break away, by
blind obstinacy, from the social life that is founded on the
convergence of minds in what is commonly apprehended as
true; it is the sin against the Holy Ghost. But it must not be
thought that we are really determined to this or that truth;
we are generally determined to truth as we are to good. Our
particular assent to a given truth must be motivated; it is
always a choice, not only of the good but in a certain manner
of the true, it is the choice of our life.

How many are there not in error, in invincible error, as
the moralists have it? This invincibility does not come about
through determinism. It comes through a series of intellectual
and volitive acts which create in us mental habits, constant
orientations, a kind of personal logic which makes us cleave to
error as to unshakable truth. We grow fond of the truths, the
half-truths and the errors believed to be truths, by which we

live and which form the permanent substratum of new voli-
tions. And these, nonetheless, are always free, rooted in an
incontrovertible personal responsibility, in the here and now
of our actions. For free will, taken as auto-initiative, as the
tendency to free ourselves from error, from evil, from passion,
as the auto-decision of our actions, as the power to review our
orientations, to correct our habits, as dominion over ourselves,
is connatural to our essence as spiritual, intellectual beings.
From this comes our full responsibility for our actions and our
failures.

We have within us a basic feeling, which of itself is un-
differentiated and can lead us either towards the good or
towards the evil. It is not a consequence of the original sin;
on the contrary, it occasioned the sin of Adam as it did the
sin of the rebellious angels. This feeling is the feeling of our
personality, which can lead us to seek truth or to fall into
error, to conquer ourselves or to become enslaved to our instincts. If it leads towards the good it is called humility, if
towards the evil it is called pride. The first says: "Behold the
handmaid of the Lord." The second says: "Ye shall be
as gods."

In a philosophic analysis of human action, we find at the
root the tendency of each man to make himself the center of
his own inner and outer activity, to expand, to realize himself
and his own faculties, to seek within himself and outside for
that which corresponds to his needs, his aspirations, his life.
Thus everything may assume for us the name and complexion
of truth and goodness, everything may answer to our thirst to
know, our need to love, in a word, for reality of living.
Humility or pride colors man's impulses, tendencies, acts.

We take the words humility and pride from the Christian
askesis. They may be translated, to make the point clearer, as

the individual's true or false appraisement of his own personality, and hence as an ordered or disordered self-love. It is
always truth and love that we seek; we can seek nothing else,
nothing else can satisfy us. The whole of reality, inner and
outer, transmutes itself into truth and love. Humility is the
surest way of attaining both; pride, on the contrary, leads us
away from them.

It is rightly said that freedom for evil is no true freedom;
what was possessed by the angels before they sinned and what
men now enjoy on this earth, is inaccurately called freedom
for evil. The object of the will is always the good. When our
personality projects itself as a single and incontested value, we
cleave to it as a finalistic good. It is then that we are not able
to resolve our being into truth and our egoism into love: pride
hinders us.

The problem should be expressed thus: the will inclines to
the good, not blindly but illuminated by the mind. Among the
different goods, that which we perceive immediately is our
own being. If we were God, in knowing ourselves and loving
ourselves we should form a fellowship with ourselves while
ourselves remaining one (the mystery of the Trinity). But we
are finite; knowledge of our ego calls immediately for a
non-ego, something outside ourselves. Love towards ourselves
is not complete unless it expands outside ourselves, towards a
necessary completion.

In this boundedness lies the whole mystery of human personality, of its operations and the possibility of its sinning.
The evil is there at the root and is called pride when we
esteem ourselves beyond our finite condition, setting ourselves
above other men and, indirectly or directly, in the place of
God. In sin there is always an implicit negation of others as
beings equal to ourselves, and of God as Supreme Being.

In the Scriptures God and the good are called truth or the truth, the devil and evil are called a lie or the lie. The good is truth, in the threefold correspondency (1) of reality with its essence; (2) of a being's degree of reality with that of others; (3) of the knowledge and manifestation of such relations before men and before God. Sin distorts this threefold truth in the practical estimation of the sinner. Thus he works a lie, for he esteems himself as an end to himself, superior to others, independent of God. The sinner lies first of all to himself. "We shall be as gods," Adam and Eve tell themselves as they eat the forbidden fruit; it is not only an error but a lie: error culpably apprehended as truth and proclaimed as such. In all our thoughts there is the inward expression, made to ourselves, of the truth or error contained in the judgment that precedes our action. A lie is error known and expressed as truth. Every inner lie arises from an excess of self-love, and produces sin, which is nothing other than the practical act of an inward pride. Whether we break the precept of loving God or that of loving our neighbor, attributing to ourselves what we have not, we produce a lie.

In order to be able to correct our lying judgment in the light of truth — for the lie has insinuated itself into us only through our pride, that is, through an inner state of mind which we can cast off — we bear the entire responsibility for our actions. Whether we consider free will as our liberating initiative, from the viewpoint of the subject, or whether we consider it, as is usually done, as a freedom of choice, from the viewpoint of the object, we have the power to overcome the blindness of pride and to guide ourselves by illuminating humility. Through the fact of free will we are responsible for our acts; we bear within us the possibility of falling every time that, loving ourselves beyond measure, we deny the bonds of fellowship with men and with God, and, yielding to pride, deny the truth and love in which is centered all natural and supernatural life.

*   *   *   *   *

If we alone are the cause of the evil that we do, the same cannot be said of the good that we may do. We coöperate in good, but it is not through our virtue that we do good. It is usual to distinguish between natural good, which comes within human capacity, and supernatural good, which cannot be done save by and through grace. As an objective analysis, abstracting from psychological and historical reality, the distinction is exact and sound. Every good action contains a beginning of truth and love; otherwise it could not be good. Anyone who gives alms as a pure act of charity, without any admixture of vainglory or other unworthy feeling, and without any secondary end, has done a good work which can hardly be accompanied except by a motion of grace. The same may be said of every other good action when it presents itself as of a natural character, like love of parents, faithfulness in marriage, the care and good upbringing of children, honesty in business, respect for the law, and so on.

The character of truth and love to be found in every good action naturally conceived, partakes in a certain manner of the value of supernatural truth and love. We are not able to do anything of ourselves, without the help of God. If any good action is rightly performed, in the supernatural state in which, potentially, all mankind is placed, the influence of grace cannot be lacking, whether it be the grace at once habitual and actual in those who have overcome sin, or merely actual, prevenient, excitant, concomitant, in those who, though in sin, do good works. What goodness can there be in human actions that are not moved by grace? In the eye of God, none. Those who do good not for its own sake but for their own advantage, to obtain the praise of men, "have received their reward." Praise and their own advantage were the ends they sought, and not the good, which was merely a pretext, an occasion, an external impulse.

In thus simplifying human action we do not mean to reduce it to absurdity. In the psychology of our actions we are more complex; we mingle noble feelings with base ones, and often we ourselves are unaware of certain instinctive feelings concomitant to our action. We need to sound the depths of the heart and scrutinize the habitual state of its inclinations and affections, if we are to judge of the value of our acts.[2] Grace does not destroy nature, which remains with its good and evil inclinations, with its freedom towards the true good and towards the apparent good that resolves itself into evil. Yet grace has taken possession of the good that mankind can do. Every good is placed under the influence of grace and is the direct or indirect expression of supernatural life.

Let no one think that I am confounding the two orders, the natural and the supernatural, or attenuating the first for the sake of the second. I remain within the traditional limits of theology, holding that since original sin man cannot without grace, either prevenient or concomitant, perform the supernatural acts preparatory to justification; that grace is demanded for the beginning of faith and for any efficacious desire for each salutary act; that man, under present conditions, cannot without grace constantly keep the whole natural law and overcome all temptations.

---

2. *"For out of the heart come evil thoughts, murders, adulteries, immorality, thefts, false witness, blasphemies"* (Matt. 15:19).

Theologians are careful to keep the supernatural order distinct from the natural, for the purpose, firstly, of affirming in every way the gratuity of grace and the impotence of nature to go beyond its own sphere; and secondly, of stressing man's responsibility, seen in the purely natural order, if he falls into sins and does not seek God, to whom he may come by the sole force of reason. Hence the complementary thesis, that even since original sin man can, without grace, perform certain morally good actions.

My position is not in contradiction to these premises. In my view morally good acts, if they are willed and performed for their own sake, as a duty of conscience, seeking the good of our neighbor or in God's honor, enter concretely into the category either of the acts preparatory to justification or of the efficacious desire of salutary acts, or of the effort to keep the natural law. In substance, they are a part of the psychological and ethical complexus of those who feel an attraction to good and a repugnance to evil, even if it be in a faulty manner through ignorance or weakness. To these acts, not only is grace not wanting, but as such and in such a setting, they cannot be conceived and realized without grace.

Theologians, considering the problem from the angle of God's goodness, repeat that "facienti quod in se est Deus non denegat gratiam." This is interpreted by Billot and others as meaning: "To him who does the good he can according to his powers and *with the help of grace,* God does not deny actual graces; and to him who does good *with such actual graces* God does not deny habitual grace." This is a gradual process, which has been presented here in schematic form in order to understand its terms. But *"the wind blows where it will, and thou hearest its sound but dost not know where it comes from or where it goes. So is everyone who is born of the Spirit"*

(John 3:8). The thesis condemned by the Council of Trent —
"that all the acts performed before justification, for whatever
reason they were performed, are true sins" — is very remote
from what is here affirmed of acts naturally good but performed without right intention, for personal advantage, vainglory, pride. They are bad, not because they lack justification,
but because they are rendered such by our will which directs
the intention. On the other hand, if our will does not make
them bad, grace works in them fruits of supernatural life.

The choice in the quest of good is not between the natural
plane and the supernatural, but between the good rendered
supernatural by grace and the semblance of a natural good,
which is not really good inasmuch as it is not even in accordance with rational nature. The purely natural good can only
by abstraction be isolated from human action, as a possibility,
a hypothetical relationship; whereas the supernatural good is
the concrete reality of all those who feel the divine vocation
and follow the impulse of grace. There is no third road.

*   *   *   *   *

Given that grace is needed for doing good — and it is this
that characterizes the good — how can it coexist with our
freedom? If, in spite of grace, we sin, it has no efficacy for us;
if, by grace, we do not sin, we have no merit in the matter.

If the problem is set thus, it becomes insoluble. The usual
answer is that God, as Author of nature, does not change its
character by conferring grace, nor has He even obliterated the
effects of the decadence of nature through original sin. This
answer notes the fact, but does not resolve the antinomy of
the terms. The same fact was noted by St. Paul: " ... *there
was given me a thorn for the flesh, a messenger of Satan, to
buffet me. Concerning this I thrice besought the Lord that it*

might leave me. And He has said to me: 'My grace is suffi-cient for thee, for strength is made perfect in weakness' " (2 Cor. 12:7-9).

Neither God alone, with His grace, nor man alone, with his free will, but God and man together, work good. We coöperate freely with God. This free coöperation was made perfect in God-made-Man. The Word incarnate united humanity in His Person so that our nature should coöperate in the redemption of all men. The freedom of Jesus as Man did not lie in the choice between good and evil. We know that not even in man is this true freedom; when we choose evil we do not take it for evil but for good, for that which at the moment of choice appears to us as the good. Our responsibility lies in the moral premises through which we come to make such a choice, which is consummated by a final cleaving to that which is in fact evil. These moral premises are not to be found in Jesus Christ, who was *"one tried as we are in all things except sin"* (Heb. 4:15) ; nor in the Virgin Mary, conceived by special privilege without original sin. Other men are the further removed from such premises the more closely they cleave to God.

The freedom of the man who enters into the kingdom of grace and who lives by grace can be compared in a certain way to the freedom of the musician who, having acquired technical perfection in the command of his instrument, does not err in a single note; yet if he wishes to make a mistake by an act of will, he can always do so, though it will actually be difficult, and, if he plays while distracted by other thoughts, he may perhaps make a mistake. Another, clearer example, because taken from the exercise of psychomoral witnesses rather than technical ones, is that of the nurse who has attained the virtue and professional habit of keeping her temper with every sort of patient, and who no longer finds herself losing it. If, for the handling of a particular case, she wants to speak sharply, she will hardly be able to manage it. Would one say that she is no longer free to choose between keeping her temper and losing it?

So it is with grace. It does not take away man's freedom, but helps him not to give way to bad impulses, strengthens his inclination towards good, transforms natural good into supernatural. When to St. Paul on the road to Damascus came the voice: *"I am Jesus, whom thou art persecuting. It is hard for thee to kick against the goad"* (Acts 9:5), it did not take away his freedom to answer the call; it made him feel the difficulty of resistance, so that he asked, trembling: *"Lord, what wilt Thou have me do?"* (ibid. 6). Does not the evidence of the evil we may have done force itself upon our minds when we are assailed by remorse? Or when remorse is aroused in us by a friend, a preacher, a father or mother? And is it not we ourselves who freely ask forgiveness and promise not to offend again?

Therefore St. Paul declares that he awaits God's reward. *"I have fought the good fight, I have finished the course, I have kept the faith. For the rest, there is laid up for me a crown of justice, which the Lord, the just Judge, will give to me in that day"* (2 Tim. 4:7-8). How would a "crown of justice" be possible if there were no personal merits? And how could there be merits without the responsibility for supernatural good works? And how could there be responsibility without freedom? And how supernatural works without grace?

It will be well here to note briefly that according to theologians, the merits imputed to us avail only to give an increase of grace and a degree of glory; they are not a title to the first grace, which is wholly gratuitous; nor to forgiveness of the sins by which all merit is lost, returning only with forgiveness; nor to efficacy of grace; nor, finally, to the ultimate grace. Merit, by the divine promise, is attributed to our response to grace; a merit which theologians call *de condigno,* inasmuch as there is a relationship between the supernatural good works and the increase of graces, and between these and the degree of glory in heaven.

To sum up: Man is naturally free; grace does not lessen that natural freedom, but is the means by which man's good actions are transported to the supernatural plane, so that he may coöperate with God and obtain the merits of good works, which God, in His justice and liberality, takes into account for increase of graces and a degree of glory. But if man unhappily falls into sin, the responsibility is entirely his and he deserves the penalty.

*   *   *   *   *

These are the terms of the problem, but the mystery remains of their union in the synthesis of the supernatural good act. Is this such because we willed it so? Yes, because we willed it, but we have willed it and performed it because a prevenient, exciting and concomitant grace made us so will and perform it. This grace theologians call *efficacious.* If instead we had merely willed the good action without performing it, or worse, if we had opposed a refusal to the summons of grace, this would not have been efficacious but, according to the theologians' terminology, only *sufficient.*

Theologians use the word "efficacious" to indicate that to such grace must be attributed the performance of the good work; whereas they use the word "sufficient" to indicate that it was not through a want in the grace given but through our will that it did not produce its effect. But whence comes the

efficacy of grace when it is indeed efficacious? The Thomists
say that it is so in an intrinsic manner, of itself, independently
of our coöperation; whereas the Molinists declare that it is
only efficacious in an extrinsic manner, insofar as God foresaw
our coöperation.

The two schools mark the two points of the mystery. The
one stresses the will of God, who gives to some the efficacious
graces and to others only the sufficient ones; the other stresses
human will, which God in the distribution of graces knows
and foresees as coöperating or not coöperating with His grace.
But this second school, that of the Molinists, does not explain
how God's will would not be limited in giving grace by the
foreknowledge of our coöperation, which would characterize
its efficacy; while the first school, the Thomist, does not explain
how our coöperation with a grace intrinsically efficacious can
be free.

The mystery deepens: our very coöperation with grace —
could it be possible without an actual grace rendering it so?
No, assuredly. Going back from grace to grace with which
we have coöperated, we reach the first, wholly gratuitous grace.
To produce the chain of graces with which we have coöperated,
the first must have been efficacious by its own virtue. If, on
the contrary, either the first was not efficacious, or the chain of
grace and coöperation was broken by a refusal to coöperate,
even if we admit that this was our fault, we may ask ourselves
why God, foreseeing our fault, did not give us an efficacious
grace. But by this we claim to know the mystery in the synthesis of the divine will, when we cannot even know the
mystery in the synthesis of the human will. We feel that we
are free to say no to God, just as we feel that we are free to
say yes, but we do not know up to what point it is our doing

or God's. Thus we shall never know up to what point God has wished to take into account our response, to which He appeals by His love for us, for He first loved us; nor how He has sovereignly made the choice and established the predestination of His elect.

It is not grace that is conditioned by our response but our response that is conditioned by grace. Grace is offered to all: the raising of mankind to the supernatural state, the redemption from original sin by the merits of Jesus Christ, the saving will of God and the vocation to salvation extended to all, are the reason of our hope; but divine predestination is a choice. The elect are the predestined. They will have responded to the graces given, they will have merited the increase of graces and their degree of glory, they will not have placed impediments in the way of receiving the ultimate grace and they will have prepared themselves for it. God has made of them vessels of election and they will have coöperated with God "to make sure their calling and election."[3] Our coöperation is necessary, on penalty of decadence, sin, perdition. But divine predestination has a value that surpasses us in the whole of our being and our workings and which, in its essential nature, cannot depend on anything but God.

This is not clear to us. It is a mystery. Just as it is not clear how creation exists and follows the laws given it by God, yet in the face of God is nothingness, for it does not limit either His infinity or His omnipotence or His liberty. Yet creation is, and coöperates with God. Thus we coöperate with God in the building of His Kingdom, but we are nothing and can do nothing without His grace, and our will avails nothing

---

3. *"Therefore, brethren, strive even more by good works to make your calling and election sure"* (2 Pet. 1:10).

save to make us responsible for our sins. Only to him who responds and in the measure in which he responds to grace will it be said: *"Well done, good and faithful servant; because thou hast been faithful over a few things, I will set thee over many; enter into the joy of thy Master"* (Matt. 25:21).

CHAPTER IV

COMMUNION

OUR vocation and predestination to supernatural life brings us beyond our earthly plane, and like Abraham we are called to a communion with God. For this, grace is the means; it is the divine gift that disposes us for eternal life. Grace is not God Himself but His gift, through which He unites us to Himself and makes us partakers of His Godhead. It is a habit infused by Baptism, which raises the soul to the supernatural state, making of it a new creature, giving birth within it to virtues such as the new life requires— the theological virtues, faith, hope and charity, the cardinal virtues of a higher order and the gifts of the Holy Spirit. It is intrinsically inherent in the soul and increases with the practice of virtues and through the continual divine helps which theologians call actual graces.

Without grace there can be no fellowship with God; the absence of grace is sin. There cannot be, in the present order, a natural stage at which there is neither grace nor sin. The dwelling of God in us and of us in God, that intimate communion of a fellowship installed by Baptism, becomes more perfect every time new grace is granted to us, either in a wholly inward manner, through our responsive love, or in the sacramental partaking of the divine *charismata*. Confession is the sacramental forgiveness of sins. Confirmation strengthens us in our profession of faith by word and works. The Holy Eucharist gives us the food of life and the pledge of glory. Extreme Unction comforts us in the pains of death

81

and prepares us for beatific vision. And, in their social character, the one hierarchic, the other domestic, Holy Orders and Matrimony give us the grace of the state to which they refer, while both symbolize the union of Christ with the Church.

Each Sacrament is communion with Christ, the Mediator, the Redeemer, the Head of the living, the Center of life, Man and God. He, in associating in Himself manhood with Godhead, merited for all the union with God by grace. In no other wise can we be united to God than through Christ Jesus and in Christ Jesus. The Sacraments are the signs and means of participation in the grace that He has merited. The fellowship between Godhead and manhood which in Him is hypostatic, personal, in us is a partaking of His very life which circulates in His mystical body, made up of all those who are in grace. The Eucharist is both the symbol and the reality of this communion, when we receive It in ourselves as our meat and drink, in a signification of ineffable intimacy.

Our human social life is necessarily founded on knowledge and love. Without knowledge there can be no fellowship. Men who have never met, who have no relationships of any kind, either direct or indirect, personal or collective, do not form a society; there must be at least a common term to bring them into relationship. Kinship, calling, city, nation, all form such links, that is, the connecting social element which brings individuals into touch for mutual knowledge of each other, direct or indirect, and which makes of them a community. Knowledge is not enough; there is need for an effective tie, for the love that unites them so as to render it possible for men to live in community. Indifference creates separation, hatred divides; love unites. What ensues is a working together, according to the needs and ends of the community; this deepens knowledge and love by works of justice, order, peace, perfection. But since we are sensible beings, it is the life of feeling that makes a community effective and practical, increasing acquaintanceship, stimulating affections, releasing energies and helping to give the spiritual basis of society the natural means of affinity and consolidation. Because of the self-seeking and perverse inclinations in each one of us, this ideal picture of human society is never realized; but the elements which nature provides and the finalism inherent in nature, lead us to picture to ourselves the ideal society.

These very characters of natural society are carried into the new and higher society of us with God and of God with us. This, too, is a society founded on knowledge and love, and made visible by sensible means which correspond to our sensible nature and that of our society. It cannot be questioned that God knows us and loves us. How could it be otherwise? Are we not His creatures? He could have left us in the natural stage resulting from our reasonable nature; He wished us to become His adopted children and partakers of His divine life. Theologians are right to insist on the absence of any exigency of grace in human nature; only so can we understand, after a fashion, God's infinite goodness to us. But this should not be made into an opposition in which the terms Nature and Grace and Nature and God are hypothetically contrasted. In excluding the idea that nature could call for grace as something it requires, nature is often imagined as set in contrast to God, as an alien and autonomous principle. This is not the case. Human nature had from God its being and its place in the world; and like all creatures finite in themselves, it is by this very fact passively predisposed to receive some other principle which, in the ladder of being, shall perfect it and make it rise a little higher towards the perfection of the First Principle.

The plant is a living being complete in itself. As such, it does not demand sensitive life, but it is presupposed by sensitive life. In the abstract, we may discover in it a "passive" disposition to sensitive life. It is the same with sensitive life in regard to human intellectual life, all in a natural order. When a being has a mind and a will to love, it has what is necessary, as a premise, for a new life to enter into it, through which knowledge and love can pass from the created order to the uncreated. The first is called *nature,* the second, *super-nature,* precisely because there is an abyss between the created and the uncreated order.

It is true that grace, as theologians describe it, is a created gift which makes us partakers of uncreated life; but grace is not an entity that can exist in itself. God exists in Himself, Grace Increate; created grace exists in us, men, angels, and the manhood put on by the Word, and makes us partakers and co-fellows of the Godhead. Therefore such grace, though created, is not of the natural order but supernatural, in that it is created outside any natural order, as an act of co-fellow-ship with God. Without created grace, it would be impossible to conceive of a real communion between ourselves and God. The want of grace would make us incapable of supernatural knowledge and love; just as he who has no eyes is incapable of seeing and he who has no mind incapable of understanding. Theologians rightly insist on the conception of created grace, to avoid the error of emanationism. Indeed, a divine emanation which left us our personality would be of an unconscious character, which the mind rejects; and if, on the contrary, the emanation gave us the divine personality, it would obliterate our own — all men would be incarnate godheads, which would lead to a most strange and inconceivable pantheism.

God has wished to leave us our whole being, our personality, our liberty, even our faults, our wretchedness, our freedom to sin. He has respected everything in us, and at the same time He has given us a divine gift, so that we may come to communion with Him. A mysterious fellowship is born between the finite and the infinite; souls become the brides of God. We say to Him: "Take possession of us." He replies that He has already taken possession of us by His grace. We ask Him to strengthen our mind that we may the better know and our will that we may the better love. He replies that He has done so by the faith, the hope, the charity which He has infused into our souls. We say then yes, we believe, we hope, we love, but we want to prove it by works. He replies that He has given us the infused cardinal virtues and the gifts of the Holy Spirit. We seek to sing the divine epithalamium, breaking into praises and jubilation of love. He reminds us that He has placed His words on our lips to praise Him and has given us wings to follow Him wherever He may go, and has prepared for us the immortal marriage-bed in an eternal glory. We then, in the ecstasy of such a union, cry that "it is not we who live, but it is Christ who lives in us"; that "our life is hidden with Christ in God"; that "in this life that which is temporal is swallowed up in that which is eternal"; that we "are changed from brightness to brightness"; that "it is the whole Trinity that dwells within us" and we "are lost in the infinity of God." Thus, now and in the future, our communion with God begins and is perfected.

* * * * *

"Everyone who loves is born of God and knows God. He who does not love does not know God; for God is love." Thus St. John in his First Epistle (4:7-8). As we meditate

on this passage in the light of Johannine thought, the connection between the three themes, "birth, knowledge, love," becomes clear. On the mystical plane they are equivalents. The knowledge of God comes through being His sons, born of Him by grace, and such sonship is through love. How would it be possible to know God without loving Him? There is no knowledge of a good as such, as desirable and pursuable, without love. The deeper the knowledge, the stronger the love; the keener the love, the more intimate and close-cleaving the knowledge.

Those who make of knowledge a purely representational faculty, those who translate it into an existential judgment, without cleaving heat or without repulsion, abstract from reality, ignoring the finalistic character of knowledge, leaving out of count the movement of sympathy towards truth, of recoil from error as such, and the desire to seek that grain of truth that every error contains. Knowledge is a principle of love; the knowledge of the true good, insofar as it is real and full knowledge, is undoubtedly love. To know God is equivalent to establishing a relationship with Him, inasmuch as we recognize Him as our Creator, our first principle and our last end. Revelation presents Him to us as Father, Redeemer, Comforter, who makes us partakers of His divine life itself. Love is the same knowledge realized in the relationship of sons to their father.

Those philosophers who conceive of a strictly rational God, as prime mover, as creator or rather as architect of the universe, reduce the relationship of man with God to a metaphysical dependency. This relationship is stripped of any cleaving will, of any sense of love; there is no communion in it. The God whom we conceive is the God to whom the prophet Jeremias said: *"But Thou, O Lord, art among us, and Thy name is called upon by us: forsake us not"* (14:9);

He is the same of whom St. Paul affirmed to the Athenians on the Areopagus: *"For in Him we live and move and have our being, as indeed some of your own poets have said: 'For we are also His offspring' "* (Acts 17:28). The presence, the participation of God, His being in the midst of us, His dwelling within us, are all approximate expressions of His intimacy with us, so that we may say that in Him is our life, our activity, our being.

Giambattista Vico, in one of his profound intuitions, declared that man does not know through "clear and simple ideas" (which as such may represent either truth or error), but by becoming after a fashion himself the cause of the true, inasmuch as he is the cause of the fact that is converted into the true. God knows all the things that He has created according to His archetypal ideas; man knows what he makes or remakes within himself and outside himself. He knows nature in the measure that he makes it his own and after a fashion remakes it to draw it closer to himself. And he knows God insofar as he can succeed in experiencing the Godhead in himself. Man has experience of God as traditional historical consciousness (the common belief of mankind); as individual consciousness (what today is called experience of the divine); as revelation individually and socially realized (the primitive revelation, that of the Hebrews, that of the Gospel).

Vico's theory carries us to the heart of our problem: knowledge is experience, it is life, it is love. We may invert the terms: love is knowledge and it is life; life is knowledge and love. Only in the synthesis of the three terms can we conceive the totality of our being, both on the natural and on the supernatural plane, not in isolation (which would not be possible) but in communion with others. The gardener in his own little garden which he has planted knows the history and needs of every plant, of every flower; he knows his garden's

remotest corners, because he loves it. If he did not love
it he would have abandoned it. Weeds would have grown
up without his knowing how, they would have stifled
the seeds once planted and forgotten, and the plants with
forgotten names would pine away. The garden would no
longer be his; it was not born of him, he would not love it
and therefore he would not know it.

*"He who is of God hears the words of God. The reason
why you do not hear is that you are not of God"* (John 8:47).
Thus Jesus to the Jews. Earlier He had said: *"The father
from whom you are is the devil, and the desires of your father
it is your will to do"* (ibid. 44). These words did not mean
that the Jews to whom Jesus spoke were not creatures of God
and were not of the seed of Abraham, but that their works
were those of men who had renounced God. This renunciation
was implicit in the fact that they would not hear God and
hence were no longer of God. The two terms are convertible:
such are not sons of God because they will not hear Him
(that is, they do not know Him as God); or else they will
not hear Him because they are not sons of God (that is, they
do not love God as their Father). Either love fails, or knowledge fails; the one leads to the other. And this failure takes
away the source of sonship, cancels the relationship of communion. It might be said to bring a change of nature, from
sons of God to sons of the devil. The devil is the lie set
against the truth, which is God. He is pride (self-seeking,
schism, heresy, idolatry) set against the charity which is God.
There thus comes about a dissociation from God and communion with Him ceases, for true love and true knowledge
have ceased.

It is because of this that at the root of such communion
stands faith. God has given us a mind to know Him according
to nature, and He gives us faith to know Him in a super-

natural way. The natural mind remains in its degree, rendered able to know those natural things that are presupposed by revelation or spring from it, but it is faith that brings us into the divine mystery. We cannot fully grasp the revealed mystery; this is beyond our forces. But we are able to know so much of its infinite reality, of its manifestation to men and of the authoritative truthfulness of this manifestation, as is necessary to allow us to enter into communion with God.

The synthesis of natural intellect and supernatural faith, of human perceptions and of revelations of infinite mysteries, is made in the heart; it is made in the cleaving will. *"Corde enim creditur ad justitiam, ore autem confessio fit ad salutem,"* writes St. Paul to the Romans.[1] Faith becomes working conviction, justifying grace; the profession of this faith gives us salvation. In the natural order the knowledge of truth is a cleaving of the will, an operative act, and it is the same in the supernatural order, from the psychological standpoint, although, through the lack of evidence for the reason, it calls for a stronger inclination of the will. And in natural life, too, the more a truth is veiled and difficult to discern, the more man seeks it and loves it. The acts of intuition revealing a hidden truth often indicate the affection brought to bear on its quest, so that we cannot discern how much in the intuition is due to intellectual research and how much to the affection of volitional sympathy.

In any form of knowledge there is a beginning of communion *sui generis* between the knower and the object known. It may be asked: Is there perchance a communion between the botanist and his collections, the chemist and his retorts, the cartographer and his maps? Under a certain aspect we might say that it is a communion with himself, a projection of his

---

1. *"For with the heart a man believes unto justice, and with the mouth profession of faith is made unto salvation"* (10:10).

own ego, of his work, of the affection he bears to the things he has produced and which receive from him the imprint of his paternity. But there is also another mysterious communion, that of things in their reality. For they are not pure matter devoid of a ray of thought but the reflection of the thought that makes them be and react, each in its own fashion, repeating secret ideal correspondences which we translate as categories, species, essences, reasons of being; believing perhaps that these are our own invention, whereas they are gleams of invisible rays that reach us. Through nature, studied or worked upon, contemplated or transformed, set in a museum or traced in drawing, we reach an instinctive communion, not reflective and almost not willed, with higher entities; we shape their symbols, their myths, we pick out their rhythms, their harmonies, we sing their beauty. Either we come through nature to God or we stop short at nature, perhaps deifying her; but our communion is with all that which, known as reality, we come to perceive as truth, truth seen as good, desirable, lovable, so that we are drawn by its beauty and fascination.

The natural order is necessarily presupposed by the supernatural. Our very faculties act with their natural possibilities even in the supernatural order. To enter into true communion with God would have been impossible had He not revealed Himself to us. That is the starting point for the ineffable communion. Our mind as such could have only a rational knowledge of God, and this neither clear nor unmixed with error; but it is God who makes Himself to us the Revealer of Himself, of His life, of the manner in which He renders us partakers of His very life, calling us His children. It is not the case of the revelation of a truth that does not touch us save as distant and indifferent onlookers, but of one that concerns us as God's communication of Himself to us. The revealing act is a social act.

When a man is told that his wife has given birth to a child, his first child, he is not given news of a speculative reality but of a new relationship, the highest and most important that exists for him on earth, that of fatherhood and sonship. A new communion exists, even though the child is not able to understand it and it is felt and enjoyed by the father alone. The same thing happens, in another order, in the Baptism of babies. God knows that this child belongs to Him, has received sanctifying grace, has entered into the lot of the children of God, even if the child does not know it, even if he will not know it for many years, even if, by chance, he will never know it. Who knows how many graces will be given him after the first grace, of which, through no fault of his, he knew nothing? or how the inner voice will speak to him of a blessed past of which he will have known nothing and of a future of peace to which he aspires without any clear knowledge of it?

What a wonderful fellowship is that of man with God! And what can be the root of such a fellowship if not a living faith, faith perfected by hope and charity? St. James in his Epistle says: *"The devils also believe, and tremble"* (2:19). But the faith of the demons is not the same as the faith of the just. The one is a dead faith, and therefore they *tremble;* the other is a living faith, and therefore they *love.* The first have no communion with God; grace is lacking to them. The second have such communion, because their faith is made living by charity. The knowledge that the demons form of God is not full knowledge; their sin to which they obstinately hold makes an impediment to the knowledge of God as a Father, of God as a Redeemer, of God as a Comforter. They know the punitive justice of God through their sin, for, while knowing God, they continue to measure themselves with Him and to wish

to be as gods. Their sin of pride is no ladder to lead to God,
it is the abyss that separates them from Him.

*   *   *   *   *

The communion which is life and knowledge is perfected
in love. God has given a commandment that we love Him.
"The greatest and the first commandment," Jesus calls it,
replying to the Pharisees. As children must love their parents,
not only by feeling and natural attraction but by the duty of
sonship, so we creatures and children of God must love Him
in response to His love, for all that we are comes from His
infinite goodness.

The love of God is presented to us as a commandment
for the sacrifice of ourselves that it implies. The attraction
exercised on us by the good in general, referred, by reason
and by faith, to the Godhead, is not wanting. But though our
mind may draw us near to Him and faith present Him to us
as the Father who first loved us, yet the more we are attached
to ourselves and for our own sakes to the persons and things
surrounding us, the more we do not feel the attraction of
His love.

That the varied attractions of earthly love should draw us
away from God is due to the weight of our humanity, which
drags us down notwithstanding revelation and grace. Hence
the character of a precept given to love of God, which should
be nothing else than the spontaneous and complete correspond-
ence of love, so that we may observe all His commandments as
embraced by the moral, natural and revealed law; these all depend on the commandment to love Him, and in it are synthesized and raised to a higher plane as the fundamental and
final reason of the whole rule of life that is given us.

"If you love Me, keep My commandments" (John 14:15).
Here is the consequence of love, the observance of the divine
commandments. The same thing happens in the human order.
Those who love their parents, their children, their husbands
or wives, their betrothed, their friends, seek to please the beloved persons, to fulfil their wishes, to anticipate their requests,
to sacrifice themselves for them. Thus, through self-surrender,
they tend to make themselves like to those they love. Every
love has its laws and its sacrifices. To enter into the communion of love means to establish this competition in self-
surrender for the other's sake, in self-sacrifice for the other's
sake, as an indissoluble nexus between love and action.

If this is not so, it is no longer a case of love between
human beings but of self-seeking; the exploitation of the
feeling of love for his own advantage in one, the servitude
of love without recompense in the other. Vulgar pleasure in-
filtrates into love, a pleasure that passes from voluptuousness
to sadism, to anger and to ill treatment, to the enjoyment of
suffering and humiliation, or to a thirst for vengeance and
blood against the one believed to be the loved person. In
human life love and self-seeking alternate, like the moments
of generosity and those of abjection. In our relations with
God such alternation means that we are still subject to sin.
Self-seeking drives out love, self-seeking is sin.

By self-seeking is meant an inordinate self-love, preferen-
tial or exclusive, which overcomes the love of God in the
practical observance of the divine precepts. An ordered love
of self is not self-seeking. Jesus Christ told us to love our
neighbor as ourself, to mete to others the same measure as to
ourselves. Self-seeking filters in when we prefer ourselves to
God and our neighbor, when in loving ourselves we do not
at the same time love God and our neighbor.

Love of our neighbor does not fall outside our communion with God; it is, we might say, an integration of it, or better, it melts into it. Jesus Christ spoke of two precepts of love, the love of God and the other, like unto it, the love of our neighbor. The precepts are two, but the love is one; the objects are two, but they resolve themselves into one. St. John writes in his First Epistle: *"If anyone says, 'I love God,' and hates his brother, he is a liar. For how can he who does not love his brother, whom he sees, love God, whom he does not see? And this commandment we have from Him, that he who loves God should love his brother also"* (4:20-21). The reason for this kind of identification of the love of our neighbor with the love of God is given by St. John in the same Epistle, where he says: *"Beloved, let us love one another, for love is from God. And everyone who loves is born of God, and knows God. He who does not love does not know God; for God is love. In this has the love of God been shown in our case, that God has sent His only-begotten Son into the world that we may live through Him. In this is the love, not that we have loved God, but that He has first loved us, and sent His Son a propitiation for our sins. Beloved, if God has so loved us, we also ought to love one another"* (4:7-11).

God, our Father; men, His children. The whole human family called to this filiation through Jesus Christ, God and Man. In His manhood our brotherhood is hallowed; the ties that through Jesus Christ bind us to God and to one another are ties of love; in each man we find the sign of the love God has for him. There is only one love, that which St. John and St. Paul call charity, the virtue that comprehends all virtues, to possess which is sanctification.

St. Paul, in his celebrated hymn to charity, does not draw any distinction between the objects to which it is directed, God and our neighbor, but he extols the qualities which refer to the practice of this virtue in the present world. Nothing has worth compared to charity, he says, neither the tongues of men and of angels, nor the gift of prophecy, the knowing of all mysteries and all knowledge, nor faith, nor the sacrifice of a man's goods and of himself (if made without love). What like is charity? *"Charity is patient, is kind; charity does not envy, is not pretentious, is not puffed up, is not ambitious, is not self-seeking, is not provoked; thinks no evil, does not rejoice over wickedness, but rejoices with the truth; bears with all things, believes all things, hopes all things, endures all things"* (1 Cor. 13:4-7). St. Paul's words can refer only to charity towards our neighbor, but the charity towards God is implicit, for it is the one charity which, united to faith and to hope, forms the theological triad of our life, of which triad "the greatest is charity." When all of this world shall have passed away, when faith shall end in sight and hope in possession, charity will remain, never to end, in communion with God.

Jesus, in order to show how love towards God lies implicit yet in its fulness in love towards our neighbor, describes the Last Judgment as founded on what each shall have done for his neighbor; this shall weigh as though done for the Son of God and King of all, Himself. The just will ask Him: *" 'Lord, when did we see Thee hungry, and feed Thee; or thirsty, and give Thee drink? . . .' And answering the King will say to them, 'Amen I say to you, as long as you did it for one of these, the least of My brethren, you did it for Me' "* (Matt. 25:37-40). And St. Paul in his Epistle to the Romans, after speaking of subjection to the authorities and summing up the duties of justice — *"Render to all men whatever is their due; tribute to whom tribute is due; taxes to whom taxes are due; fear to whom fear is due; honor to whom honor is due"* — continues: *"Owe no man anything except to love one*

*another; for he who loves his neighbor has fulfilled the Law.
For 'Thou shalt not commit adultery; thou shalt not kill; thou
shalt not steal; thou shalt not covet'; and if there is any other
commandment, it is summed up in this saying, 'Thou shalt
love thy neighbor as thyself.' Love does no evil to a neighbor.
Love therefore is the fulfilment of the Law"* (13:7-10). In
these last words the negative essence of love is given: to work
no evil to our neighbor; and as though to recapitulate the
whole teaching of the chapter, St. Paul concludes: *"But put
on the Lord Jesus Christ, and as for the flesh, take no
thought for its lusts"* (ibid. 14). To put on Jesus Christ,
according to St. Paul, is to become like to Him, to be per-
meated by His grace, which is charity. The final recommenda-
tion, not to arouse the lusts of the flesh, touches the root of
the spirit of self-seeking which quenches charity towards God
and towards our neighbor, the pride of the flesh.

Theologians, considering the character of the obligation in
our relations with our neighbor, distinguish between what is
due in justice and what is due in charity. This analysis leads
to a differentiation between the two virtues, and in this case
charity is not taken in its universal value as supernatural love
of God and our neighbor (including love of ourselves as children of God), but as the moral virtue of doing good to others
(beneficence). Those of a secularizing turn of mind on the
European continent have preferred the word "philanthropy"
to "charity" (in the narrow sense), to take away its traditional
Christian implications. From a higher and wider standpoint,
any good done to our neighbor, even that which is his due
in justice, should be animated by love and thus, objectively
speaking, embrace the act of love. Justice, too, not in the
juridical but in the ethical and supernatural sense, is animated
and quickened by love.

This universality of love in our supernatural life and its specific nature as communion with God have led some to identify charity with habitual grace. From the metaphysical and objective standpoint, the two should be kept distinct, inasmuch as habitual grace is a habit created by God to make us partakers in the divine life. But from the mystical standpoint, grace and charity melt one into the other, for *"God is love, and he who abides in love abides in God, and God in him"* (1 John 4:16).

Here is the central point: God is love. He is substantial Love, we are partakers in such a love. He is absolute Love, we live by this love. True love of ourselves and of our neighbor resolves, perfects, engulfs itself in the love of God or it is no longer love. If we think that we love ourselves and others as ourselves, while leaving aside the love of God, or else having no reference to God, or worse, denying any such reference, our love will no longer be true love: the essence of love will be lacking.[2] Love by its very nature seeks to become absolute, and for that very reason it seeks God, is transformed in God, has peace in God alone. When God is lacking we seek the absolute love in ourselves or in something extraneous to complete ourselves. But any such attempt must fail.

A man and a woman in loving each other believe in their love as unfailing and eternal. They seek the data for its perpetuity in the family they create, the children they expect, in a future that will continue after death. If all passes and the moment of love does not return, then the memory of a happy past takes the place of an unhappy present, or a better future gives the hope of a return of love. How small a disappoint-

---

2. There are some Good Samaritans who work very disinterestedly and energetically for the poor, though they do not have religious faith and are not thinking of God; but they implicitly and unconsciously love God Himself in their neighbors.

ment shatters their illusions! And how easily their love changes into hatred! The need for the absolute had not found its complete satisfaction.

It is from a similar need that men are led to give a dis-proportionate value to the social group as a substitute for God — the family, the clan, the tribe, the nation, the race, the State — to which they attribute perpetuity and even an absolute quality. These are not taken as convenient names for the various social relationships, but rather as extra-per-sonal, self-subsistent realities, which are even deified, with attribution to them of mind, will, power. Thus the love of the group comes to be celebrated as an absolute, demanding the sacrifice of ourselves and others (by instinct, rather of others than of ourselves); personal self-seeking and an arro-gant sense of dominion are confused with the quest for the collective welfare. The social group thus conceived is the negation of a human brotherhood extending beyond the group; it is the selfish exaltation of those who are part of it. In such a conception the absolute is transferred from God to the social group; there is no room for God. Those who would have made humanity an absolute substituted an abstraction for the concrete group. The true absolute cannot be an idea; it must be a reality or it is not absolute. Love of humanity which is not a love of our common brotherhood in the Father-hood of God loses itself in sentimentalism.

The true absolute is God. If he were merely a physical or metaphysical principle, the logical primary, the unmoving first mover, we should have no communion with him that could induce us to love, no love that could arrive at com-municative union. But our God is personal, in His mysterious Trinity-in-Unity. He has given the proof that He loves us in creating us, in revealing Himself to us, in sending us His Son to redeem us, in communicating to us His Spirit, who is Love. We have not seen God, but we see our brethren, and our first Brother is Jesus Christ. *"Nor does anyone know the Father except the Son, and him to whom the Son chooses to to reveal Him"* (Matt. 11:27). Who will that be? *"Come to Me, all you who labor and are burdened, and I will give you rest."* And then? *"Take My yoke upon you, and learn from Me, for I am meek and humble of heart; and you will find rest for your souls. For My yoke is easy, and My burden light"* (ibid. 27-30). What can it be, this easy yoke and this light burden? It is the law of love. *" . . . The charity of God is poured forth in our hearts, by the Holy Spirit who has been given to us"* (Rom. 5:5). And it is the same Holy Spirit who dwells in us. Since He is substantial love of God, to Him must the love poured forth in us be attributed. And as love makes reality an experience, so the Holy Spirit who is the Spirit of Truth makes us love by knowing and know by loving, in an ineffable communion of life in which, when it is the true life of love, *"the Spirit Himself gives testimony to our spirit that we are the sons of God"* (ibid. 8:16).

To deepen such life in communion with God and with men in truth and love is to find the absolute goal of our most intimate aspirations. All creation, then, is resolved into that life; there all events have their center, that which is without is brought into our inmost soul, where we find the Spirit of God to illuminate, guide, excite, warm, inspire, perfect. Then by the virtue of charity we come to that true union with God and with men for which Jesus prayed the night before His sacrifice on the cross, turning to the Father, saying: *"The glory that Thou hast given Me, I have given to them, that they may be one, even as We are one: I in them and Thou in Me; that they may be perfected in unity"* (John 17:22-23).

CHAPTER V

MYSTICAL UNION

B Y THE raising of humanity to the supernatural life and by our vocation to salvation, we are all potentially in union with God. By the communication of sanctifying grace we are habitually united to God in mystical communion. By the acts of combined faith, hope, and charity we render such union actual. Through the gifts of the Holy Spirit and the Sacraments, we increase the grace and the theological virtues that hold us united to God, as we advance in the way of perfection. The mystical union is thus at the beginning and at the root of our supernatural life, which must move towards its consummation.

In the whole of actual supernatural life there is mystical union with God, since there is sanctifying grace, making us "consorts of the divine nature," and the charity which contains in this present life both faith and hope, bringing us into the communion of love. We call this union mystical because it is a participation in the divine nature; it is distinct from natural union with God as Creator, Disposer, Providence and End of mankind. We call it mystical because it is hidden and dark to our reason and to common experience, but revealed by faith and indirectly experienced in the practice of virtues and in the way of perfection.

In a strict and special sense, mystical union is the name of the infused contemplation in which union with God is experienced in an almost habitual manner. While it is esteemed a privilege (not useless for us who have not the privilege, because by knowledge and desire we may in a certain manner have a part in it),[1] such union in infused contemplation is founded on the union through sanctifying grace. The difference between the baptized child and the saint who has reached the apex of perfection is not one of nature but of fulfilment, of development, of degree. Both are mystically united to God, both have in themselves the title to salvation and the seed of the beatific vision. Yet what is fitting for the sucking babe is not fitting for the grown man; the first has not the exercise of his faculties, is not exposed to the trials of life, has not to fight and overcome temptations. As in natural life, so in the spiritual life: there is a preparation, a fulfilment, a development towards the degrees of perfection.

The union with God which is given as a free gift cannot be preserved nor increased without our coöperation. A first and basic law is that of the fecundation of such union. Like the buried talent in the Gospel parable it cannot be left barren under pain of loss. The other law is that of development and is like to the first: those who have reached a certain degree of union cannot turn back without harm. A law of fecundation, a law of development. Through the first we may not remain idle — *"Why do you stand here all day idle?"* (Matt. 20:6). Through the second we may not turn back — *"No one, having put his hand to the plow and looking back, is fit for the Kingdom of God"* (Luke 9:62). The two laws interpenetrate in the divine precept: *"You therefore are to be perfect, even as your heavenly Father is perfect"* (Matt. 5:48). The whole of the spiritual life is a striving for perfection. The mystical union is realized ever more intimately and fruitfully the more we become like to the Father.

---

1. St. Paul says: *"The manifestation of the Spirit is given to everyone for profit"* (1 Cor. 12:7).

Theologians observe that in this life there can be no perfect state but only a process towards perfection, not only because imperfections and venial sins are not always avoidable but also because the two chief factors of perfection, grace and charity (and both whether habitual or actual), may always indefinitely increase in the soul. That grace as the principle of supernatural life is also the principle of perfection and that the fulness of grace is perfection itself, is self-evident. The angel's salutation to Mary — *"Hail, full of grace, the Lord is with thee. Blessed art thou among women"* (Luke 1:28) — is significant heavenly testimony. Moreover, there is no charity without grace, nor grace without charity, nor union with God without grace and charity. Perfection is the continuous increase in grace and charity of all the virtues.

If perfection in this world is never complete but always growing, sanctity may be considered as the summit of perfection characterized by the attainment and practice of the theological and moral virtues in a heroic degree. This is not a static conception, for sanctity too has its endless ladder rising towards God, so that it too means a continuous development in perfection. In the philological sense of the words, which influences the formation of ideas, perfection is a fulness of life, sanctity a consecration to God. In the supernatural life the two are at root equivalent; but whereas there is no sanctity that is not perfection in a heroic degree, there is a perfection which, because it does not reach the heroic degree, cannot be considered sanctity.

Two points must be retained as basic to the idea of spiritual perfection: that all the other virtues whether as habit or as practice, are means for the conservation and increase of grace and charity; and that a constant tendency towards perfection and a desire to attain and deepen it are implicit in the effort to conserve and increase grace and charity. It is by two points that we should appraise what is known as the *askesis*[2] of the spiritual life, both in those who are dedicated by religious vows and in those who live in the world.

Askesis, in the current common usage of theologians, means the method of reforming and perfecting the spiritual life through active application of the will in the observance of the Christian precepts and the practice of the counsels of perfection, by each according to his state. It is distinct from *mysticism,* which concerns a higher state of union wherein the soul, by a special gift, lends itself to the mysterious operations of God. This distinction is simply an analytical one, to indicate the differences in the use of the words, or to serve as a didactic method of classification. If we are to understand the true nature of spiritual *askesis* and of *mysticism,* we must go deeper in our analysis of what separates them and what unites them.

In regard to the attainment of moral virtues, the Christian *askesis* has the same biopsychological basis as the Stoic or naturalistic *askesis.* By both man may succeed in acquiring the habit of virtues, of abstinence from fleshly pleasures, of renunciation of ease and wealth, of patience and gentleness, of silence and recollection, and so on. But the specific natures of the two schools, the Christian and the naturalistic, are altogether different, for the Christian *askesis* means a deepening of the supernatural life, which is love of God, whereas the other arrives only at the conception of a human perfection. Any Christian *askesis* is thus mystical by its very nature. The perfective effort is either in union with God, that is, mystical,

---

2. With the narrowing of the sense of the word *ascetic* we have in English no word that corresponds to the Italian *ascetica.*

or it is not Christian. We call it unitive and mystical because either it is united with charity (habitual and actual grace), or it is directed to regaining charity (penitence) ; otherwise it has not a Christian character.

I have said elsewhere that any act of virtue if performed with purity of intention, that is, without a secondary aim bringing separation from God, is either an act of supernatural virtue or leads towards the supernatural state. What is said here is not contradictory, but is the other side of the problem. If virtue is willed for its own sake, as an end in itself, whether it be poverty or chastity or abnegation, then an ascetic effort is certainly present; but because the mystical root which would give it life is lacking — that is, the union with God which alone confers a supernatural character on moral virtue — such virtue remains detached from the center of life, unquickened by the divine sap, the shadow of virtue only, in spite of all the spiritual striving that has gone to produce it.

That is why I have said that perfection consists, not in the attainment of virtues as such, but in the deepening of our union with God, for which the attainment and increase of virtues are means — either necessary, like the theological and cardinal virtues, or useful though not necessary, like the state of poverty, chastity and obedience, to which not everyone is called.

The mortification of the will, of the intellect and of the senses, the practice of spiritual and corporal penance, are ascetic means for acquiring self-mastery, for overcoming our passions, for becoming capable of elevations of the spirit. But if such practices do not pass from the natural plane to the supernatural, they will increase our vanity and pride in a more subtle and treacherous form, producing moral self-complacency and even self-worship.

The first fruit of a Christian *askesis* is that of detachment from sin and love of sin, from the world and love of the world. This cannot come about without the love of God; the ascetic means will have value only insofar as they are animated by love. It is because sin denies the union with God through love that it is the death of spiritual life. *"He who does not love abides in death,"* says St. John (1 John 3:14). It is because the world loves sin and causes sin to be loved that the world is the enemy to be fled. Therefore the sons of God, the followers of Jesus Christ, the faithful Christians, "are in the world" but "not of the world." This was the testimony of Jesus to His Father on the eve of His sacrifice.[3] To be in the world but not of the world demands detachment from sin and from affection for sin; it means to be with the Father through Jesus Christ, "sanctified in the truth," against the lie represented by the world and by the prince of this world. To be "sanctified in the truth" is in this sense a sacrifice, as Christ's sanctification was a sacrifice: *"For them I sanctify Myself, that they also may be sanctified in truth"* (John 17:19). And He adds: *"I have made known to them Thy name, and will make it known, in order that the love with which Thou hast loved Me may be in them, and I in them"* (ibid. 26). Here is the true spiritual perfection and the mystical union in its full process, reaching a kind of unity between man and God, a complete consummation: *"ut sint consumati in unum."*[4]

*   *   *   *   *

------

3. *I have given them Thy word; and the world has hated them, because they are not of the world, even as I am not of the world. I do not pray that Thou take them out of the world, but that Thou keep them from evil. They are not of the world, even as I am not of the world. Sanctify them in the truth. Thy word is truth"* (John 17:14-17).

4. *". . . that they may be perfected in unity"* (ibid. 23).

In order to describe the perfective process, theologians
usually note three stages or ways: the way of purgation, the
way of illumination, the way of union. Others in more formal
terms distinguish the stages of the beginners, of the progressed
and of the perfect. From the standpoint of the process towards perfection the second classification is the more suitable,
while the first indicates better the prevailing characteristics of
the three stages. I say the *prevailing* characteristics because
at bottom in all three stages we find purgation (by active
penance or by passive trials), and knowledge or illumination
(by faith and the gifts of the Holy Ghost), and union with
God by charity and grace. But from the standpoint of the
perfection sought, each stage has its own character. The way
of purgation leads to detachment from all that is sinful or
that may lead to sin or that in a certain fashion tends to lead
away from God insofar as we remain attached to ourselves
and to creatures. The way of illumination has as its special
character an opening of our minds to spiritual knowledge,
not in a theoretical or abstract manner but through understanding, experience and actuation. The way of union is not
only based on the union by habitual grace, but it is, I may
say, its living actualization, forming a special habitude of
union of mind and will with God, a continuous presence of
God in us, a nearly uninterrupted contemplation, even in the
midst of the work and exigencies of outward life; our will
cleaving ever more closely to that of God, so that we can say
that the will of God is in us.

Turning this classification into practical guidance, mystical writers usually place in the first stage those who have but
lately turned from sin to God — not those whose conversion
was a miraculous transformation, as in the case of St. Paul,
but those who in their conversion carry with them in the
ordinary way the residue of past passions and evil habits,

which must be vigorously fought against. To the same stage are assigned the lukewarm: those who, while they have progressed spiritually, do not make enough effort to avoid habitual venial sins. And finally, this is the stage of those who have not taken pains to go forward, confining themselves in the normal way to avoiding grave sins.

In substance, all these may be called only beginners.[5] They may lack the idea of perfection, the sense of having to go forward if they would avoid backsliding, or an exact conception of what perfection demands. For the most part, they are the people too much taken up with family or professional matters, with the business and anxieties of outward life, so that they neither find time for inward recollection nor have acquired the habit of it, being too readily dissipated among many things. Yet if the effort to avoid grave sins is real and constant, if after a fall they rise up at once, seeing the abyss of sin and feeling supernatural sorrow for it, if frequentation of the Sacraments and daily prayer are among their good habits, it may be said of them that they are in the way of purgation and on the first stair of the ladder of perfection.

In the Psalms and the prophets this idea is clear: not sinning is likened to well-doing, and God does not fail to give His help and comfort.[6] Ezechiel places this criterion on the Lord's own lips: the man well-pleasing to Him is he who fulfils the duties of justice, who has not been an idolator, nor

---

5. Bishop Mario Sturzo writes: "If a religious or even a lay person makes no progress in praying and mortifying himself, his soul does not remain in the first steps of the spiritual life, but withers, as Father Garrigou-Lagrange says" (*Orazione e Adorazione,* Torino, Editrice Piemontese, 1939).

6. Ecclesiasticus says of the rich man: "*Blessed is the rich man that is found without blemish: and that hath not gone after gold nor put his trust in money nor in treasures. . . . He that could have transgressed, and hath not transgressed: and could do evil things, and hath not done them. Therefore are his goods established in the Lord . . .*" (31:8, 10-11).

an usurer, nor a calumniator; who, in conclusion, *"hath walked in My Commandments and kept My judgments, to do truth: he is just, he shall surely live, saith the Lord God"* (Ezech. 18:9). Thus does Jesus speak to the adulteress: *"Go thy way, and from now on sin no more"* (John 8:11). Thus does He speak to the paralytic at the pool: *"Behold, thou art cured. Sin no more, lest something worse befall thee"* (John 5:14).

To avoid sin and to keep the law and the precepts is in itself the beginning of the perfective process, the first stage in the life of union. But it is not possible to avoid sin and to keep the divine commandments without prayer and the use of the Sacraments, at least in explicit or even implicit desire for those who cannot actually partake of them. Thus in most cases these points are stressed for the faithful living ordinary lives, since otherwise it would be impossible for them to live an initially supernatural life and to move forward towards the degree of perfection to which each has been called.

There is in fact a vocation to perfection and it is the vocation of all. And there is a particular vocation that is bound up with all the spiritual conditions of our life, with the course of our activities, the way in which we follow the impulsions of good — in a word, with our response to grace. This is an important point for our supernatural life. God knows to what degree of perfection He has predestined us, and gives us the graces to reach it; we are under obligation to respond to them. This is a general obligation, failure in which does not translate itself into sin unless we actually fall into sin; but neglect of the voice of God, of His impulses, of His illuminations, leads us astray from our path of perfection and salvation.

The ways of God to lead us to perfection are inset in all the conditioning factors of our life. They often remain hidden from us because we do not see the spiritual sense underlying what happens to us and around us. We do not succeed in hearing the voice of God, often as soft and light as the breath of a little wind upon our faces; if we are not attentive we fail to note it, and it has gone. That is why we need from time to time to leave the occupations and preoccupations of earthly life, to bring back our mind to God in prayer, to acquire the habit of seeking God in all happenings and of cleaving to His will.

The prayer that Jesus Christ taught us is not a magic formula nor a collection of devotional phrases, it is the synthesis of our life of union with God, the prayer of every instant. Calling upon God as our Father, we unite ourselves to Him with the affection of sons. The hallowing of His Name embraces all our duties of worship, subjection, adoration. In calling for the coming of His Kingdom we call for the triumph of good, of justice, of love, over the kingdom of Satan, the world, injustice, hatred. And in the fulfilment of the divine Will is our humble and loving cleaving to the providence, mercy and justice of God. The realization within us of the Name, the Kingdom and the Will of God, leads us to requests nearer to our personal and social life — the daily bread that sustains us, the forgiveness of sins (which we extend to our brethren, each to the rest), the forestalling of temptations and the liberation from every evil.

This prayer is life, it is the realization of life, it is friendship with God. Any prayer either is life or it is a vain sounding of words and wandering of thoughts; it is the life of actual and act-ful union with God, in consideration of the divine mysteries, in adoration, in thanksgiving, in offering, in petition. The intimacy with God which is gradually gained by prayer impels us to pass beyond the stage of occasional, sentimental prayer, often made under the pressure of painful hap-

penings or of earthly hopes, towards a meditation on the
mysteries of the Redemption, on our wretchedness, on our
final destiny, in which a deepening of our understanding
mingles with the affective prayer of the heart, and finally
burgeons as the flower of a true piety.

Yet another step towards a higher goal. Affective prayer
leads us to contemplative prayer, in which the understanding
of the divine mysteries becomes loving intuition. The affections, passing beyond the stage of feeling, becoming a cleaving to God. Intuition and cleaving grow into contemplation,
in which discursive thought disappears, the passage from one
affection to another is arrested. The contemplation becomes
focal, tending towards an absorbing quiet, in which there may
be even that instantaneous obscure experience of God, as
when the heart for a moment pauses in its beat and then
returns to its usual rhythm.

This process of prayer is part of the process of perfection: both because there cannot be a perfection that is not
obtained with prayer, nor a response to divine graces,
that is not corroborated by prayer, and because a spiritual life
in daily relationship with God and with our neighbor — a
relationship of love — cannot be achieved unless its flame is
kindled by prayer. And thus prayer is in fact a necessary means
of supernatural life, and not only a means, but itself a vital
and perennial act, just as breathing and the beating of our
hearts are our very life and their cessation is death.

It may be said that prayer sums up our spiritual life and
is the sign of our union with God. It is based on two fundamental and intrinsic acts — purity or rightness of intention
and cleaving of the will. By the first we exclude any end
that is not related to God, His glory, union with God, the
love of God and in God of our neighbor, and that is not
completely subordinated to Him. By the second, cleaving to

the will of God we carry it into ourselves to fulfil it in our
lives. These two acts are presupposed by prayer, they are
prayer, they are the fruit of prayer. It is true that on this
earth we cannot maintain such an intention and such a cleaving constantly and actually without a privileged grace, but it
is enough that they should be virtual in all our daily acts
and renewed when necessity arises and as often as possible,
for them to become a habit of mind and will, the rule of all
our actions, a reminder in time of temptation, a solid groundwork for the further process towards mystical union.

* * * * *

Right intention draws all our activities nearer to God, it
makes us seek Him for Himself, it orders and coördinates in
Him all other ends, human and spiritual. Right intention is
not something extraneous added to our activity from without;
it is on the contrary its interiorization, the carrying into the
supernatural plane of the whole of natural life, as we ourselves
are carried by a gift that becomes the very value of our life.
*"Whether you eat or drink, or do anything else, do all for the
glory of God"* (1 Cor. 10:31). This Pauline precept does not
alter the direct and natural ends of our actions, it at once
embraces and transcends them. In the Epistle to the Romans
we find a polemical passage concerning the dispute between
the Judaizing and the Gentile converts over the use of certain
foods and the days of the traditional Hebrew rites, to which
the former felt themselves especially bound while the latter
did not mean to be held by them. St. Paul wishes to lead both
beyond the spirit of attachment or conflict which creates a
particular finalism at the expense of the higher finalism, the
intention to God. He uses one of those happily chosen, comprehensive formulas which has resounded through the ages

as a perpetual recall to realities: *"For one esteems one day above another; another esteems every day alike. Let everyone be convinced in his own mind. He who regards the day, regards it for the Lord; and he who eats, eats for the Lord, for he gives thanks to God. And he who does not eat, abstains for the Lord, and gives thanks to God. For none of us lives to himself, and none dies to himself; for if we live, we live to the Lord, or if we die, we die to the Lord. Therefore, whether we live or die, we are the Lord's"* (Rom. 14:5-8).

Theologians rightly note that a good intention does not make a bad action good, but it makes an indifferent action good and adds goodness to a good action. The intention must be directed to God as Supreme Good and Last End, and it is this that illuminates the intermediate ends, making them means in respect of the last end. The intention is what the Gospel calls the "eye" — vision of the end, cleaving to the end.[7] The idea that a right intention could coexist with bad means (the theory of the end's justifying the means), or that a right intention could render good an action in itself evil, springs from two fundamental errors. The first is, that the intention is something superadded to the action, whereas the intention is the action itself realized in its spiritual inwardness; the second, that there is no objective morality, that is, that the agent is a norm to himself.

Right intention does nothing other than render actual and efficacious, in all particular actions, the supreme end of man, which is God; it is in substance an act of love, the fundamental motive of our life. Particular ends, even if good in themselves, may detain us as intermediate stations and withhold us from going further in the way of perfection and of

7. *"The lamp of the body is the eye. If thy eye be sound, thy whole body will be full of light. But if thy eye be evil, thy whole body will be full of darkness"* (Matt. 6:22-23).

actful union with God. The practice of right intention breaks away from all that misleads, perturbs, distracts, retards or lessens the fervor of the way of perfection. The Gospel precept, *"If thy hand or thy foot is an occasion of sin to thee, cut it off and cast it from thee"* (Matt. 18:8), indicates the process of detachment from all things insofar as they are or may be a motive drawing us away from God, a detachment which only right intention can render effectual and constant.

Yet another step. Right intention as the light of our action and the goal of our will is not enough. The will of God must become our will. Here is the complete fulfilment of the obedience to God of which Christ gave us the example, *"taking the nature of a slave and being made like unto men. And appearing in the form of man, He humbled Himself, becoming obedient to death, even to death on a cross"* (Phil. 2:7-8).

The precept of conformity to the will of God is fundamental. The prayer of the Our Father centers in the *"Thy will be done."* Jesus Christ, at the moment of facing the sacrifice of the cross, prays in Gethsemane: *"Father, if Thou art willing, remove this cup from Me; yet not My will but Thine be done"* (Luke 22:42). This is the confirmation of the new kinship established by Christ for His disciples: *"Whoever does the will of God, he is My brother and sister and mother"* (Mark 3:35). This kinship means the following of Christ. Therefore, to the disciples who said to Him, *"Lord, let me first go and bury my father,"* Jesus replied, *"Follow Me, and leave the dead to bury their own dead"* (Matt. 8:21-22). He spoke thus not because He did not recognize the duty of sons to care for their dead, but to show the spiritual detachment necessary from whatever might dissuade or withhold men from following Him.

It is therefore fundamental for our life of union to know what the will of God for us may be. *"For this is the will of*

God, your sanctification," St. Paul would write to the Thessalonians; *"that you abstain from immorality; . . . that no one transgress and overreach his brother in the matter. . . . For God has not called us unto uncleanness, but unto holiness"* (1 Thess. 4:3, 6-7). And to the Ephesians he would write: *"For you were once darkness, but now you are light in the Lord. Walk, then, as children of light (for the fruit of the light is in all goodness and justice and truth), testing what is well-pleasing to God; and have no fellowship with the unfruitful works of darkness, but rather expose them"* (Eph. 5:8-11). To search out what pleases God (*quid sit beneplacitum Deo*) should be the care of each one of us, in our personal life, in our inmost conscience, in our outward activity; we should seek an ever closer conformity to the divine will, not external and formal, but as a compenetration of life. This is St. Paul's thought where he writes to the Romans: *"I exhort you therefore, brethren, by the mercy of God, to present your bodies a sacrifice, living, holy, pleasing to God — your spiritual service. And be not conformed to this world, but be transformed in the newness of your mind, that you may discern what is the good and acceptable and perfect will of God"* (Rom. 12:1-2).

Both passages mark the connection between our earthly life, the use of our body and of material goods, and the knowledge of what is pleasing to God, what is good, what is His will in us. Those who conform to the manners of the world, who have a disordered care of the body, who live in darkness, cannot succeed in knowing the will of God, nor in fulfilling it. Jesus said: *"Blessed are the pure of heart, for they shall see God"* (Matt. 5:8). To see God is not only the final goal; it means also to know Him in the darkness of this world as the light of truth, to feel Him as the attraction of love, as the will to be fulfilled. Purity opens a window on heaven from

which a ray, passing through the gross and opaque things of
the world, reaches the soul. Immediate experience of truth,
contact with the good, with that which is pleasing in the
sight of God, is possible only in detachment from what is
impure and worldly. Thus each will be able to know and fulfil "that which is pleasing to God," that is, the will of God
applied personally to himself.

It is usual to speak of doing the will of God when we
are overtaken by disappointment, sickness, private or public
misfortune, by things which at bottom go counter to our
wishes and to the human will, individual and collective. It is
then that we remember Gethsemane and the prayer of Christ,
and end by accepting, difficultly and painfully, the will of
God. This disposition is so habitual that usually the idea of
the divine will as providential order, as redeeming economy,
as love universal and particular towards all creatures, as a
giving out to us of the supernatural life, is lost sight of.
The idea of our cleaving to the will of God as coöperation
in love, as actful and constant union of our life with His,
I will not say escapes us, but does not take root.

At bottom, resignation in time of sorrow, acceptance of
our moral and physical crosses, shows whether our cleaving to
the will of God is truly complete, or whether we cannot succeed even in repressing the movements of revolt; whether,
worse, we do not seek to console ourselves by cleaving im-
moderately to created things, forgetting God and His law;
or whether, on the contrary, we seek to penetrate deeper into
the mystery of the divine will by complete and perfect acceptance of what it wills of us. In this last case, there comes about
a *catharsis,* a transforming passage of purification, a going out
of ourselves to enter into God and to live in the orbit of His
will. To follow Jesus on the way of the cross means a progressive purification in detachment from ourselves, from our self-

complacencies, from that self-love to which, alas, we tend at
every moment, even in the spiritual life.

Therefore we distinguish between God's will and His
permission in regard to the free activity of intelligent creatures and the effects of their freedom of choice. It may be
said that all evil is due to our fault and all good to the will
of God, inasmuch as it is we who, refusing to fulfil the will
of God in ourselves, seek good in error, in deviation, in self-
centeredness. This cannot be said to be willed by God. He
cannot will self-centeredness, hatred, injustice, but on the
contrary must condemn them. Yet He has willed this moral
order in which free and intelligent creatures may even revolt
and do evil. But so that nothing should remain that is not
ordered to good, from the evil that created beings may commit He draws a greater good, not only in the order to come
but even in the present order. This divine dialectic, drawing
good from evil and reducing all evil to good, is nothing other
than the fulfilment of the sole and sovereign will of God,
who has made and ordained all to His glory.

To this sovereign will we are subject, though preserving
our character of intelligent and free created beings and acting according to our own dialectic. Only the cleaving to the
will of God, whether it guides us to action for good, or
whether it follows the action and makes us hate the ill done,
unfetters us from the dialectic of evil by a higher liberation.
The *catharsis* of our purified will is accomplished, in every
happening, in the fulfilment of the will of God. It is in us
conformity and resignation, patience and penance, union and
love. Because of this even our faults and spiritual failings,
which we hate as an offense to God and which we strive not
to repeat, may be for us motives of good, insofar as they urge
us to a more actful and constant union with the will of God.

The acceptance of the will of God, thus conceived, does not in any way rob us of initiative or coöperation or activity. It takes from us only our self-centeredness, as a motive of action or as complacency in having acted. This self-centeredness is, in the language of spiritual writers, pride; the cleaving to the will of God is its counterpoise, humility.

It is not easy to gain an exact idea of the virtue of humility, and still less easy to practice it. If all the virtues either resolve themselves into charity or are not true virtues,[8] this is especially true of humility.

Humility is founded on truth, for it makes us understand the infinite distance between creation and the Creator, and draws us closer to our fellow-men in brotherly solidarity in which no one may believe himself better or higher than the others. It makes each one of us appraise truly the place he should occupy in creation, casting out the lie of pride, of vanity, of self-complacency, and every injustice that makes us set ourselves above others and before God Himself. Some believe that humbleness consists in an outward affectation of speech and manner which takes away from each personality its own character and enfeebles the affirmations of the individual conscience. No! Such humility is false, nor was it ever practiced by Jesus Christ, who "humbled Himself." He vindicated the rights of truth, those of His divine and human Personality, those of His initiative in proclaiming the Good News and in bearing witness to the Father.

Humility, too, is founded on charity. Truth and charity are correlative and in their synthesis express the will of God, for it is truth and charity in His infinite act. Thus St. Paul

---

8. I do not say this in the sense that some have given to it, i. e., that there are no virtues distinct from charity, but in the sense that every virtue, while having its own character, cannot pass as true without the breath of charity.

shows the union in Jesus of humbleness, obedience and the act of infinite charity in giving His life for us: *"He humbled Himself, becoming obedient to death, even to death on a cross"* (Phil. 2:8). For us proud and sinful men it is needful to overcome that self-esteem, that vain and lying valuation of ourselves over others, which forms the root of our self-centeredness and pervades even our spiritual life. In every sin there is implicit a preference of ourselves to God, and of ourselves to others — it may even be explicit; sin is an act of pride that contains in itself lying and egoism, a triple negation of truth, charity and submission to the will of God. Even the imperfections of the spiritual life have the same source as the sins, grave or minor, into which we fall.

The mind seeks to know, but, as St. Paul warns us, we should "know with soberness," within the bounds of humility, recognizing that mystery surrounds us and the infinite absorbs us, that knowledge by itself "puffs up," whereas "charity edifies." The will seeks mastery, but here too bounds are set: *"Let . . . him who is the chief [become] as the servant"* (Luke 22:26). Government is not dominion, but ministry. Subjection is not servitude, but obedience and coöperation. Thus humbleness is not feeble-heartedness, just as obedience is not passivity. Humility and obedience are qualities of action; they accompany the responsibilities of initiative, the effort to overcome obstacles, to bear witness to the truth, to practice charity, to cleave to the will of God.

The social relationship between inferior and superior, between child and father, between pupil and master, is nothing other than spiritual. It is our relationship with God extended to human relations. It is our subjection to God making us subject to others in that order which is the divine will. Thus Jesus, speaking of the Pharisees, who claimed to be called fathers and masters, directed: *"Call no one on earth your father; for One is your Father, who is in heaven. Neither be called masters; for One only is your Master, the Christ"* (Matt. 23:9-10). In this command Jesus made it understood that subordination to another man is such only insofar as it is a subordination to God; that discipleship of one man to another is such only insofar as he teaches what Christ taught. And Christ declared: *" ... I am He, and of Myself I do nothing: but even as the Father has taught Me, I speak these things. And He who sent Me is with Me; He has not left Me alone, because I do always the things that are pleasing to Him"* (John 8:28-29). Thus the fellowship between the Father and the Son, between God and the Messias, a fellowship of intimate union (which is the Spirit of Truth and Charity) is prolonged in a way in the human relationships founded on truth and charity. The relationship of teaching and of obedience (the divine will to be communicated to the world and fulfilled in it) is that which exists between the Father and the Son made Man and obedient unto death. We should fulfil in all our actions this will of God, doing, like Jesus, "always the things that are pleasing to Him."

To cleave to men as such, taken as fathers and masters, is untruth, division, pride: *"For whenever one says, 'I am of Paul,' but another, 'I am of Apollos,' are you not mere men? What then is Apollos? What indeed is Paul? They are the servants of Him whom you have believed — servants according as God has given to each to serve"* (1 Cor. 3:4-5). Thus St. Paul reproved the Corinthians. To declare oneself for a man, for a faction, for a school, is to pride oneself on an empty name; it is to seek a share in dominion through divisions and schisms made in the mystical body of Christ, as divine sonship and human brotherhood. To be of God, to hear the voice of the Master, to follow Jesus, is an act of

union, of truth, of humility, of acceptance and obedience to
the divine will.

When it is said that obedience should be blind, it does not
mean that he who obeys should not inquire into the authority
in whose name he is commanded, or the spirit animating the
order and the object set for him. Otherwise we could not
repeat, with Peter and John: *"Whether it is right in the sight
of God to listen to you rather than to God, decide for yourselves"* (Acts 4:19). This does not come from a spirit of
pride, but corresponds to the Gospel precept: *"If anyone comes
to Me and does not hate his father and mother, and wife and
children, and brothers and sisters, yes, and even his own life,
he cannot be My disciple"* (Luke 14:26).

It is commonly stated as part of a certain individualistic
conception of society that obedience to other human beings —
parents, masters, religious superiors, civil authorities, magis-
trates, military leaders — lessens the responsibility of the subject. This is because authority is conceived of as self-subsistent,
outside the limits of moral order and of supernatural relationship, outside a constant and single reference to the divine
authority which, providing for the coexistence of the two
orders, natural and supernatural, wills that both should be
fulfilled within us. To separate human authority from the
relationship of responsibility to God is to vitiate both these
orders, producing irresponsibility and often immorality in
commandment, flattery and feeble-heartedness in obedience.
All the human relationships of both personal and collective
life need to be carried back to the cleaving to the will of
God, as universal authority, as indefectible truth, as infinite
charity.

This cleaving is perfected in the abandonment of ourselves to God. By the practice of this virtue we may come to

the state of abandonment that Père de Caussade describes thus: "a continual dependence on the Spirit of God and His grace, which makes the soul no longer seek in herself to occupy herself [with God] . . . but to hold herself before Him in simple readiness; to accept gladly from moment to moment what He may will or may not will, . . . not by a certain eagerness and wish for action, but solely so as to hold herself ready for action. . . . "[9]

The practice of abandonment is an *askesis,* a purification. The state of abandonment is its fruit, the mystical pacification. We must overcome what the world of time brings us of perturbation, anxieties and distractions, by a serenity beyond time; the spiritual present swallowed up in God. The past is no longer in our hands: it belongs to God's mercy. The future is in the hands of His providence. The present alone is ours — the act of love, of union, of trust in God, of cleaving to His will, of awaiting His coming, His inspiration, His grace, so as to be able to say, with St. Agatha: "My heart is firm in God." What counts in the life of the spirit is the present, where past and future meet in the single living reality. De Caussade says truly: "What comes to us at each moment, by God's order, is what is holiest, best and most divine for us," for "God's order, His divine will, is the life of the soul, whatever the appearance under which the soul applies it to herself or receives it."[10] The ever present, that which is life for us, must be transported from ourselves to God; no longer the present of ourselves to ourselves but the present of God to us, indeed, the presence of God within us.

9. *L'abandon à la Providence divine,* posthumous work, Vol. I, Avant-Propos, p. x; Paris, Libraire Lecoffre, J. Gabalda et Cie., 1934.
10. Ibid., Vol. I, Livre Premier, ch. 1, §§ IV, V.

To make this presence of union plain we have only to refer it to the experience of our lives, not as an imaginative and stimulating adaptation, a beneficent autosuggestion, but with the cleaving of faith, of hope, of charity. It is the supernatural reality that comes to transform our daily life with its trials, sufferings, aspirations, desires, activities, into an awaiting of God within us in a state of ineffable and total abandonment. It is not at all a cessation of all our initiative, which would be error and deception, but a disposition of the soul which transforms our initiative, making it no longer ours but God's, and making our action depend no longer on our will but on that of God. Our attentiveness to discern within us the presence of God will be as that of Elias to discern the presence of God in the little wind that breathed upon his face; that we may feel at every moment God's proposal to us and our quickness for response, transform our inner activity into passivity or better, receptivity, attentiveness, docility to the voice of God, and translate our outward activity into the self-surrender of obedience, humility, holiness.

St. Paul tells us that all our actions should be done in the name of God, since from Him they have their beginning, in Him their meaning, for Him their end. And he says also: *"In all things give thanks; for this is the will of God in Christ Jesus regarding you all"* (1 Thess. 5:18). Time and again he repeats these promptings, to show how the events of daily life, the trivial actions, the petty trials, enter a transforming atmosphere at the touch of grace which illumines them; just as the dust suspended in the air is illumined at the touch of the sunbeam, or, better, as the atoms of our body are made partakers of the vital breath of the soul. Such atoms have, so to say, their autonomy, their movement, a kind of atomic individuality, a world of their own, but this world can subsist and live only through the vital influx of the soul, cessation of which scatters them, bringing death.

To reach the state of true abandonment to God we must shed our egoism, we must pass through the phase of self-disintegration. We think of ourselves more than we know and more than we would wish. As we carry self with us throughout our life, the sense of our own person, of our own thought and will, of our own activity and satisfaction, is naturally keen. It accompanies us everywhere, even into the sanctuary, in our hours of meditation, in our most sacred moments of surrender and sacrifice for others and for God. In prayer itself we often speak too much and speak of ourselves, we listen to ourselves even when we strive to listen to God. Both the prayer which we find welcome and that which repels us often take us from God and give us back to ourselves. Disintegration of our egoism can be attained by the practice of abandonment to God. Then nothing can disturb us from the outer world, which we shall esteem as being for us what God has willed; nothing will attract us save God Himself; everything, every happening, will be for us the image, the touch, the revelation of God. We shall forget the world around us, our thoughts and desires, our wills and aspirations, to live by what God sends within of thoughts, desires, will, aspirations. The future? It is God who makes it; when it comes it will be as willed by God. Death? Let it come how and when God shall permit. Purgatory — the reward? They are accepted and willed in the divine will. Through abandonment in God we do not consider the reward in itself, for our satisfaction, but as unconditional, complete, total cleaving to the will of God, as the transformation in Him in whom all things are comprehended and engulfed in pure faith and pure love.

In order to characterize the state of abandonment in God, spiritual writers describe it as a passive state of the spirit in which the initiative is left to God purifying, activating, creating within us a new heart. To be exact, the initiative in our sanctification is never ours but God's. He first loved us, as St. John says. Revelation, sanctifying grace, actual graces, infused virtues, gifts of the Spirit, the Sacraments, the Church of which we are part, are all gifts freely given, divine initiative. If we can do nothing of ourselves — and the Gospels say so and St. Paul so teaches — and can do all things in God through Christ, we must above all seek to subordinate ourselves to the divine initiative and the divine work in us.

But sanctification is not only the work of God; it is also our work, as the response of love, the will to serve, to obey, to follow. All this may be looked upon as our activity. Though our acting is not of ourselves or for ourselves, in God and for God it is still our will, our effort, our coöperation. We thus share in the work of God, though often mingling with it the faults, the vanities, the resentments, the impurities, the pride, of which we are made up. This is the bundle of wretchedness bound up with our fallen nature, and left us as a motive for humbling, mortifying and purifying ourselves. To this end two methods may be applied, according to our needs and our stage of progress towards perfection, the active and the passive. The first, known also as the ascetic method, is to strive for detachment from ourselves and from the world by the practice of virtues, by the mortification of base instincts, by spiritual and bodily penance. This method is not complete. The second, or passive, method is not its opposite but an advance and a completion. When a stage of perfection has been reached in which our faculties are rendered more docile and obedient to the empire of will, cleave more closely to the moral values of the law of God and of the Gospel counsels, are more detached from earth and more united to God through the continual renewal of acts of presence and through habits formed in this perfective *askesis,* then our passive qualities will develop better. These are not pure passivity but also action.

The prevalence of what are known as the passive states gives its chief character to the phase of higher life which we call mystical in the strict sense, and which fulfils itself in contemplation, whereto it tends as its inner exigency. Therefore it is usual to distinguish in the spiritual life between active and contemplative. It must not be thought that in the active life there is not at least a beginning of contemplation (any form of true prayer is an initial stage of contemplation), nor that the application of the active method is wanting in every stage of contemplative life, which would be absurd. But in the one contemplation prevails over action, and in the other action over contemplation.

Needless to say, the words are not being used here in the sense in which they are currently applied to the religious orders, which are classified as contemplative, active or mixed. These terms show the monastic or apostolic character of the different congregations, and not the inner spiritual life of each of their members. One man may reach the highest degree of contemplation while being a member of an active order, such as the Jesuits, or, on the other hand, a member of a contemplative order like the Trappists may have remained at the practice of the active virtues without contemplative progress. We find great contemplatives even among laymen and laywomen living in the world, and we may fail to meet them among monks and hermits.

That for which Jesus gently rebuked Martha was not activity in the service of the house, but lack of unification: *"Thou art anxious and troubled about many things; and yet*

only one thing is needful" (Luke 10:41-42). Many things
instead of one thing, the necessary one; so the Master concludes: *"Mary has chosen the best part, and it will not be
taken away from her"* (ibid. 42). To talk with Jesus is the
best part. This can be done, as many spiritual souls find,
while they are looking after the house, doing the cooking,
tending their children, caring for the poor, even pursuing
business, but holding fast in God to the best part, where all
is unified and transformed into an aspiration of love, in a
union not only habitual and subconscious but a living part
of experience. Little by little a manifold and distracting
activity becomes unified activity, through right intention
habitual and ever-renewed, through cleaving to the will of
God. This cleaving assumes the character of abandonment
to God, first as an exercise of virtue, then as a state of soul
developing our receptive and obediential qualities under the
influx of divine action.

This ineffable passivity, which does not remove us from
our activity but which detaches us from it insofar as it detaches
us from the outer world and from our own inner world, is
signalized by contemplation. And since any effort we may
make at detachment cannot avail to render it effective, it is
God Himself who works in us if we are ready to receive in
docility, trust and abandonment His mysterious action in the
contemplative process.

Normally, detachment begins to effect itself in us when
we truly understand the mystery of pain, through adversities,
disappointments, sicknesses of body and spirit, misfortunes
in our undertakings, when we are wounded in our affections,
or in the life, whether social, political or religious, in which
we share. This normal way of the cross, this summons to
daily sacrifices, little or great, is the lot of all. He who understands that the summons is from God, makes it bear fruit

in life; he who does not understand, fails to do so at the cost of his own spiritual death. Yet even those who understand that the summons to the cross is from God, though accepting it with resignation and suffering it with patience, do not reach an entire detachment from themselves and from the world without the direct action of God received in a state of complete abandonment.

* * * * *

Contemplation is the flower of the mystical life in its various stages, which run from affective meditation up to the direct experience of God. Prayer is defined as speech with God — *colloquium cum Deo* — and as a raising of the mind in God — *elevatio mentis in Deum.* There cannot be speech with God without a raising of the mind, nor can there be any real thought of God which does not develop into a colloquy. Any really living thought translates itself into meditation or into action, that is, at bottom, into a communication of ourselves to ourselves or to others, a colloquy that becomes communion. Otherwise it is not a living thought, but only a fleeting motion of the mind or a useless dreaming. Hence the distinction between mental and vocal prayer is only formal. A true prayer is always mental; it will be called vocal inasmuch as it may be said or sung, but if it is prayer it is made with the mind and with the heart, it is at once elevation and colloquy.

In vocal prayer we may pass from one sentiment to another, as the words that we say or sing guide or remind us, though we may also hold our minds fast to a particular and central consideration. In mental prayer we stay unwaveringly at the consideration of a divine mystery or of a principle that unites us to God, and as our affections move the prayer becomes an intimate colloquy, often without words. In both ways of prayer we are drawn away from the things of earth, from the practical concerns of ordinary life, and are given the means of feeling ourselves in touch with God, as the Father in whom to confide, as the Lord to be adored and praised, as the End towards which to strive. And this in union with Jesus Christ, our Redeemer and Brother, the Beginning and the Center of our salvation; in union with Mary, Mother, Co-redemptress and Mediatrix; in union with the saints and angels, with our guardian angel, with the whole world of our faith and of our hope, to which we are bound in charity.

In periods of lukewarmness prayer may become so wearisome that we are unable to go beyond the outward formalism of the rite, save in exceptional moments. In time of intimate pain it brings comfort, if this is not an illusion when faith is too weak. In the period of conversion, of penitence, of fervor, prayer is truly a spiritual consolation and is hungrily sought. But during the stage which is usually called the second conversion, when we pass out of the way of purgation into the way of illumination, or, better, when from beginners we become proficients, God usually intervenes to purify us of our spiritual sensibility by depriving us precisely of the consolations of prayer. This is now called by all the night of the senses. Each one will know it according to the inward experience that he may have had in the spiritual life, the gifts and qualities that may be his, whether supernatural or psychological (grace though it raises nature does not suppress or distort it), his acquired dispositions, and the trials which God Himself permits him to undergo in the measure of his strength, for God does not try us beyond our possibilities.

The night of the senses is the privation of those attracting spiritual sweetnesses which have their seat in natural sen-

sibility, affection, bliss, comfort in sorrow, transports of love.
Periods of dryness and comfortlessness come, there is a sense
of emptiness, fear of the future, the torment of human
wretchedness, anxiety, dread of eternal reprobation. It is thus
that God removes us from the satisfaction of spiritual allurements which might be sought for themselves and the enjoyment they bring, and which might arouse in us feelings of
vanity, complacency and egoism. The practice of meditation
becomes difficult, prayer often a torment, outward actions are
made without any actual reference to spiritual motives, till
it seems that in our inner life there is no longer any unification in the quest of supernatural ends, nor any recall to God,
who gives us the impression that He has gone far from us.
Whether this night of anguish is long or brief, it is a trial
of detachment, preparing us for a purer contemplation of
the divine mysteries, for a more disinterested contact with
God, for a loftier life of love. The contemplative prayer that
follows the first dark night is tranquil prayer, a foretaste of
a period of quiet that will come later. It is a simple looking
on supernatural things with restful affection, without reasoning about them, without the arousing of tumultuous affections,
without warmth of imagination — *the raising of the mind to*
God by the simple intuition of ardent affection. The mind is
fixed on God as on an attractive darkness, a twinkling orientation. This experience is a quest, an aspiration, a finding by
one who knows not fully that he has found, feeling that he
holds Him, that he possesses Him, without yet being able to
feel Him in himself and to have mysterious and real contacts with Him.

This form of contemplation is normally an acquired contemplation, a practice of the presence of God with the ever-
growing detachment from self and from the world, a mortification of the natural faculties and of personality by a total

abandonment in God in humbleness and trust. It is an initial contemplation, which opens out from time to time into the prayer of quiet, which may be for fleeting periods raised to the degree of infused contemplation, but which may often return to being simply affective meditation or even discursive meditation, according to the inner oscillations of a spiritual life which has its crests and troughs, its riches and its poverties, and which is experienced accordingly as we respond to the impulses of grace.

In acquired contemplation we may reach a certain general and confused attentiveness to the presence of God and a sense of adoration and love without acts of particular virtues. The knowledge of God as of an Infinite Being comprehending all the perfections our mind can conceive, deepens without the help of imagination. Any manner, positive or negative, of reaching God by contemplation, gives us only a sense of sinking ever deeper into an unknowable infinity, into an inapprehensible presence which we know by faith to be near us and in contact with us.

*   *   *   *   *

The true contemplation of which the mystics speak is that contemplation infused, by a special gift of God, through which the soul reaches an immediate intuition of the divine truths and an experience in a sure though dark manner of the presence of God. Whether this gift is a new and extraordinary habit derived from the gift of wisdom, or whether it takes the form of an intellectual species infused by God into the soul so that it may thus have a superhuman (we should say angelic) cognition of Himself is a question debated by theologians. To the present writer it seems more accurate to say that the

contemplative state attaining the experience of God is of itself
a privilege. While not exceeding the complexus of the supernatural founded on grace, such a privilege may be considered
a foretaste of the beatific vision. All know that sanctifying
grace is the seed of the beatific vision. The union with God
in this world through faith, hope and charity is a participation in the divine nature, to be consummated in the vision.
Infused contemplation may bring temporary and obscure
glimpses of what such a vision will be. It is the splendor of
Thabor which yet has before it the Passion of Jerusalem. When
and if God wills, there comes the second night, called the
night of the spirit. God, who works out our perfection, God
gives Himself — and the soul, though feeling Him present,
not only derives no sweetness from it, but suffers a boundless
pain, a burning and purifying fire like that of purgatory. The
will is stretched out to God and feels that it loves Him. The
mind has intuition of His presence. But the whole soul suffers
by it in dryness, comfortlessness, desolation. For how long?
It may be even for long years, as with St. Teresa of Jesus,
St. Paul of the Cross, Sister Mary of the Incarnation.

Infused contemplation is usually differentiated into three
steps, according to the mode of the experience of God. The
contemplation of quiet is the first step, known as imperfect
union. The second is perfect union, either simple or ecstatic
(the latter in a transient manner). Finally there is the third
step, union or experience of God in a lasting manner, which
is usually called transforming union. The soul in this last
phase gains consciousness of her participation in the divine
nature. As knowledge, it remains obscure, but the certainty
of the presence and intimacy of God is ineffable. *Divine
touch, experience of God, divine intimacy,* are poor words to
give us an idea of what human tongue cannot tell.

All the ardent language of those who have had the privilege of the transforming union cannot reveal to us what they really see. We only understand that in them the thought of their own *I,* the reference of even their supernatural life to their own personality, ceases — a state expressed by the words *annihilation, nothingness;* they are swallowed up in God. Yet the world of earthly relationships has not vanished as though lost in the infinity that absorbs the mystic; it is refound, but in a different way, for it is refound in God. Thus the mystic pours back upon his brethren the flame of love with which he burns, and becomes, even without knowing it, an apostle, a luminary, a lighthouse for the many who creep like worms on the earth without wings to fly. And he pours it back, too, upon the rest of creation, animals, plants, inanimate things, on which falls a ray of spirituality revealing the imprint of the Creator.

Even the highest degree of mystical experience does not rob the privileged person of his own personality, in his psychological, cultural, moral activity. It does not take him out of his historical environment. He is that particular individual and no other. Thus we note the diverse and always personal characters of the mystics, so that not one is a copy of any other, but each is just what the complexus of his human and spiritual life has made him. Between the mystics of the early centuries, those of the Middle Ages and the moderns, we easily note the differences of period. And what differences between the mystics of Germany, Spain, Italy, France, Britain! A St. Francis de Sales, and still more a St. Francis of Assisi, would be inconceivable in Germany or Spain! But even among the inspired writers, the mysticism of St. Paul is wholly impregnated with the divine Personality of Jesus Christ, Head, Center and Life of the Church; while St. John the Evangelist makes Him live for us in His intimate life with the Father and in the outpouring of the Spirit, so that the dogma of the Trinity and that of the Incarnation are revealed to us in the supreme expression of love.

The whole varied and manifold mystical experience of twenty centuries of Christianity is the unfolding of the mysticism of the two great apostles, which embraces in a burning love God and their brothers in Jesus, the Center of all creation. How could it be otherwise? It is indeed Jesus who has reunited us to the divine Trinity and has made of two one — manhood and Godhead in the personal unity of the Word, in hypostatic union in which the beatific vision was granted to Him as man, from the first instant of the Incarnation.

The mystics have different experiences of the divine according to the dispositions of their spirits and the special grace with which they are privileged. One will turn his eyes to the Godhead of Christ, another to His manhood, another to the mystery of His earthly Life, Passion, Death; others to the Eucharist or the Sacred Heart. Jesus can never remain extraneous to the mystical experience of a Christian. He does not even remain extraneous to that of those who have not known Him. A Moses, an Elias, an Isaias, had experience of God, not of the historic Christ; but they knew of the Messias, they awaited Him, they prophesied His coming, they partook of the sanctifying grace that Christ would merit for all. Even in the mystical experience of non-Christians, Christ cannot be absent. Just as without knowing it they are of the invisible mystical body of Christ, so in the obscure experience of God they have the experience of salvation and of the Saviour. And without presuming that they have a personal revelation of the mysteries of the Trinity and the Incarnation, we think that if they are truly in mystical contact with God, they have that secret touch in which the mystery, neither unveiled nor revealed, may be felt in an ineffable obscurity.

There are some who believe that they find in St. John of the Cross a unitarian mysticism which, going beyond the mysteries of the Trinity and of the Incarnation, reached contact with God: the unity absorbing into itself all distinction, whether that of the mystic as one with God, or that of all creation as lost in God. But this would be an experience of semi-pantheistic aspect, in which the mind would outrun every other faculty, so that the love that should be the supreme expression of the transforming union would be supplanted by the intellective union. That there may be moments of pure intellective experience is perhaps not to be denied. Unfortunately, from the vague expressions, from the stammering words of the mystics, it is possible to gain equivocal impressions and to deduce inconsistent theories. But it must be denied that the true mystical experience stretches out to God as one without stretching out to the Trinity, or that in Christian economy such experience does not include in a positive, actual and efficacious manner the experience of Christ, God and Man. Again, any pantheistic sense is to be excluded. His own wretchedness, his own nothingness is the more deeply felt by the mystic the higher the degree that he has reached in the transforming union. The annihilation of self and of creation in God does not make self and creation God, but might be said to blot out all sense of relative and communicated reality for a spirit engulfed in the Reality that is Increate and Absolute.

* * * * *

Such is the essential position of the mystic who has reached the highest degree of infused contemplation, and it is also the position of the saint who has reached the highest degree of perfection. We must keep the mystic and the saint in two distinct categories, so as to ascertain the characteristics of the two types. It is not necessary for every saint to be a mystic in the strict sense, that is, for him to have obtained extraordinary graces such as visions, ecstacies, raptures. Many martyrs attained the heroism of giving their lives in witness to their faith without having passed through the mystical stages. Their perfection of faith and love was accomplished in the moment of decision of the will to prefer death to apostasy. What may have happened in their souls in the moment of this heroic decision, God alone knows. From certain accounts which history and legend have brought down to us about the martyrs of the early centuries, we know that the hours and days before their martyrdom were filled with divine comforts, illuminated by visions, like those told in Acts of the first martyr, St. Stephen: *"Behold, I see the heavens opened, and the Son of Man standing at the right hand of God"* (7:56).

Visions, ecstacies, miracles, are not necessary gifts for either the highest mystical grace or the perfection of sanctity. They are, for us, motives for belief, helps to hope, urges to love. Thus did Jesus reply to the disciples of John the Baptist: *"Go and report to John what you have heard and seen: the blind see, the lame walk, the lepers are cleansed, the deaf hear, the dead rise, the poor have the Gospel preached to them. And blessed is he who is not scandalized in Me"* (Matt. 11:4-6). If these gifts normally are given only to the saints, it is because the saints are in union with God in a heroic manner, so as to be witnesses to the truth, examples of virtue, apostles of good. But not all receive the same gifts; to some some, to others others, as God may judge fit. Of certain saints we know that they did not receive mystical gifts, or these did not appear, yet none the less they were saints, having attained heroic perfection. Others, instead, favored by God with infused mystical gifts (and such graces found in them psychiconatural conditions that were a preparation), have not attained the heroic degree of perfection, or at least that degree was not recognized and proclaimed by the authority of the Church.

But God knows well to what degree of grace and glory He has predestined each one of us, and though He wills all to be pure and perfect in His sight and does not give His beatific vision without the complete purification from every stain (and in purgatory faithful souls expiate what they have not purified on earth), yet not all will have the same degree of perfection and of merits, on earth or in heaven. A hierarchy of degrees and a stair of celestial beauties will form that eternal glory in which all will sing praises to God and all will be fast in Him, in the infinite Trinity-in-Unity to whose life humanity is united by the Incarnation of the Word. With this life will be associated as adopted sons, through the gift of the divine nature of which they will be made partakers, all those whom the Father gave to the Son and whom the Son saved by His merits, in truth and charity. This truth they shall see and by this charity they shall live everlastingly, in an even closer and deeper union, from brightness to brightness, while their triumphal hymn sings forever the infinite glory of God.

CHAPTER VI

THE GLORY OF GOD

I N ONE of the great scenes of the Apocalypse, St. John saw the vision of God sitting on a throne, with four and twenty elders with crowns of gold about it, and seven lamps burning before it, and four beasts full of eyes before and behind. Amid the lightnings and the thunders and the sound of voices that proceeded from the throne, the four beasts said: *"Holy, Holy, Holy, the Lord God Almighty, who was, and who is, and who is coming"* (Apoc. 4:8). And the four and twenty elders threw themselves down and cast their crowns before the throne, saying: *"Worthy art Thou, O Lord our God, to receive glory and honor and power; for Thou hast created all things, and because of Thy will they were, and were created"* (ibid. 11). Such scenes are repeated, and all are full of this exaltation of praise and glory to God, in joy and the singing of Alleluia — moments of adoration in the harmony of all created things.

The fundamental theme of this hymn of glory is the relationship of creatures to the Creator — "for Thou hast created all things." In truth, all things have their being from God. If they are, it is the will of God that fulfils itself in them. If they are as they are, it is the mind of God that has ordained how they should be. As for what they are, it is the divine ray that shines in them. The perpetual and joyful confession of this dependence is the hymn of praise and glory to God which all creatures owe Him in the measure of their capacity.

137

The divine thought is reflected in the whole of creation. Each creature reveals it in its own fashion; there is nothing that remains mute. But while subhuman creation, in progressive order and widening comprehensiveness, prepares the conditions for the appearance of thinking mind, its thought alone is able to grasp the message of creation and give it forth anew in praise to God. Thus man is by his nature a priest, who lifts up his mind and heart to God, giving Him glory and praise and love and thanksgiving in his own name and in the name of all beings. And he calls upon all creation to praise God as did the three young men in Babylon: *"O ye heavens, bless the Lord: praise and exalt Him above all forever. . . . O all ye waters that are above the heavens, bless the Lord. . . . O ye sun and moon, . . . O ye stars of heaven, . . . O every shower and dew, . . . O all ye spirits of God, ... O ye fire and heat, . . . O ye cold and heat, . . . O ye dews and hoarfrosts, . . . O ye ice and snow, . . . O ye nights and days, . . . O ye light and darkness, . . . O ye lightnings and clouds, . . . O let the earth bless the Lord: let it praise and exalt Him above all forever"* (Dan. 3:59-74).

The sharing by the universe in the praise that man offers to God is not only a manner of expressing a surge of joy, a glow of charity, a mystical exaltation, but implies the community of all being, inasmuch as we all are God's creatures, we have all within us the reflection of the divine thought and in a certain way we are His thought. Without that mirrored reality we should not be, creation would not be, matter would not be. Nothing is devoid of the value of thought, and it is this value alone that gives reality, being, life. Nothing can exist apart from the influx of the divine thought, unfecundated by it, without the Spirit that hovered when *"the earth was void and empty, and darkness was upon the face of the deep"* (Gen. 1:2).

The reality that lives in the whole of creation is the divine
Archetype, as the ancients called it, the creative Idea in its
realization. To this Idea we all belong, in ascending order;
the order too is creative Idea. When this order arrives at
man, it expresses itself in a thought conceived by a created
being. His natural, instinctive, primordial thought is joy in
living, a joy that reflects itself in all the outward life that
surrounds him, "joy-thought" that comes to understand itself,
to widen and to reëxperience itself as mirroring anew the
created world to which it has communicated itself. Reflection
and communication continue to alternate in widening circles,
with deeper meaning and in more vivid tones, till man is
able to grasp the origin of this joy-thought and of the joy-
reflecting-thought, as the sunbeam is traced to the sun. Then
does joy become praise, a song of praise, a sharing of knowledge and of life. Then does man feel himself the true representative of creation, in whose name he, interpreter and
priest, sings to God the hymn of glory.[1]

Lucifer fell with his hosts because he sought for himself
the glory due to God: *"I will ascend into heaven. . . . I will be
like the Most High"* (Is. 14:13-14). Adam fell with his mate
because they sought the glory due to God: "You shall be as
gods." Man was redeemed by Him at whose birth the angels

---

1. Epictetus knew this truth, when he wrote: "Well then: because
the most of you are blind and insensible, was it not necessary that
there should be someone to fill this station, and give out, for all men,
the hymn to God? For what else can I, a lame old man, do but sing
hymns to God? If I were a nightingale, I would act the part of a
nightingale; if a swan, the part of a swan. But since I am a reasonable creature, it is my duty to praise God. This is my business.
I do it. Nor will I ever desert this post as long as it is vouchsafed
me; and I exhort you to join in the same song" (*Moral Discourses,*
translated by Elizabeth Carter, E. P. Dutton & Co., Inc., New York,
1937; quoted with the permission of the publisher).

sang, "Glory to God in the highest," by Jesus who repeated all His life through, "I seek not My own glory."[2]

What is the glory of God, of which He is thus jealous? and which Jesus faithfully vindicated on all occasions, with words full of self-surrender, reserving to the Father alone as source of the Godhead all honor, excluding that He Himself as Man and Son of Man could usurp it for Himself? Men seek and love glory. This means for them the fame of their deeds or of the works of their minds, the recognition of their merits, the honor due to them as persons or to their dignity. But there is no human glory that is not contested, no fame that does not wither, no honor that may not change into dishonor. Jesus as Man on earth had His hour of glory when He entered into Jerusalem amid a crowd crying, "Hosanna to the Son of David," and bearing palm leaves and olive branches in sign of jubilation. But a few days later, and Jesus was condemned to the death of the cross, forsaken by His disciples, insulted by the crowd, mocked by His executioners.

Men may also be feasted, honored, glorified through adulation, through fear, with the lips and not with the heart, for politeness' sake, the mind denying the honor that is outwardly paid. Such is often the glory of the mighty. True glory means a recognition of true merit, with the love that such recognition begets in us, together with a sense of inferiority, of dependence, of subjection. Where there is envy there is no glory, nor where there is pride. In such cases any glorification is a fiction, a contradiction, baseness.

The glory that we owe to God is founded on the knowledge that we have of Him, and is hence an act of truth and justice.

---

2. In St. John's Gospel we read: *"Among the rulers, many believed in Him [Jesus]; but because of the Pharisees they did not acknowledge it, lest they should be put out of the synagogue."* And the evangelist notes: *"For they loved the glory of men more than the glory of God"* (John 12:42-43).

Of truth, inasmuch as we set in their proper spheres of value God and ourselves, the Creator and His creation; of justice, inasmuch as we render to God that which is His due, the recognition of His power, infinity, goodness, Godhead, and, what this implies, our own submission, honor, praise.

It is also an act of love to give glory to God, for conformity of will is the response to the love which He first manifested towards us. Faith opens to us the treasures of the divine mysteries and raises us to a more intimate knowledge of love, bringing us into the sanctuary of the Trinity: the Father Everlasting, Unbegotten, who *ab aeterno* begets the Son, *"the brightness of His glory and the image of His substance"* (Hebr. 1:3) ; the Father and the Son who, loving One Another, breathe forth the Holy Ghost, the substantial Charity of God. The three Persons forming the divine Trinity are one God: *"to the King of the ages, who is immortal, invisible, the one only God, be honor and glory forever and ever"* (1 Tim. 1:17).

Who could feel envy of God? Who could raise himself up in pride to contest the glory that is due to Him — knowledge of His Godhead and love responsive to His charity? *"He who speaks on his own authority*[3] *seeks his own glory. But he who seeks the glory of the one who sent him is truthful, and there is no injustice in him"* (John 7:18). Thus spoke Jesus to the Jews. Here is the initial point for one who would deny the glory of God: to speak "of himself," "on his own authority." He who does so commits an injustice. St. Paul says: *"there exists no authority except from God"* (Rom. 13:1). To wish to find among men or in nature a principle unsupported by a higher principle, and to give to such a principle the character of absolute authority is to deny God,

---

3. Vulgate: *"Qui a semetipso loquitur."*

to lay hold of the glory due to the Infinite Truth, giving it
to what is false.

The Hebrew who gloried in Moses and in the circum-
cision as in an original honor, who by separating the chosen
people from every other people made it something absolute,
an authority subsistent in itself, was rebuked by St. Paul as
seeking a vain, purely material glory, without reference to
the Spirit of God. The same can be repeated from age to
age whenever peoples, emphasizing their differences and
stirring up their envy, make of the collectivity a principle
of glory, of domination, of tyranny. This glory they seek
in arms and in victories, in breadth of possessions and in
wealth, in superiority of race or culture; often they transfer
this glory to their leaders, fabulous or real men, who become
for them deities, made into gods by a subjection unrestrained
by moral laws, without consistency of ideas or dignity of conscience, and even by the rites of religious worship. Such
speak "of themselves," seeking "their own glory," and are
unworthy of faith, for in them there is a fundamental injustice.

It is Jesus Christ alone who rightens the bent of men to
make themselves into gods, He who was made Man to carry
out the will of Him who sent Him, to obey His commandments, to recognize His authority and to seek His glory. All
men, especially those who are set up in dignity and authority,
are sharers in the mission of Jesus Christ, they too are sent
by God to recognize the divine authority and cause it to be
recognized; still more are those who by the Christian faith
are united to Christ as Head, sharing in His priesthood, as
St. Peter says: *"You, however, are a chosen race,*[4] *a royal priesthood, a holy nation, a purchased people; that you may pro-*

---

4. Vulgate: *"Genus electum."* Rheims English translation (1582):
"a chosen generation."

*claim the perfections of Him who has called you out of dark-
ness into His marvelous light"* (1 Peter 2:9).

He who seeks his own authority is untruthful. He founds
himself on the lie of his own authority, falsifying truth and
violating the rights of God. On the other hand, he who does
good and seeks justice, obeying the divine commandments,
relating everything to God, seeks indeed God's glory and not
his own. He is in truth and not in untruth, in light and not in
darkness. Not only with his voice but with his mind, his will,
his works, he sings the angelic hymn of "Glory to God!"

*   *   *   *   *

Among the deepest feelings of the human soul are the
conviction of impurity as we draw near to God, the fear that
He strikes in our inmost conscience by His judgments, the
sense of the need for purification, for justification, the knowledge that it is necessary to propitiate Him by sacrifices and
to temper His anger at our sins. That with these feelings are
mixed other naturalistic ones springing from our life of sense,
unconscious animal instincts, rituals distorted from a primitive
tradition, an erroneous conception of nature and of life, is no
cause for wonder. Man is a being that has fallen from his
primal justification.

The sense of impurity which we feel in drawing near to
God is not only the sense of sin. Even when we know that
sin has been forgiven and that our soul has been made once
more white as snow, a sense of impurity not only remains but,
we might even say, increases: the confusion of creatures face
to face with the Creator, with the need for an ever greater
humbling of ourselves, so that even the saint repeats St. Peter's
words: "Depart from me, for I am a sinful man." Even in the
single case where the consciousness of sin was wholly absent,

the Virgin Mary "was troubled" at the words of the angel
Gabriel, and humbled herself at the announcement of her
vocation to divine motherhood.

The thought of God's majesty arouses in us a special
kind of fear, which is reverence, humbleness, awe. We understand that there is no proportion between Him and ourselves,
we feel our helplessness, we know that we are nothing. This
complexus of feelings has been well described as the sense
of creatureliness in the face of the "numinous" — we the
creatures, God the Numen. To bridge in an actful relationship the abyss that separates these two terms, is the whole of
religion. But the abyss cannot be bridged unless we first gain
a deeper awareness of the distance between God and us, unless we appreciate what our nature is in relation to Him, unless we come to feel ourselves as the dust that is blown by
the wind, the flame that a breath quenches, the worm that a
foot can crush. And even this is not enough. There is infinity
between Him and us. All images fail, we must think ourselves
as nothing. And still we have no exact term; we may speak
of a consciousness aware of itself as the impure that cannot
by itself be made pure: *"not of blood, nor of the will of the
flesh, nor of the will of man ..."* (John 1:13).

Thus there is born in us the sense of terror in drawing
near to God, and at the same time the need that compels us
to Him the more deeply conscious we are of our nothingness.
It is not the flight "from the face of the Lord" which drives
afar the hardened sinner, like Cain — *"My iniquity is greater
than that I may deserve pardon.... I shall be hidden from
Thy face, and I shall be a vagabond and a fugitive on the
earth"* (Gen. 4:13-14). Nor is it the suicide of Judas Iscariot,
who despaired — *" 'I have sinned in betraying innocent blood.'
... And he flung the pieces of silver into the temple, and
withdrew; and went away and hanged himself with a halter"*

(Matt. 27:4-5). The sense of the numinous brings us near
to God in holy awe, in the humility of annihilation, in the
fascination of infinity.

But how can we draw near to God? Sacrifice in all its
forms and in all its rites has a common basis in the recognition
of our creaturely nature, of the impurity of sin, of the infinite
distance between us and the Godhead. A sacrifice demands
a victim, that we may approach God in a spirit of holocaust.
Whatever may have been the original idea of offering a victim
to the Godhead, whatever the significances attributed to it by
primitive peoples, whatever the innumerable perversions of
the practice, it is certain that human tradition has created the
custom of offering a victim as a means of propitiation and a
symbol of union with God.

The first offering to God by the first man, Adam, is
bound up with the first divine revelation. The offering was
man himself in the consecration of his whole being to God.
The symbol of the offering was every outward act that man
performed in union with God, whether eating or resting,
contemplation or labor, knowledge or action, at the rising
or at the going down of the sun, by day and by night, in
enjoyment and in slumber. In everything. Symbol and reality
were united, as heaven and earth were united in the first communion of man with God.

The fall of Adam and Eve broke this communion. The
voice of God speaking of condemnation and redemption was
heard in fear and trembling, in remorse, in anguish — and in
hope. Abel and Cain offered to God the fruits of the fields
and of the flock. God still communicated Himself to men,
inwardly in their consciences, and distinguished with outward
signs what was acceptable to Him because offered with a pure
heart, and what He rejected because the heart was impure.

All symbolized feelings have expressed themselves through the ages in rites, prayers, songs. The offerings of animals and fruits which became ritual among all peoples, should not have led them away from what they signified as self-offering, self-surrender, communion. The meats that were consumed by fire were to signify the total offering of self, those that were eaten, communion. But their material quality was a cause of deviation. Thus we read in the Psalms: *"I will not reprove thee for thy sacrifices: and thy burnt offerings are always in My sight. I will not take calves out of thy house: nor he-goats out of thy flocks. For all the beasts of the woods are Mine: the cattle on the hills, and the oxen. . . . Shall I eat the flesh of bullocks? Or shall I drink the blood of goats? Offer to God the sacrifice of praise: and pay thy vows to the Most High. And call upon Me in the day of trouble: I will deliver thee, and thou shalt glorify Me"* (Ps. 49:8-15).

But is it possible for impure man to come to God and to be able to glorify Him, without first having obtained of God that purification of which the sacrifice should be the symbol and the means? And how could we ever understand that God has made us pure, save through a new sacrificial communion with Him? The whole of Christianity is concentrated in this mystery. Man cannot raise himself up to God by his own strength, his sacrifice cannot propitiate, his offerings cannot avail to bridge the abyss that separates him from God. It is not possible for fallen mankind to purify itself of itself, nor to offer its merits to God to obtain purification from Him. For neither man as a creature, nor man as fallen from his original justification, is able to give to God the glory that is due to Him, if he is not placed by God Himself in a condition to share in the hymn of glory that is celebrated *ab aeterno* in the inward life of the Godhead.

The Father begets the Son, in all things like to Him save that He is the Father begetting and the Son is begotten. The Son is the Word, who in perfect likeness celebrates the Godhead, the Eternity, the Infinity, the Goodness, the Beauty of the Father. And this celebration is nothing other than Love, it is the Spirit that the Father and the Son breathe forth together as the sole Principle of Love. Thus the glory of God is the very knowledge and very love of the Three Persons in unity of nature. All is accomplished and perfect in this pure and infinite trinitarian act — life, knowledge, love.

And of life, knowledge and love God made man partaker when He spoke the ineffable word: "Let Us make man to Our image and likeness." This image and likeness mean the knowledge and love in living beings capable of them and as such sharing in the glorification of God. *"The Lord hath made all things for Himself,"* it is said in the Book of Proverbs (16:4). Nor could it be otherwise. Thus from the moment that man thought himself an end unto himself and fell, he ceased to share by knowledge and love in the divine glorification — until *"the Word was made flesh, and dwelt among us. And we saw His glory — glory as of the Only-begotten of the Father — full of grace and truth"* (John 1:14).

The sacrifice of Jesus on the cross, and its continuation in the Mass, is the sole means of bridging the abyss between us and God and of making us once more sharers in the divine glorification "by Him and with Him and in Him." The Word Incarnate has become the supreme Priest, the sole true Priest of all creation. He has taken man's place in the office of interpreter of nature in the glorifying of God. Uncreated Wisdom has brought into the world His eternal praise, making human nature a sharer in it.

This human nature put on and hallowed by Him is the victim offered to God in propitiation for the sins of men.

Jesus Christ has appeared "in all things like as we are," and we can draw near to Him as to our Brother, with the same trusting faith as Mary Magdalene, as the Phœnician woman, as Bartimeus, as the leper, as the paralytic. At the same time we see Him as the Victim of divine justice, nailed upon the cross, giving up His spirit for the glory of God and for our redemption. The veil of the temple is rent, the earth trembles, the sun is darkened, nature shares, in a mystic sense, in the consummation of the sacrifice of the one Victim worthy of God. And the glory of God is revealed in the Resurrection and Ascension of Jesus Christ, as illuminating the perennial mystery of death and life, in the continual confession of divine justice and charity, in the hymn made of it by Jesus Christ for all men.

*   *   *   *   *

There would be no way of explaining how, through the Incarnation of the Word, the abyss was bridged that separated man from God, if we had not had the revelation of the mystery of our rebirth in Christ "by water and by the Spirit," of our communion in the merits of Jesus Christ, of our absorption into Him as living members of His mystical body, in spiritual brotherhood with Him, in the same divine sonship. Christ is the supreme, the true, the perpetual Priest of the glory of God, and we are priests with Him. Christ is the holy Victim without blemish, offered to God in propitiation and reconciliation, and we are offered with Him.

All the created world is in itself an offering to God; otherwise it would be meaningless. The creature with understanding must fulfil this offering in adoration, recognizing that all is of God and for God. This cannot come from the understanding creature of his own initiative, or he would be equal to God.

It comes about because God grants it to him, giving him the strength and the will. But when man sets up a refusal, by sin, it is the Son of God who takes his place, uniting human nature to His Person and offering it to the Father. The Incarnation has its inmost value in the sacrificial offering. We cannot explain the mystery, we seek to penetrate it and to make it ours and to share in it, as it is given to us to do, in the sacrificial offering. This has been made plain to us through the death of Christ.

That God for His glory should have willed the bloody sacrifice of Jesus, is also a mystery. We feel all its tragic profundity without understanding it. "By sin death" entered into the world, and Jesus had to overcome sin and death, the first on Golgotha (*consummatum est*), the second at the Sepulcher (*resurrexit*). The God of the living and not of the dead, as Jesus proclaims Him — *"He is not the God of the dead, but of the living"* (Matt. 22:32) — created a new society of the living, in the full and complex sense of the word. He did not destroy human nature but raised it up, still as human nature. Immortality would have been granted to Adam, by the eating of the tree of life — a natural immortality which was at the same time a sharing in the divine — but after his sin, God forbade that this should be. *"Behold, Adam is become as one of Us, knowing good and evil: now, therefore, lest perhaps he put forth his hand, and take also of the tree of life, and eat, and live forever . . ."* (Gen. 3:22).

Thenceforth, the idea of death prevails over that of life. There is no concept of eternity. The bodies of the dead pass away, the souls wander more as shadows than as realities. Do they expiate? Will they have another life? It is not known if and how this might be. The error creeps in that souls, too, will die. There is the attempt to save the idea of immortality, combining it with that of expiation through the transmigra-

tion of souls into other bodies, of men, beasts or plants. The
goal is a final happiness, but how can this be attributed to
the wicked? For these, a final unhappiness. When St. Paul
spoke of a risen Christ to the Athenians on the Areopagus,
"some began to sneer." The Hebrews themselves came only
late, and with difficulty, and after many centuries of ripening
of the truth revealed, to awareness of a complete immortality
awaiting man, and containing implicitly the idea of the resurrection after bodily death.

It is in the message of the Gospel that Jesus reveals
clearly both the resurrection of the body and the fulness of
immortality that has been granted to us with everlasting life.
But it would not have been possible to make this truth wholly
understood if Jesus Christ had not risen again, not at the
end of time as has been established for all men, but hardly
three days after His death. He rose again, not like Lazarus
or the daughter of Jairus or the son of the widow of Naim,
nor like the child of the Sunamite brought back to life by
Eliseus, or Tabitha brought back to life by Peter. All these,
risen for a little while, lived this mortal life till the grave
received them again. Jesus Christ rose immortal, clothed in
His glorified body.

Thus He overcame death and gave us a sign how we shall
overcome death; not on the natural plane but on the supernatural, soul and body reunited so that the whole of man
in his very nature should be saved. If Christ had not
died, He could not have risen again. And if He had not
died men might have doubted whether His manhood had been
like our own — whether truly He had been "in all things
like to us." Again, if His had been a natural and not a violent death, there would not have been the public expiation
of human sin, the visible sacrifice according to the sacrificial
tradition of the peoples, which responded to a fundamental

symbolism of death and resurrection. Jesus not only does not
refute that symbolism but He hallows it. He accepts the tradition which can reach the minds and hearts of all — not
only of the cultured who are a small and often proud minority,
but of all.

Baptism is the beginning of the Christian life; in it
we are dead, buried and risen with Christ. It is the rebirth
"of water and the Spirit." Why water? The symbol of a
washing away, an obliteration of stains and filth, a new beginning, fresh strength, renewal. But it is the Spirit that
inbreathes life, giving to the symbol of water its real value.
The sacramentary origin is in the bloody sacrifice of Christ.
The blood He shed is a sign of utmost love: *"The Good Shepherd lays down His life for His sheep"* (John 10:11). But
at the same time it is the sign of the victim, the complete and
irrevocable offering to God, the complete annihilation. Nor
in this annihilation is there lacking the communication to all,
in the sacred meats to be distributed among the priests and
those who share in the sacrifice. The Host is consumed and
the sacrificial meats, real and symbolical, are distributed
through the ages, the Eucharistic Bread that is the very body
of the Lord, the consecrated Wine that is His very blood,
to be renewed forever.

Sign and reality alternate and blend. Here are no imaginative symbols for impressing on the mind the value of the
reality, nor intellectual symbols directed to its understanding,
but vivifying symbols, for the living of a life. The symbol does
not create the life, but the life is given by means of the symbol
that contains it. The symbol is matter quickened by the Spirit.
The water is the matter, the Spirit is life, the water and the
Spirit together communicate life. The bread and the wine are
the matter, the quickening word is the Spirit, the two together
are the divine meat and drink. And human nature is the

matter, the Spirit of Christ offers it up, and it becomes a host, a holocaust, a victim acceptable to God.

The sacrificial liturgy of the Mass is a vital and life-giving symbol. It is the rite of the single sacrifice, repeated daily, hourly, in every corner of the earth. It is not simply a commemoration, it is a perpetual renewal, everlasting as the union of human nature in the Word, as the Christ who lived and died, rose again and is in heaven. The everlastingness of the sacrifice of Christ is not only temporal, from the day that He was lifted up on the cross on Golgotha; its value suffers no boundaries of before or after, yesterday or today, it is always actual; before His coming as since.

"Now while the Pharisees were gathered together, Jesus questioned them, saying, 'What do you think of the Christ? Whose son is he?' They said to Him: 'David's.' He said to them, 'How then does David in the Spirit call Him Lord, saying, "The Lord said to my Lord: Sit Thou at My right hand, till I make Thy enemies the footstool of Thy feet"? If David, therefore, calls Him "Lord," how is He his son?' " (Matt. 22:41-45). And again in more precise form, Jesus tells the Jews who contest His Godhead: *" 'Abraham your father rejoiced that he was to see My day. He saw it and was glad.' The Jews therefore said to Him, 'Thou art not yet fifty years old, and hast Thou seen Abraham?' Jesus said to them, 'Amen, amen, I say to you, before Abraham came to be, I am' "* (John 8:56-58). The two passages quoted refer to the Word in its Messianic function, seen in its eternal aspect. All sacrifices, from that of Abel, of Abraham, of Melchisedech, of Aaron, of the Hebrew priests, could have value only through the one true sacrifice, that of Christ. All the ritual celebrations of men, in every time and place, if performed in purity of heart, directed to the Godhead as adoration, offer-

ing, surrender, propitiation, petition, can and shall have value
through the sacrifice of Christ.

He is placed at the center of creation, above the angels,
sole expression of praise acceptable to God both in His own
name and for all creation, sole homage of glory worthy of
God. The whole cosmos celebrates this glory in its own language, as knowledge and love, but only through the Mediator, Redeemer, everlasting Priest, Jesus Christ, God and Man;
for He alone has this right in its fulness from all eternity.
This is the teaching of St. Paul in that wonderful page of
his Epistle to the Colossians: *"He is the image of the invisible
God, the Firstborn of every creature. For in Him were created
all things in the heavens and on the earth, things visible and
things invisible, whether Thrones, or Dominations, or Prin-
cipalities, or Powers. All things have been created through and
unto Him, and He is before all creatures, and by Him all
things hold together. Again, He is the Head of His body, the
Church; He, who is the beginning, the Firstborn from the
dead, that in all things He may have the first place. For it has
pleased God the Father that in Him all His fulness should
dwell, and that through Him He should reconcile to Himself all things, whether on the earth or in the heavens, making
peace through the blood of His cross"* (Col. 1:15-20).

* * * * *

Theologians justly distinguish what they call essential
glory from what they call accidental. The first is nothing
other than God Himself inasmuch as He knows Himself and
loves Himself — essential, unutterable act, which is the Trinity
of Father, Son and Holy Ghost. The Three Persons are the
very act in which God knows and loves Himself, inasmuch

as this ineffable act is God Himself, with neither succession, nor variation, nor composition, but unity, simplicity, infinity.

What can we know of this? And how can we approach so dazzling a truth without being blinded? The divine glory is sung by the Three Persons in their reciprocal mode of knowing and loving Themselves, in the being of God as One and Three. Nothing can be added by creatures to such glory, for they add nothing to the divine knowledge and love. Does the light of the sun reflected from the planets add anything to his generating and inexhaustible force? But if the comparison were to have any aptness, we should say that the light is the essential characteristic of the sun, and that it is his own light which, reflected on the planets, returns to him as faint outward attestation of his luminous essence. It is thus that we imagine the whole of creation, with the very humanity of the Word, mirroring the glory of God, inasmuch as sharing in this glory in diverse ways according to the special potentiality given by God to each created thing.

But God wished to add to the light of nature the light of grace. This, which is the seed of glory, is nothing other than a supernatural sharing in the nature of God, and we send back to Him the same light that He has given us, praising His glory. He has given Himself to us in the revelation of His mysteries, in the Incarnation of the Word, in the bloody sacrifice of Golgotha, in the outpouring of the Holy Spirit, in the Church, in the Sacraments. He sets on our lips the fundamental prayer taught us by Jesus, the Our Father. He prescribes for us the actions that please Him, the law which we are to follow, and He gives us strength to do so. The whole complexus of our supernatural life, vocation, predestination, communion, mystical union, are nothing other than a sharing in the divine glory, through Christ, with Christ and in Christ. If Adam had not fallen, it would not have been necessary to ransom

us by the bloody sacrifice of the cross. Yet the Incarnation of
the Word for the greater glorification of God not only is not
excluded by some theologians but, as a hypothesis, gives us an
illuminating vision of the mystery; for in Christ all is epitomized, and all is placed under His dominion.

In Jesus Christ the substantial glory and the accidental are
expressed together in the hypostatic union: the first is identified, through the Person of the Word, with the divine unity;
the second is the eminent, unique epitome of all the glory that
creatures may give Him, now and forever. This eminence of
glory, knowledge and love in Jesus the Man is the most perfect
possible, through the beatific vision which the soul of Christ
obtained from the first moment of the Incarnation, and which
through the merits of Christ extends to all the saved when
they too shall be able to share in it. And this vision not only
is the completing and perfecting goal of our supernatural
elevation, but is the most eminent glorification of God, for
in it He is known directly *sicut est* and loved with a complete
cleaving of the will.

It may be debated whether the beatific vision is intrinsically an intellectual or a volitional act, but the result is integral. In God there could not be knowledge without the
begetting of the Word like to the Father, nor could there
be love and knowledge between the Father and the Son without the procession of the Holy Spirit. And in the same way,
in creatures lifted up to the beatific vision, there cannot be a
beatifying knowledge without there being, at the same time
and for the same reason, love.

The whole of the supernatural life lived on earth tends
towards this term of bliss for us and glorification for God,
God known and loved for Himself, giving Himself to us in
His infinite reality *face to face*. The call to us to be perfect
"as the Father is perfect" is made so that we may share in

the divine glory the more perfectly the higher the place of glory assigned to us and merited by us. This call epitomizes the striving of our whole life in daily increment tending towards the mystical union.

Notwithstanding the work of grace, there is always imperfection in us, springing from error or weakness. The mind is not pure enough to know all the truth. The will is not sufficiently fortified to cleave completely to God and to overcome all the movements of its own egoism. Complete self-surrender, pure and purifying, is of the few; we move in an outer and inner world that renders the crystal clarity of grace opaque to us. Therefore we are succored by purifying pain, self-inflicted or voluntarily accepted, which detaches us from the outer world and from our very "I," and which gives us, in a bounded but effective manner, the experience of sacrifice. This Christ had during His life, as a lot appointed to Him, not to purify His soul as gold in the crucible, but to fulfil in Himself the sacrifice of the whole of mankind, that our actions and our pain might become in Him meritorious and in His sacrifice be sanctified.

Thus was established in Him that form of solidarity between the justified and sanctified known as the communion of saints, so that we all share in the merits of Jesus Christ and of His followers as in a common treasure. The communion of saints stretches into the other life, reaching the souls in purgatory through prayers and indulgences, till the trial of purgation is complete. The mystical body of Christ in heaven is taking shape, as the continuation and perfection of the mystical body on earth. The mystical body on earth is animated by grace, but is in its spiritual childhood — exposed to the storms of temptation and the disturbances of error, troubled by evil, perturbed by events. Little by little it develops, grows, consolidates itself in an ever more overflowing vitality, in a ripeness of sanctification. A Jacob's Ladder is stretched between earth and heaven, and the angels, God's messengers, descend and ascend in continual alternance of contacts; from below rise prayers, aspirations, tears, cries, rejoicings, hopes, from above come messages of grace, words of comfort, invitations, exhortations, pledges of salvation. Death cuts away earthly life and the redeemed souls fly up to their eternal feast.

The more they have sought in this life to share in the glorifying of God, the greater will be their part in heaven in the glorifying of God in vision and love. For all men there is one law of salvation — the glorifying of God through truth and love; one law of beatitude — the glorifying of God through sight and union. To all men the way has been opened, in Christ all are called to life. From Adam onwards all could and can respond to such a call, through that share of divine light that is granted to all and the graces that are offered to all. And the hymn of glory is sung by the whole universe and is everlasting and perfect in Christ, yesterday, today and forever.

The Gospels reveal an end of the world, a universal judgment with a special glorification of Christ. Mystery envelops this truth. When it will come to pass is in the hands of God; it is not known even to the Son, that is, to the humanity of the Word. But what we can understand is that this nature on which is built the supernatural, must accomplish its journey as one, and must know itself unified in Christ, confess Christ as its Head, be judged by Christ.

God having made Christ the Head of all mankind, and having given to man the possibility of being redeemed by Christ, has established the second Epiphany of His "beloved Son," as if to render justice to very Man, to the Mediator, the Head, before rendering it to all men severally, so that all, even the wicked, may recognize Him as such. The glorification of Christ before the Father is full and complete. The glorification of Christ in chosen souls is in relation to their participation in grace. In the Church as His Bride it is an everlasting source of life till the fulfilment of time. But mankind as such, with its good and its evil, must recognize Him in a new light in which the mystery of the manhood put on by the Son will be torn away.

Mount Thabor showed how the humanity of Christ contained the divine splendor; Golgotha, how that same humanity could become the victim of salvation; the Mount of Olives, how humanity had risen again and ascended into heaven in a new reality of glory. But the Valley of Josaphat will show, not to a few witnesses of Judea and Galilee but to the whole of mankind, the reality of the humanity of Christ the Judge, in His universal power. This mystery contains implicitly that of our freedom for evil, of our choice of reward or penalty, of the justice and mercy of God in eternal woe or in eternal joy.

We are not able to understand the co-existence in the same divine act of liberty and predestination, justice and mercy, love and condemnation. Yet the whole rings out in the necessary unification in God of His glory, as a single hymn of knowledge in love and of love in knowledge, in which all is recapitulated and all exists and nothing can exist that is not and does not reduce itself to *Glory to God in the highest.*

Part Two

FROM EARTH TO HEAVEN

CHAPTER VII

EVIL

I N STUDYING our spiritual life, from vocation to mystical
union — contact even on this earth with the glory of God
— we have seen that there was always a shadow, a back-
ground of darkness, that gradually faded before the splendor
of the Godhead. This shadow is in the fullest sense of the
word evil, which makes us unhappy in this life.

For many the path described in the preceding pages is
incomprehensible, or they think it unfeasible, and they reject
it. Whether because it is outside their knowledge and experience, or because they have not understood its depth and goodness, or because of the difficulties and steep passages they may
have encountered, they stand aside from it. Such separation
is not free from sin, for in every spiritual degree there is a
wilfulness, implicit or explicit, in rejecting the gifts that are
offered to us and the vocation that has unfailingly summoned
us. An inverse process shows itself in not a few souls — that
which leads from the shadow into deeper and deeper darkness, from the sense of good to insensibility towards evil. Such
a process is not fated, nor due to a deterministic urge. It is an
involute process, with pauses and recoveries; but if it is not cut
short in time it leads towards spiritual death, through the
atrophy of those faculties that could have brought the rebirth
of life to which our inmost aspirations always tend.

In order to understand this process towards spiritual death,
which affects both individuals and communities, as well as

161

society as a whole, we must clarify our ideas on evil, its characters and its mystery.

*   *   *   *   *

Evil, which expresses a negative idea, cannot be defined
save by its opposite: all that is not good is evil. As the idea
of good comprises under different aspects all that exists as
reality, or may exist as an ideal, the idea of evil cannot indicate
anything else than limitation, privation, negation of good.

If this philosophical conception fails to satisfy us, it is
because we translate the idea of evil in terms of our living
experience. We find ourselves so bound and encompassed by
evil that it seems to us a living reality, an enemy always in
ambush, indeed a motive of unhappiness inseparable from
ourselves. If we strike the balance of good and evil, we are
inclined to say that we have had more experience of evil
than of good.

Philosophers, distinguishing three kinds of evil, physical,
metaphysical and moral, start from the first, considered as
pain or an injury felt as pain. But pain is not an evil in itself,
it is the sign of a bodily ill, it is a warning to us to seek a
cure. The evil lies in the disorder that occasions the pain,
which may be a disease or a passing disturbance. The same can
be said of any other impression that occasions pain. What is
more, not every pain is evil. The surgeon's knife causes pain
but brings healing, whereas not seldom the absence of pain
may leave us without warning of a disease undermining our
health, or of the imminence of death itself.

Physical pain is a necessary condition of our sensitive being.
Whether we regard it as an evil or accept it as a good depends
on our reasonable nature. What may be described as physical
evil is not the pain but the lessening of the fulness of our

faculties and of our bodily vitality, and finally, death. What brings us to death, or what makes us unable to enjoy sensible life, is therefore classed by us as an evil. But since in us there is not only sensible life, but also intellectual, moral, social, political, religious life, in a word, the life of relationship, all that impedes the expansion of life towards an ideal fulness, though actually unattainable, must be classed as evil.

Thus the idea of evil is rooted in that of good — the good that we desire if we have it not, the good that we wish to preserve and fear to lose. It is the ideal perspective that forms the groundwork of human desire (which was believed to be the root of evil). Hence the evil is in the present, which limits our strength, lessens our energies, modifies our aspirations. The good, instead, however it be conceived, is in the future, and we desire and seek to conquer, possess, enjoy it. If what seems to us evil is translated into an urge to master it, it will become a means for the good on which all our energies are bent. If, instead, the evil presents itself to us as an insuperable obstacle, then either we wear out our strength without overcoming it, or else we seek other goods that may be reconciled with the present evil.

Under these aspects, evil may be considered subjective, a spiritual disposition of man in considering his activity and in seeking the goods that he finds it possible to attain. Evil would thus become the unsatisfied desire, the unsuccessful contest, the unfilled lack; it would cease to be evil when man had overstepped the boundary and vanquished the obstacle.

Our life is conditioned by the physical, historical and social elements which bound us. It is not given to all those who are poor to become rich, and it happens that many who are born rich are reduced to poverty. If riches are a good, they are not granted to all. Those who have not the means of educating themselves will usually remain in ignorance. Those who might have become the foremost in a propitious environment will remain in the second place, or even the last, thrust aside by the world. Thus the problem of individual evil and good, in regard to the enjoyment of natural life in all its aspects, cannot be solved from the outside, which restricts and conditions, but must be solved from within each one of us, and from our own experience.

Three answers may be given us in regard to natural pleasure — that of the epicurean, that of the stoic, that of the ascetic. The epicurean seeks to find a balance in his personal experience between the enjoyments accessible to everyone, so as to tame the sharpness of desire and lessen the sense of pain. The stoic feels himself superior to evil; he exalts his own personality, disciplining it to a superb indifference which has no care for outward goods. The ascetic seeks to diminish desire through abstinence, grief through patience, anxiety through oblivion, his own personality through absorption in nirvana or in God. All three give a partial, incomplete answer, but one containing the beginnings of a solution in the three grades of life. The epicurean remains in the world of matter, seeking only the equilibrium of the senses; the stoic reaches higher, to the level of the mind; the ascetic passes beyond things and thoughts and takes for his own direction the will to self-abnegation. In each one of us the epicurean, the stoic, the ascetic alternate, combining or clashing according to the phases of our life and its prevailing ideals.

Everything tends to organize itself for the sake of a prevailing end or of concomitant and coordinated ends. What may be discomfort in a lower order may become even enjoyment in a higher. The toil of the farmer is often very heavy. He bears it for the sake of the fruits to be garnered from it, and he finds a compensation in country life, in home intimacy, and finally, in the satisfaction of the harvest. So it is with the student seek-

ing knowledge, with the artist, the soldier, the politician, with
whoever sets before himself (and he cannot fail to do so) a
practical purpose for his life.

The more closely the purpose corresponds to the aspirations
of his being, to his inner visions of the good to be won (goal
and good are convertible, in the sense that there would be no
goal if the object of striving were not apprehended as good,
and it would not be a good if it were not willed as a goal),
the more resolutely the will seeks it. Nor could the will seek
it if its object had not been known by the mind as a good
to be desired. It is then that there arises in us that sense of
cleaving that we call love. This is a tendency to unite ourselves,
to identify ourselves with the end to be attained, with the
object willed.

Love is a basic affection for good, which succeeds in overcoming evil either by avoiding it or by transcending it. A
Sicilian proverb says: *Qu' pati p'ammuri nu'n senti duluri*
("He who suffers for love feels no pain"). Pain is transcended
by love. It is not that he who loves becomes insensible, but
that through love he acquires such energies as to be able to
face the suffering. Christopher Columbus for the sake of his
cherished ideal of finding the western way to the East, faced
every kind of danger. Thus it is with all generous-minded men,
who by their sacrifices for noble ideals, or ideals they hold to
be noble, face pain and overcome it.

Personal experience shows us that we tend to coördinate
pain with higher ends, when these can be attained through the
energies we may put forth in reaction against the pain itself.
Even when the pain is deadening to our faculties, if there are
still real possibilities before us, if we have still a margin of
choice left by the options with which life presents us, such
coördination is possible. How many men mutilated in the last
war found, in the necessity for a new physical adaptation, that

they could put forth energies they never thought they possessed! *Vexatio dat intellectum.* With a change in the physical conditioning of our life comes a change, too, in its practical orientation and its immediate end.

The moment will come to each one of us when any coördination of life for practical ends will be impossible, when we pass from sickness to impotency, to the dissolution of the body, to death. The coördination then is no longer in activity, but within, in a vision of spiritual realities, in the remembrance of duties fulfilled, of affections merited, in reconcilement with ourselves and with others, in the religious ideal, in the trust for the future of the departing soul. The curtain of death falls. Is it an evil?

*　*　*　*

Man is not isolated, but in society with his kind. The sufferings of each and the sufferings of others continually meet and blend. The efforts to overcome evil and to find good are multiplied in social life, with diverse results. Society itself invents and multiplies evils, such as slavery and war, and provides the means for overcoming them, such as the family, the economic system, law, education, political order, organized religion. Without society there is no life. Pain is personal, as thought is, and like thought it is at the same time social. Neither the experience nor the overcoming of pain are so personal as not to be at the same time a collective experience, a collective victory.

On the social, and hence on the historical, plane, we cannot speak of physical pain but only of limitation in the fields of our life of relationship. This limitation implies, now absence, now lack, insufficiency, defect — all negative, or more exactly, privative ideas to signify objectively what subjectively would be pain. The life of each one of us and of all social groups is characterized by a fundamental deficiency that is an urge to us to overcome it. This we may do either in appearance only, or effectively. In the first case, the problem is aggravated and not resolved. In the second, this same problem of deficiency and limitation is carried on to another plane, where it calls for a new effort to resolve it, and so on indefinitely. A cycle of woes and labors, of mitigations and rests, of satisfactions and joys — such is life. If we do not look beyond the plane of physical needs, we cannot succeed in solving one of the problems that pain sets to individuals and limitation to collectivities. What we may call a "critical cycle" is overcome by passing to a higher "critical cycle," and so on, in a continual relationship between individuals in the singular and society in the whole. The interweaving of personal life into collective life brings, I would say, a fusion of all the pains and all the deficiencies. Mankind and its history cannot be conceived outside pain and limitation, in the continual effort of confronting them.

The limitation that we call evil, as a generic term in opposition to good, is merely a quality of reality, a modality of being, one of its relative sides. Could the collision of one star with another, supposing them uninhabited, be esteemed an evil? But if the crash were with the earth, engulfing all the living, then it would seem to be for us a grave evil. And yet, if mankind were transported bodily into "new heavens and a new earth," we should find, ideally, that the crash had been a wonderful solution of all the evils that at present afflict us.

We say that it is an evil when hail destroys the wheat, not for the wheat, to which it makes no difference whether it ends by hail from heaven or by the sickle of man, but precisely for the man who through the hail loses his labor and money. If because of the enjoyment we found in a plot of flowers, it is an evil for us that it is destroyed, this can be said of the flowers themselves only in a figurative sense. For them it is the same if they lose their beauty when a storm scatters their petals, or when the hand of man has plucked them, or even if they remain on the plant to wither.

Evil is a human conception. What man estimates as evil is always so in relation to a particular order, which through given causes has been disturbed. Thus what we call evil in relation to one order may even be called good in relation to another. The deaf man has an organic deficiency which, in relation to his sensible life, may be said to be an evil. But if the deaf man is Beethoven, who through this defect can better interiorize his musical creations, and through his sufferings can leave his fellow-men an inestimable patrimony of beauties, he and we may esteem that sensible evil as a good in the higher order of art. Does this mean that Beethoven did not suffer? On the contrary, he suffered as no other man less gifted could have done, in being deprived of the power to hear his music with his physical ears, and in having to content himself with what he heard in his mind. And how much did not Dante owe to his exile for his *Divine Comedy!* Thus evil is transformed into good.

Leibniz was the first to speak of *metaphysical evil,* in regard to the boundedness inherent in nature, whereas physical evil would be the want of a good that by nature is due. That the human eye cannot see beyond a certain distance, or anything smaller than a certain size, would, according to this theory, be a metaphysical evil, whereas if it fails to see through disease or defect, this is a physical evil. The first is according to the order of nature, the second against the perfection of nature. Yet the physical evil itself enters into the order of nature (and resolves itself into metaphysical evil), if we consider that both pain and disease or imperfection correspond, they too, to natural causes and to the normal vicissitudes of life. They too, as we have seen, are a limit, a natural contingency. The difference between the two is here conceptual: metaphysical evil is considered objectively, while physical evil is apprehended and appraised subjectively. The first is cosmic, not merely human, whereas the second concerns man and all that is near to him through the projection of his sympathy or through his anthropomorphic tendency.

We may then ask, why should man attribute the character of evil to what is in the order of nature? If the idea of evil is opposed to that of good, it cannot be applied to what in actual fact is a reality, an order, and hence a good. A limit is inherent and essential in nature, it is reality itself, its condition, its activity, its purpose. Space and time are finite, the rhythm of life is a limit, matter and spirit limit each other, individuals and collectivities cannot be conceived of without limits. The illimitable cannot be multiple. Is all this an evil? An illimitable nature would be a monstrosity! Is it even conceivable?

Limitation is an intrinsic datum in the idea of creatureliness and in the complexus of creation itself, as in any possible shape and number. One alone has no limits, the Creator. Those who, excluding the idea of creation, identify the absolute with nature, are then obliged to classify its temporal and spatial manifestations as epiphanic actuations of what is intrinsic reality. A masked dualism here reveals itself. The infinite cannot be confounded with the contingent. All cosmic monism resolves itself either into incoherent multiplicity, or into a more or less crude form of pantheism. Limitation is the sign of the coexistence of the multiple, which is created nature, and of its contingency, which speaks of relationship to its Creator.

To say that limitation is a metaphysical evil, that is, metaphysically considered, is to say that nature is evil under a metaphysical aspect. This is an error. The idea of limitation implies coexistence, gradation, solidarity, development, purpose. All this reveals a creative order, which cannot be other than a good, as creation is a good. And this good cannot be and is not anything other than a participation in the divine goodness, which is here manifested as design, reality, order and finality.

The pessimistic tendency in man which drives him to seek the principle of evil in nature, now as pain, now as limit, is not appeased by the words of Genesis: *"And God saw all the things that He had made, and they were very good"* (1:31). Man has recourse to various hypotheses to justify to himself the existence of evil, for he sees in nature a divergence between his own ideal of perfection and reality, or rather, a certain individual and partial reality.

This is often explained by reference to secondary causes, which are or may be faulty, not corresponding to the natural qualities of perfection of each creature. A tree that lacks water grows badly and does not fruit; from diseased parents are born sickly or defective children. If the whole end of nature were enclosed in such partial results, we could accuse it of innumerable deficiencies. But it is precisely the secondary causes that activate the whole development of creation according to its own potentialities. We must not think either that God should correct defects by a preternatural intervention, or that He has not foreseen all this, or that, on the other hand, He did not will or was not able to give to every being a fulness of natural forces according to its proper order.

Nature is what it is, with the secondary causes (which are all natural causes) which may not give full and complete results — let us say ideal results — in every individual thing in its concrete existence. But why should they give such results? We are anthropomorphic in our conceptions of nature, and this leads us into error.

Therefore let us consider nature either in itself, as
something outside man and without man, or else with
man as part of it, within the orbit of its activities. Let
us pause at the first case, to reflect that the nature which escapes
our action does not on that account escape our observation.
Shall we say that the spots on the sun are an evil or a deficiency? Shall we think that it is a defect in certain stars
if their light has not yet reached us? How can we tell whether
the secondary causes operating in the sun and moon and the
whole firmament are as evil as those that produce a mangy
sheep or a stunted tree?

Let us pass on to the nature that belongs to us. Insofar
as we exercise on it our power of transforming it to our advantage, we may appraise it as useful or harmful (to call it
good or bad would be an improper use of words); for we
bring into it our activity as intelligent beings, and, I would
almost say, humanize it. When, instead, it is not in our power
either to approach it, or to know it, or to make use of it, it
may belong to us as a mystery that we seek to penetrate (experimentally and scientifically) or as something presumed as
hostile that we seek to conquer. How much does the science
of which we are so proud not owe to this mystery of nature,
felt as an enemy!

Good or evil nature is a human relationship, exclusively
connected with our action. Or rather it is a relationship that
we create, classifying it as good or evil inasmuch as, here and
now, under a particular aspect in regard to our persons and
our interests or needs, or even our tastes or ideals, a given thing
proves useful, useless or harmful, while at the same time the
same thing for other persons may be reputed the opposite.

In substance, it is the natural conditioning environment
of our life and activity, in the corner in which we live, in the
time of our particular existence, which gives us the possibility

of fulfilling, with varying degrees of difficulty, our earthly life. From this standpoint the usefulness or harmfulness of things cannot be classified as good or evil save in view of what we desire to obtain from them, in an inner relationship between our needs and reality considered only as a means of satisfying them. Thus, for one who needs warmth, cold is held to be an evil because it brings the annoyance or discomfort which heat brings to others.

We have seen how from this standpoint every pain and every limitation translates itself into good for him who is able to make it the motive for the raising of his tenor of life, better development of his activities, their coördination to serve ever higher ends. But even objectively speaking, all that may seem to us as wanting in nature is either only apparently so, or is so only from a particular point of view. This must be subordinated to a wider view, and so on continually, till we come to a total and integral vision of the universe. St. Thomas writes: "Corruption and defects in natural things are said to be contrary to some particular nature; yet they are in keeping with the plan of universal nature; inasmuch as the defect in one thing yields to the good of another, or even to the universal good."[1] The expression *dicuntur contra naturam particularem* indicates the human judgment, which in fact is anthropomorphic; so much so that we apply it currently to the objects which belong to us or which we have made our own, or which we feel to be near to us and like us, such as plants and domestic animals, while we do not usually apply it to nature in general.

But when we pass from the subjective to the objective, from the human to the purely natural, from the particular to the universal, and consider the cosmos in its full reality, then

---

1. S. Th. I, Q. XXII, art. II, 2.

the idea of evil flies from us. It is the idea of good that we
associate with the grandeur and beauty of the sun, the immensity of the firmament, the infinity of stars, with the earth
in its variety and even in its history — a history that we search
out from age to age, to see how it could have become our own,
rendering human habitation possible, and how it can be made
to respond more and better to our strivings and our needs. So
we may conclude by reputing the whole cosmos good, ordered,
endowed with an inexhaustible energy, releasing beneficent
energies, working together for a purpose in which we cannot
but see the creative imprint.

*   *   *   *   *

I say "a purpose in which we see the creative imprint," because this purpose raises, unifies and reveals nature. Much has
been written against what is known as the final cause, because
its import has not been understood. It was taken for an arbitrary addition to reality, an intention of our own attributed
to non-intelligent creatures through anthropomorphic tendency.
But the "final cause" (which I prefer to call finality) is nothing other than nature itself, looked at in its inward depths by
an intelligent being able to perceive them.

Those who do not conceive of nature as predisposed to
knowledge will not understand our meaning. Starting from
the notion of a God as Creator, we cannot conceive of creation
without a thought pervading it, an idea of which it is the realization in all the phases of its becoming, as something incomplete that completes and surpasses itself, not by a blind tendency but by virtue of Him who gave existence and set creation
on its journey. Just as everything that is made is known by its
maker and manifests the thought that moved him to make it,
so in an eminent, unique manner creation is known by God.

Nothing can exist without this initial thought, which, translated into creative will, is also love.

What purpose can nature have other than to realize the thought and will of Him who created it? He fixed its limits, giving to the whole cosmos, to all the groups of beings, to each individual, appropriate characters and qualities in their essential unity and multiplicity. The whole of subhuman creation, the world of beings that, without consciousness themselves, yet live by a thought implanted within them, is at once the necessary premise and the practical conditioning environment of the existence of man on the earth, and of the other intelligent beings in all habitable stars. In these are reflected, by a knowledge derived from without or divined within themselves, the purposes of the created world as in a mirror that receives and understands. The finalistic ordering of things to man is not an idea of our complacent vanity, but a reality of which we become aware the moment we understand the chain of purposes that forms the cosmic solidarity. And since man alone (as far as we know) has a mind able to understand nature and make his own that part of nature that serves the fulfilment of his life — to the point of sharing in the creative transformation of nature — thus man alone can consider himself one of the stages of purpose where the process of the solidarity of creation pauses, as at a halting place. And man for his part, through intellectual intuition of reality, comes to knowledge of the Creator, and feels in himself, and through himself in the cosmos, the inward ordering of all things to God as Author, Providential Sovereign, and Ultimate End.

As a whole, nature presents three finalistic aspects: that of the solidarity of coexistence in every order of reality in the cosmic unity; that of a process of thought intrinsic to reality, leading to the flowering of conscious thought as active intelligence, for which unconscious creation is the preparation, the conditioning environment and the means of development; finally, the aspect of creaturely subordination, recognized by the intelligent being and actuated by him as interpreter of the whole of nature. The creative imprint reveals itself in all the degrees of being, but man alone understands, proclaims, glorifies it.

Those who sunder the solidarity of the cosmos because they do not see all its links and note what seem to them limitations, gaps, conflicts (which we call evil), are not able to understand its value and its finalistic texture. They fix upon the individual as if the individual were or could be comprehensive of the whole of reality. Or else they confine themselves to a concept of particular life, as if such could fulfil the task of cosmic life. Others arrest the process at a given point of the chain of real existence and isolate man from it; or rather, not man, but certain men, of a given period, of today, as if the journeying of beings could be finished or could stop at our stage. The unceasing flow of life, which seems to us as if it should never end — for we, though knowing that on this earth we are mortal, feel a kind of illusion of unending life — must still go on, towards new manifestations of the creating thought, towards further fulfilments of the purposes imprinted in nature.

All this shows the finite quality of single existences within the indeterminable space and time of the cosmos, in cycles beyond our knowledge yet none the less effective, such as those that went before in past ages and will continue in the future. The past is actualized in the today, in that which exists and lives. Human and natural history tell us the why of the present. That past which no longer exists is only the detritus that had to perish, the individual existence that has given place to others, transforming its matter into a conditioning factor for those to come after. Amid the ceaseless renewal, transformation or variation of beings the finality of the cosmos is perpetuated, its reason for being, the one true reality that outlives what passes away, since it is the everlasting value of the divine thought and order.

* * * * *

In this setting, what can evil (or rather, the opposite of good) truly be if not that which is contrary to the nature-with-its-purpose wherein the divine thought and order are revealed? Evil, what is really evil, is nothing but moral evil, the only thing that can intentionally work against the existence of good and lead men and things away from their proper creative purpose.

Evil finds its way into nature through the free action of an intelligent creature. Apart from such action there is no evil nor can there be. It is in the act, not as activity but as intention, that evil consists. If an action that is judged evil is performed without the intent of evil (such as killing a man by accident), it is not evil.

None of the natural ends — cosmic solidarity, the conditioning of human existence, the ordering of all things to God — can be frustrated. The mere attempt to frustrate them is evil. Indeed, the intention to frustrate them is enough to constitute evil, which has its seat in the mind and will. Theologians, in order to bring out the objective nature of evil, distinguish material evil, the evil action taken in itself, from formal evil, the conscious and wilful intention of an evil action. The distinction has an analytical character (and we shall see its usefulness), but it is not to be found in the order of nature and its inherent purpose. In this order, which is that of the metaphysical reality of creation, only formal evil has the character of evil.

Indeed, the problem of evil should be examined in the relationship of man with God as Author of nature and its purpose, and with human society, as one of the special forms of the cosmic solidarity — the choicest because constituted by conscious beings in whom the subhuman reality is resolved and sublimated. The same may be said of any order of created intelligences. In the relationship with God the intrinsic finalism of creation is expressed by man as creaturely dependence, as the homage of servitude, as worship and adoration, as the carrying out of His will, the keeping of His laws. In all this there is an order, a solidarity and a purpose, of which we perceive the existence and feel the empire. It is a higher voice that speaks to us. If we rebel against it, it is through a sense of pride.

The clash between natural purposes and the laws that guarantee them, on the one hand, and the spirit of selfishness in each individual on the other, creates the conflict between good and evil. Self-love has a natural foundation in good, giving us the urge to evolve our own personality, to affirm its rights, to satisfy its needs, to overcome the obstacles set in the way of our individual fulfilment. Self-love is inherent in us and is a duty. It exceeds the measure and becomes selfishness when it refuses to submit to the law of solidarity, defined by Christianity as love of our neighbor. It is this law that reveals to man his relations with God, in whom is the source of every right and wholesome love.

Organized society is, under this aspect, a mediate and practical revelation of the natural ends of men among themselves and in relation to God. It fixes the laws of human coexistence, not in an arbitrary manner, but as the outer experimental realization of innate human purposes. It is true that the manifold actuations of society often fail to correspond to our inmost nature and its exigencies, while principles and their applications are distorted (as in the case of slavery). But in this continuous experimentation, the endeavor to grasp the values of nature and to fulfil their purposes has never ceased nor will it cease.

Here we find ourselves faced with a very arduous problem, that of the coexistence in society of institutional evils which it seems impossible to abolish; or which, if they are abolished by virtue of external laws, give place to other social evils which in their turn gnaw into the social body. But of this I shall speak elsewhere. What I wish to bring out here is that we do not come to perceive the evil of offense to God save through the evil which we commit in society with other men towards members of that society. This may seem a daring thesis, but it is necessary to pursue it more deeply in order to understand it in its full inward significance.

The law of the relationship of man with God is not visible save through our conscience, which is itself a very personal activity. But there is no activity, not even thought, which does not project us into society; which is not effectively social.[2] It is through being mirrored in others that we are able to perceive a law that limits us in action as in thought, and insofar limits us as it fulfils in us our natural ends. Thus we learn the laws of the family, those of our calling, those of our status as subjects or citizens, as universal laws in the same way that we learn a truth or truths in their universality. Whereas the particular relationship is individuated by the group to which it refers, the universality is sanctioned by a principle that transcends individuals and groups, that is known now as law, now as duty, and recalls us to the Godhead who translates order into law and imposes the duty of observing it. Thus the Godhead which through nature is known as the Creator,

---

2. Luigi Sturzo, *Essai de Sociologie,* Chap. I, 5, 6.

through society is known as the Lawgiver, and in either manner is mirrored in our consciousness as duty.

And it is in our consciousness that the will ripens to rebel against God as finality (cosmic order) or against His moral laws (human solidarity). The act of rebellion is such when it is known and willed, violating in intention both orders. Thus formal evil (sin) is what is opposed to God. Society punishes the evil that violates social solidarity in its character of outward order. If the evil turns out to be formally willed, the responsibility of him who is guilty is greater and the penalty should correspond; but society deals also with material evil in its objective character and seeks to prevent it because it is harmful to others and because it may hide in its recesses the formal intentionality, while it may also provide a motive for imitation. For social ends material evil, too, has the character of evil and must be repressed. It has this character also for subjective ends, for it may give an impulse to formal evil and to further offenses.

Direct offences against the Deity, whether negative, like wilful ignorance, omission of prayer and worship, or positive, against His name and authority, are considered as offences neither deriving from social solidarity nor referring to it. This is exact only if we would characterize such offences metaphysically; in their psychological process they too have their social character and offend against human solidarity. Negations and offences spring from an act of rebellion which practically is concerned with social authority, collective life, the laws imposed, the habits and traditions, against which the individual believes he has a motive for resistance, whereas it extends to the Deity or to a given positive religion as the cause of the bonds which he seeks to break or even of disorders which he would wish to abolish. Thus any form of irreligion is at

bottom practical and not theoretical; and, as practical, it is
not only individual but social.

"*If anyone says, 'I love God,' and hates his brother, he is a
liar. For how can he who does not love his brother, whom he
sees, love God, whom he does not see?*" (1 John 4:20). In
this question there is the profound sense of the transition from
brotherly love (that which on the organic plane we call
social solidarity) to the love of God. We read in an earlier
chapter of the same Epistle: "*He who hates his brother is in
the darkness, and walks in the darkness, and he does not
know whither he goes; because the darkness has blinded his
eyes*" (ibid. 2:11). The idea of hatred embraces all the en-
mities and injustices that mar the common life of society. The
violation of the moral laws is darkness, sin is darkness, hatred
is darkness, offence to God is darkness; all are an aberration
from the creative purposes, which are light because they are
divine thought. St. John speaking of God writes: "*God is light,
and in Him is no darkness*" (ibid. 1:5). Evil, hatred in the
complex sense of separation from men and from God, is opposed to truth and opposed to love. It is the negation of good
and of every perfection.

If we compare the concept of moral evil with those that
usually underlie the appraisement of physical and metaphysical evil, we shall find such a disproportion and irrecon-
cilability that we are unable to embrace them all in a single
general category. Moral evil affects the soul in its intimate
relationship with God and tends to disturb the purposes of
creation. The basis of physical evil is not analogical with that
of moral evil; it is to be classified among the conditioning
factors of existence. The link that may be found between the
two is that pain may provide occasion for sin; but so may
pleasure, for given the close solidarity of soul and body, all
bodily sensibilities may provide motives now for good and

now for evil. If pain and death followed the fault of our
first parents as punishment, this was not through a vitiation
of nature, but through the privation of the preternatural gifts
granted to Adam.

Metaphysical evil is a disputable philosophical conception
which the writer does not admit, inasmuch as the limitedness
of the creation is its very nature and corresponds to its intrinsic
ends. It is we ourselves who reflect upon our bodily nature
and upon the surrounding outer world the good and evil which
are part of our inner life as intellectual judgment, tendency of
will and activity. While "for the pure all things are pure,"
and "all things work together for good to him that loves God,"
and limitations, sufferings, pains, martyrdoms accepted or
rightly borne transform themselves into "perfect joy" — on
the contrary nature itself and its goods, mind and will, are a
motive for pessimism, anguish, lewdness, rancor, pride, to
those who are bad at heart and who live in hatred of God
and of men. Thus through moral evil they come to feel and
apprehend as evil what nature presents to us as limitations
and sufferings, and even as joys, without being able to raise
themselves to the sublime ends of creation.

CHAPTER VIII

THE WORLD

U P TILL now we have been studying the problem of evil mainly under a philosophical aspect. But in the reality of human life there are the indisputable facts of spiritual decadence, the inclination towards evil, the outward prevalence of evil over good. If these are considered on the natural plane, it is impossible to find an adequate explanation. The solidarity of evil which accompanies man has a twofold source, the one rational, the other mysterious, bound up with the idea of original sin. The first is the same as that of the actual sin of Adam and Eve, of the actual sin of Lucifer and even of our own actual sins — excess of self-love, making us prefer ourselves to God and to our fellows.

It is true that the actual fault remains exclusively personal, and inasmuch as it is personal, does not create any bond of solidarity with others. But through the social character of any human activity, even a personal fault has social effects. Cain after killing Abel feels that he deserves a chastisement corresponding to the offence: "Every one that findeth me, shall kill me." There is something that, from remorse, as recognition of guilt, passes without; it is the reality of the evil committed. Either it is repentance manifested by self-punishment, or it is the repetition of the offence in the quest of further satisfactions. These are effects that overflow from the personal into the social. The cleaving to the offence (the weight of which we are unable to throw off of ourselves) leads to fresh offences, in a hardening through which the voice of remorse

182

is no longer heard nor the need for repentance any longer felt. The offences neither purged nor amended of several persons living together in a family or in other agglomerations, form a maleficent environment which tends more and more to suffocate the growth of good and to foment evil passions. It is impossible for the personal offence to remain shut within itself, not to expand socially creating either a reaction against the evil or a consent to it, or both together.

This, which is obvious in a merely natural view of human actions, must be conceived within the mystery of original sin. Our first parents from the earliest moment of their existence were raised by grace to the supernatural life and endowed with preternatural gifts such as knowledge, immunity from lust, preservation from disease and death. Transgression of the divine precept meant that the effects of these gifts ceased, together with grace, without any right to their restoration. Adam and Eve thus formed for their offspring the first environment of sin. Without any need to paint too black a picture — as is sometimes done on the strength of certain emphatic expressions used by the Fathers, and especially by St. Augustine — it is sufficient to characterize the mystery of original sin as the loss, for the whole human race, of grace and the preternatural gifts. By the mercy of God through the merits of Christ, the original grace was restored to us as redeeming grace, whereas the preternatural gifts were withheld from us forever. Yet here too Christ Himself brought the remedy, for on the one hand He taught us the knowledge of the Gospel, and on the other He gave us the example of suffering and death turned to matter of merit and the means of sanctification.

What characterizes the state of decadence, making us aware of our wretchedness and causing us to feel the extreme need for divine help, is on the one hand the loss of the immunity from lusts (taking the word in its widest sense of uncontrolled and unwholesome desires), and, on the other, the dominion of the devil over guilty men as the tempter who conquered his prey when he induced Eve, and Eve, Adam, into disobedience. These two permanent effects of original sin, combined with the psychological and social effects of actual sins, are the dominant spirit of what the New Testament calls comprehensively "the world."

In many passages of the Scriptures we find this word used as signifying the opposite of the Kingdom of God and of His love, or moral evil, sin in its roots, in its inward and outward incentives, in society in the concrete, in its conspiracy against God. St. John in his first Epistle writes: *"Do not love the world, or the things that are in the world. If anyone loves the world, the love of the Father is not in him; because all that is in the world is the lust of the flesh, and the lust of the eyes, and the pride of life; which is not from the Father, but from the world. And the world with its lust is passing away, but he who does the will of God abides forever"* (1 John 2:15-17).

The world is at once reality and symbol — the reality of earthly life with all its allurements and seductions, inciting to love of the present which passes away; the symbol of opposition to God and His love; the reality of our unwholesome lusts, which show themselves outwardly in the fulfilment of the desires of the flesh (against St. Paul's precept),[1] and in ostentation of power and riches ("the pride of life") ; the symbol of the vanity and fleetingness of this life compared to the eternal life given to him "who does the will of God."

There is another aspect in the idea of the world, which concerns the personality and the mission of Christ, of His disciples, of His Church. *"He was in the world, and the world was made through Him, and the world know Him not"* (John

---

1. Gal. 5:16.

1:10). More, it has hated Him: *"If the world hates you, know that it has hated Me before you"* (John 15:18). Indeed, it has hated Christ in His disciples; but separated from Christ, no longer His disciples, it does not, cannot hate them, for they are its own." *The world cannot hate you, but it hates Me, because I bear witness concerning it, that its works are evil"* (John 7:7). And such hatred reaches to the Godhead. *"He who hates Me hates My Father also"* (John 15:23). This hatred is begotten by the refusal of love, by deafness to the Word of God made flesh, by the ignoring of our adoption as sons of God and the acceptance instead of the domination of the devil — "the prince of this world" — thus becoming his sons. *"The father from whom you are is the devil, and the desires of your father it is your will to do"* (John 8:44).

It is the mission of the Holy Spirit to show what is the world. *"He will convict the world of sin . . ."* (John 16:8). This conviction by the Spirit of Truth is the evidence of evil: the sin of refusing to believe in Christ. It is the judgment of the "prince of this world."

This principality indicates not only the prey of the tempter, but sin in act ever since the beginning, the sin that is propagated in the world: *"He who commits sin is of the devil; because the devil sins from the beginning"* (1 John 3:8). His is the first sin, which continues; it is an immanent sin, it is constant rebellion. Adam confessed, repented, submitted to the penalty. Not Lucifer, who remained the rebel by malice, hardened in his malice. He is the symbol of the immanent sin. Men sin and repent, and God forgives them, as He forgave David, the adulteress, Mary Magdalene, Zaccheus. To those who repent God gives the grace to be His sons. But the others, the sinners who cleave to sin, are of this world, which in its entirety, as St. John says, *"in maligno positus est"* (1 John

5:19) :[2] forming the kingdom of evil, creating the solidarity of evil, which takes concrete shape, is objectivized and perpetuated from generation to generation. Thus the world is opposed to the Father, hating Christ and His followers, and has for its father the devil.

* * * * *

In order to penetrate more deeply into the mysterious symbol of evil which is the world (and which we in Baptism declare that we renounce, together with the flesh and the devil), we must first pause briefly to study the structural formation of society. We must start from the idea, which is often forgotten, that man is at once individual and social and that society is nothing but the projection of single activities in the interweaving of all activities. All that crystallizes outwardly as language, traditions, institutions, laws, all that incorporates itself with places — towns, streets, labors, monuments, records, temples or churches — or with forms of costume, of intercourse, of living, all that is expressed by works of thought and art, and that which develops with time, namely history — all are the personal activity of man, soul and body, individual and society. The whole is born of his free initiative, its comprehensive and objectivized outcome.

In this elaboration both good and evil tendencies are exteriorized and consolidated. Hence in any social reality we find at once the imprints of the good and of the evil that stir in the heart of man, now of wise men, men of great goodness and intelligence, now of the licentious, the wicked, the oppressors.

------

2. *"The whole world is in the power of the evil one."*

Since man seeks first of all driven by the twofold instinct of preservation of the individual and preservation of the species, to satisfy the needs of earthly life, the complex social construction, with its traditions and laws, hierarchization of classes, and public power, has for its direct purpose the satisfaction of such needs. This satisfaction, in its elementary form, becomes the necessary conditioning of any further activities. Works of thought and art, scientific research, legal, philosophical and theological speculation, become the task of a limited class as compared with the complexus of the material activities of life. If there were not certain factors intrinsic to natural activity which ennoble it, mankind would fall into an insuperable utilitarianism. Personal *labor* is one of these factors, even when it is burdensome; it gives man the sense of his right to exist and to share in social goods, it gives him the sense of his own personality. The *family* gives, together with the joy of parenthood, a sense of mutual completion in the wedded pair and a real responsibility towards life which passes from the individual to the social nucleus. The formation of *law* makes society assume a rational, human aspect and creates the limits and the guarantees of the liberty of individuals within the common life of society. *Intellectual speculation* and *artistic creation,* though reserved for the few, radiate out into the whole of society and contribute to the cultural uplifting of each and all. Finally, *religion,* the expression alike of natural morality and of divine worship, coördinates all the partial purposes in a spiritual elevation, in the sense of duty and of justice, which begins and ends with the knowledge and adoration of God.

Against these factors of good, which every society naturally contains and concretizes, we must place the others springing from ignorance or from unwholesome lusts, which encourage not only personal offences but what such offences produce as objectivized in the social structure. Society is made up of inequalities. These are of nature, hence the strong should help the weak, the learned should teach the ignorant, the rich should share their riches with the poor. Society should tend to lessen or overcome inequalities by recognizing and guaranteeing the rights of the person, by co-partnership and coöperation in economy, and by the moral solidarity of its members. Solidarity, whether among individuals or among peoples, is a law of nature. But as actual sin in its character and its effects is a breach of solidarity (and hence a violation of rights, an infringement of justice, a refusal of coöperation), it projects itself and takes concrete shape in social institutions as dominion of the stronger, caste division, slavery, oppression. Contests for wealth and power engender hatred, strife, deportations, wars. The thirst for sensual enjoyment leads to the exploitation of the weak, of women, of children, to polygamy, prostitution, the white slave traffic. The refusal to bear domestic and social burdens creates inhuman practices, such as the exposing of newborn infants, child murder, abortion and birth control.

There is no period of history in which we do not find traditions, usages, institutions, conflicting with the principle of natural solidarity and with the fundamental laws of morality, or in which the tendencies to evil have not their widespread common social concretization. It is the task of the various forms of authority in the social nuclei to strike at the evil when it assumes external form and to limit the excess of passions by establishing wholesome laws and intervening with opportune sanctions. And although often the men placed in authority are themselves personally guilty and abuse the power given to them for the social good, yet as a whole organized society does set a barrier to the predominance of evil, whether by criminal justice, or by preventive legislation, or by upholding paternal and maternal authority and encouraging educational, moral, charitable and religious enterprises. When on the other hand the laws are not good or are not carried into effect, when the rich are more favored than the poor, the collusion of the men in power with the depraved, the dishonest, the corrupters becomes general, and demagogic revolts and unjust wars drain the blood of countries and kingdoms — these are the signs that the evil is worsening and that society is set on the wrong road. But even when measures are humane and good and the authorities do not fail in their duty, there yet creeps into the social complexus that sense of pride and ostentation, that "pride of life," which is occasioned by power and wealth and which, together with the whole complexus of evil objectivized and socially fecundated, constitutes what is called "the world."

This is the world of which the Gospel warns us, with its pomps, riches, powers and perversities; of which Jesus had an awful vision in the third temptation, when Satan led Him onto a high mountain and showed Him *"all the kingdoms of the world and the glory of them,"* saying to Him: *"All these things will I give Thee, if Thou wilt fall down and worship me"* (Matt. 4:8-9). The temporal structure into which the human spirit is projected and in which historical reality takes concrete shape, shows always the aspiration "to be as God, knowing good and evil": the same as that of Lucifer, who therefore claims dominion over it. Pride mingles in all the good and all the evil that man accomplishes on earth, and it is pride that makes the world the antagonist of God.

We must not confuse the structure of society with the spirit of evil circulating within it, nor see them as one. The first is made up of that matter which is given to the activity of men driven by the need to live together in organized groups. The spirit of evil breathes within it as an element of destruction of all the good that is always contained in the activity of men moving towards their proper ends. This spirit, known now as pride, now as lust, is a spirit of rebellion against the finalistic order of creation. From every individual it passes into reality, is "socialized," so to speak, becomes collective, circulates in institutions, speech, traditions, laws, in the various social manifestations, and, consolidating itself externally, translates itself into a conditioning of human activity and into an objective obstacle to the actuation of good.

It may seem strange, but the spirit of evil is so inherent in the social structure that often it confounds itself with "the established order," with "the traditions of the elders," with the *faits accomplis,* in a word, with all that is stabilized in man's name. Hence the continuous need to promote reforms, to affirm ideals even if up till now they have never been realized and perhaps cannot be realized, to proclaim the kingdom of peace: it is all an effort of liberation from evil. Every mystical current, like the angel in the Gospel, stirs the waters of the pool round which the sick and feeble wait so that at least the first to be touched by them shall be healed. This current is permanent in society, but it is not able to develop unless there is a sentiment, a holy, noble and lofty ideal, an angel indeed in the widest and symbolical sense of the word, a divine messenger, to touch and polarize it.

The liberating current is threefold. The first is natural, the movement of rationality away from the stabilized past towards a better future. Every historical concretization contains that something of the rational or pseudo-rational that made men seek it as a good under given conditions, but which, through changed conditions or through decay in the good won, or for other psychological or historical reasons, at a given moment no longer responds, in part or in the whole, to what reason recognizes as good. If against it is set a better ideal, or one that is believed to be better, then the mystical current which is inherent in the social body finds its orientation towards a liberating effort.

The second current is that of art — the vision of the good in symbols, in sentiments, in aspirations expressed by art. Every art of itself works a cathartic purification in minds that penetrate its value and enter into communion with it. This does not mean refined and intellectualized art, but true art, including primitive and popular art, that which is able to express ideals of beauty and which as such contains the true and the good. Art does not awaken reforming currents but it infuses and diffuses a sense of education and civilization, of loftier life and religious feeling, so that it may well be compared to the peristyle of a temple, leading to the altar of God.

The third is the religious current, revealing truth and goodness and liberating from the evil of sin. It is the contact with God which renews the heart. Without this current it would be impossible to restore the human solidarity shattered by the spirit of evil, or to give back to each individual the sense of true and harmonious purposes leading to the Supreme Good. In it the rational and the artistic currents are completed and transformed, and through it they breathe forth the perennial breath of goodness bringing new life to a society divided and oppressed by the spirit of evil.

It is thus that we can explain the coexistence of the two senses of "world" in various passages of St. John's Gospel, and typically in verse ten of chapter one. The "world" that was made by God is creation as willed by Him, principally man, and society as the human structure and the condition of man's existence on earth; though fallen, it must return to Him. Thus Christ said: *"I have not come to judge the world, but to save the world"* (John 12:47). But the second "world," that which "knew Him not," is the one of which He said: *"Not for the world do I pray, but for those whom Thou hast given Me, because they are Thine"* (John 17:9). The world for which Jesus does not pray is that which accepts the spirit of evil, that in which the charity of the Father does not dwell, the world that is opposed to God.

*   *   *   *

Our inquiry cannot pretend to explain the mystery of evil, whether actual sin or original sin, but it merely seeks to bring out how moral evil becomes objectivized and socialized. The mystery remains, indeed it deepens, when we see that the world has as its followers nearly all men, and that even those who do good are not wholly detached from worldly attractions and exigencies; so that for every age it could be said that Satan not only is the prince of this world, but that he can dispose of earthly kingdoms, as in the third temptation of Jesus in the wilderness.

This appearance is one of the characteristics of evil. The world is that which appears and that which passes away, and it passes away insofar as it is an appearance. What remains everlastingly is "the truth of the Lord." This too is in the world, though not of the world. Those who stop short at the appearance do not see this truth. They see the evil, they see it often as a good, and they are no longer able to see the true good that is in the world.

This is the consequence of the original fall. It has darkened our spiritual sight, has bound us more closely to sensible life, because it detached us from the inner reality of things which lies in the character imprinted on them by God, as His hallmark, His thought, His purpose. Lust has magnified for us the allurements and seductions of sense. Such an effect is connatural to sin, which has its origin in a transposition of values, setting up ourselves, through egoistic pride, as the end of our actions. The vitiation is radical. Those habituated to sin, the miser, the murderer, the loose-liver, the defrauder, the tyrant, look upon themselves and upon others, upon their own activities and the effects that ensue, with a clouded, distorted eye. In Scripture this is indicated in the passage in Genesis wherein Adam and Eve, after their sin, become aware that they are naked, and hide themselves at the voice of God: *"Who hath told thee that thou wast naked,"* God said to Adam, *"but that thou hast eaten of the tree whereof I commanded thee that thou shouldst not eat?"* (Gen. 3:11).

Once the balance between spirit and sense has been shattered by sin, it is the sensible life that prevails in us. In order to regain the lost balance we need at least a gradual liberation from the dominion of ignorance by truth and from that of evil lust by the love of good. Our spiritual restoration is not and cannot be the work of man, but of God. For sin grace is offered to us; the Kingdom of God is counterposed to the world. Sin is visible, grace invisible; the world is the sensible semblance, the Kingdom of God the spiritual reality. The dualism is fundamental. The dominion of the semblance will seem the deeper and the stronger the more a man is engulfed in evil. Whereas the man who has freed himself from it will have the inner sight of the reality of the spirit.

In the personal life of each of us, as in the collective life of groups, the two moments alternate and also interpenetrate, that of the lure of the semblance as reality and that of the overcoming of the semblance for the true reality, obscure though this may be. The two moments do not correspond, in their objectivity, to those of evil and of good, but if the semblance is appraised and accepted as immanent and total reality, it is evil; if the semblance is estimated as transitory, since the true reality lies beyond it, it is good. Therefore St. Paul did not write to the Corinthians that they should not make use of this world, which for the greater part of men would be impossible. Instead he wrote: " . . . *the time is short; it remains that those who have wives be as if they had none; and those who weep, as though not weeping; and those who rejoice, as though not rejoicing; and those who buy, as though not possessing; and those who use this world, as though not using it, for this world as we see it is passing away*" (1 Cor. 7:29-31). Such detachment could not be attained if the vision of the world drew to itself all our attention and our heart, if it were taken as permanent and immanent, if of it and in it our knowledge and our love found their sustenance, if the world of which the Gospel speaks were truly our portion.

On the contrary, those who overcome the worldly semblance are sharers in the Kingdom of God; it is they whom Jesus Christ calls blessed: *"Blessed are the poor in spirit. . . . Blessed are the meek. . . . Blessed are they who mourn. . . . Blessed are they who hunger and thirst for justice. . . . Blessed are the merciful. . . . Blessed are the pure of heart. . . . Blessed are the peacemakers. . . . Blessed are they who suffer persecution for justice' sake . . ."* (Matt. 5:3-10). The Kingdom of God is on this earth and is "in the midst of us"; it is in Christ and through Christ. The "just," the "blessed," the "saints" (in the wide, Scriptural sense of the word), coöperate to make up the mystical body of Christ, the new society, the Kingdom of God. They partake of the life of grace, which circulates in the souls redeemed from original sin and washed clean of actual sins. And the life of grace is the seed and beginning of the life of glory, where the Kingdom of God is made perfect and triumphs.

Who can discern on this earth the mystical body of Christ? Has grace perhaps a worldly appearance? Yet, the Kingdom of God has its visible formation on this earth, the Church.

That is, men chosen and sent to preach the Word of God, Sacraments as means and signs of grace, congregations of the faithful in union with authorized heads and "sanctified," the Holy Spirit communicated by the laying on of hands and revealed in the gifts of prophecy, of tongues, of miracles, and in the works of charity. The Church is a visible society and, thereby, has also its own worldliness. It is in the world and takes from the world elements for its outward structure and activity. Hence not all those who are in the Church belong to the mystical body of Christ, if they have taken of the world that which the world has as its own, and which is contrary to the Kingdom of God.

This fact is symbolized in the parable of the weeds. The enemy sows the weeds where God has sown the wheat, in His Church itself. The good grows with the evil, the Kingdom of God is infested by the maleficent products of the world "and those who work iniquity." Good and Evil, Reality and Semblance, Grace and Sin, are mixed together in human life, in society, in history, and it is they that form at once the Kingdom of God and the World. They are allowed to *"grow together until the harvest,"* and the Master *"at harvest time . . . will say to the reapers: Gather up first the weeds, and bind them in bundles to burn; but the wheat gather into My barn"* (Matt. 13:24-30, 36-43).

The parable shows us that the Kingdom of God is prior to the world even in time. It is what God has willed, it is His planting. The enemy came later, at night, in the darkness, by guile and corruption, to sow the weeds. Original sin was above all the actual and personal sin of Adam and Eve and, in the mysterious disposition of its effects, was the cause of human evils and sins and, through them, of that visible penetration of evil into the social structure, which is described as "the world."

There are theologians who ask: given that God in creating Adam foresaw his fall, and He could not but foresee it, through what mystery did He bind with it, in the decree granting supernatural grace, the fate of all mankind? The Christian liturgy answers by the hymn of Holy Saturday: *O felix culpa!* "O happy fault that merited for us such a Redeemer!" The mystery remains still darker for us if we ask, again with certain theologians, whether Adam's sin truly altered God's plan, or whether Adam's sin did not enter into God's plan. In the first hypothesis, man would have hampered the will of God, and in the second, it would have been God who preordained Adam's sin. The dilemma is untenable.

It would be outside the scope of the present work to enter into theological hypotheses, nor does the writer think by his reasonings to penetrate such mysteries; what he is seeking is light on the present theme. Notwithstanding the mystery in which the truth is veiled, it is certain that neither did Adam alter the divine plan, nor did God place Adam's fall in His plan of redemption as preordained by Him. What entered into God's plan was the creation of a free and intelligent being. Without freedom man could not be raised to the state of grace. Created free, his will was in his own hands. God foresaw that Adam would sin; He preferred to create him, to sanctify him before he sinned and to redeem him afterward: such is the plan of God.

Those theologians who hold that, supposing Adam had not fallen, the Word would have been incarnated for the greater manifestation of the glory of God and as the most sublime of the *ad extra* works of the Trinity, render a great service to the smallness of our understanding in its speculation on the divine mysteries. They do not add anything to the infinite reality of the Incarnation and to its finalistic value as indicated in the Creed: *"propter nos homines et propter no-*

stram salutem"; but they make us understand better how the divine plan was not spoiled by Adam's sin. The Incarnation is the theocentric end of the whole creative work of God, and in Christ the whole universe is epitomized. Christ is not only for men, but for all creatures, for the angels of heaven, for the intelligent beings that have lived or live in the stars, or will live ages hence. Thus we may apply in the widest sense the pregnant and mysterious words of Paul to the Colossians: *"He is the image of the invisible God, the Firstborn of every creature. For in Him were created all things in the heavens and on the earth, things visible and things invisible. . . . For it has pleased God the Father that in Him all His fulness should dwell, and that through Him He should reconcile to Himself all things, whether on the earth or in the heavens, making peace through the blood of His cross"* (Col. 1:15-16, 19-20).

Here is unveiled the whole divine plan in its reality, with at the center Christ crucified for the fall of Adam. But this historical reality is filled with the light of a function transcending the earth and the men who dwell on it, to become universal in the primacy of Christ over all creatures visible and invisible; all enter according to their nature into God's primordial plan, revealing His glory. The World which Jesus came "not to judge but to save," is the men who cleave to the Kingdom of God of which He is King; and this the world that is not seen, whereas that which is seen is the world that passes away. As St. Paul says, *"the things that are seen are temporal, but the things that are not seen are eternal"* (2 Cor. 4:18).

CHAPTER IX

HISTORY

GOOD and evil, the world and the Kingdom of God, embrace the whole of human activity on this earth, in a continuous process which we call history. This activity, begun in time, has never been arrested, never turned back, never repeated itself, but has gone forward. It is not evolution, like a life unfolding from a germ by fixed laws, nor progress, in the sense of movement towards a term and of gain necessarily implicit in such movement. Both these are inadequate and oversimple ideas for indicating the nature of human activity. I have called it a process, and so it is: continuous activity, outward succession and inward unfolding — a process in which progressions are never more than partial nor evolutions more than relative, and in which liberty is the source of movement, idea of whatever is actualized, invention of all that is created.

Indeed it is human activity that makes history. It is not determined *ad unum,* but free in its ways, its options, its particular purposes. And although human activity is at the same time subject to the conditioning forces of material and social reality, this conditioning is not the same for all, it is not compulsive. It is a fetter and it is an urge; it is a starting point and it is something to be surmounted. So that the more the will to act is free and strong, the more do the conditioning factors cease to be a bond and an obstacle and become a means and a coefficient of realization.

All that is not individual initiative may be considered as its conditioning. But human activity is at once individual and in common. The two factors of individuality and community so intertwine that it is hard to distinguish them and impossible to divine them. It may seem that only individual activity is free, and that the more it is detached from activity in common the freer it becomes. This is an error in perspective. In communal activity, too, freedom is complete, even though there is the sense of a mutual conditioning. If this sense is less present in individual activity, and it is not always so, this comes from an unreflecting apprehension of reality. The individual activity that stands out from that of others and opposes others looks like an energetic surmounting of all the conditions imposed. Actually, it is a choice of unusual ways of acting, which therefore encounter different conditioning.

The interweaving of initiative and conditioning factors makes up man's experience in his striving for any immediate goal. Every activity is performed through associated groups, and in spite of the barriers set up by nature and man, tends to communicate itself to the whole earth, while it prolongs itself in time, even though death mows down over a hundred thousand lives a day and in less than a century the generations alive together are three or four times renewed.

Not all human activity can be called history, although all contributes to its creation. The word history has so many uses that we must clarify its prevailing meaning and its essential content. History does not mean here a mere narration, oral or written, of single events, *rerum gestarum;* this is the part that we give to memory and to imagination too, to link us with the past. Every people has its memories, its feats, its name. The narration of these is born with the language; it mythicizes origins, shapes traditions and projects in great and fantastic forms the first strivings of a social group to attain a personality

of its own. Early leaders are recorded as doing good or evil for
the benefit or injury of all, and as forming the spine of the
group's history. Such history makes us think of a collectivity
as a person living for long ages through the physical persons
who succeed each other from generation to generation. Is this
a reality or a nominalistic hypostasis? We find both in it, according to our standpoint. What lies at the root of the social
entity is the individual consciousness, which, interreflected
among the members of the group as thought and action, forms
the collective consciousness and through it the social personality. History may thus be regarded as the processual projection of this consciousness-personality.

Let us pause a little at this idea. An aristocratic family that
can go back two, three, five, nine hundred years, recalling
glorious deeds, warriors and men of law, reformers and saints,
has its own consciousness and personality and preserves it in
living by it so long as such a family is bound up with a social
function of its own and a public tradition. But if, as today in
many civilized countries, the aristocracy has ceased to have any
true social function, if the economico-feudal basis of the past
no longer exists and big estates have either been broken up or
are loaded with debts, then the aristocratic family's group consciousness loses its consistency and its personality vanishes. The
past is no longer alive in the present and the memory of ancestors is no longer for the group a history of its own, but a
catalogue, a picture gallery, or at most a moral example.

The same happens with peoples. Ancient Greece was not
reborn in the new Greece created in the nineteenth century.
Though the latter is more or less the same in territory, speaking a tongue that has resemblances with the old and preserving
the names, monuments, works and memories of classical history as those of its own forebears, yet the collective consciousness of today is not and cannot be animated by that of the

past, for as a group-consciousness it no longer lives in the present. In spite of all the rhetorical efforts and imitations, the Rome and the Italy of today have not the collective consciousness of Republican and Imperial Rome, and they do not continue its personality. The historical process of ancient Greece and ancient Rome found its outcome, through the mediation of Christianity, in the classical culture that shaped the minds of succeeding ages, and it is impossible for that past to return as the active consciousness and the nationality of the modern peoples living in Greece and Italy, who, through their origins, have a personality entirely of their own. The group consciousness is formed by that past which lives in the present and which is the present as source of life and collective activity.

*   *   *   *   *

The essence of history is the very activity of a social group in its process. The personality of the group is really living, with a unity not psychological or mechanical, as certain sociologists imagine, but moral-historical, founded on an intercommunication of consciousness. Even within such limits it is impossible that a personality should not have a function of its own and should not move towards ends that transcend single individuals. Such personality gives birth to a collective finalism which is the welfare of the group and its members, and which, taken as a whole, transcends the exigencies of individuals and even present life, pressing forward into the future.

Therefore the future is seen as better than the present. The present is faulty, insufficient; it is felt and resented as an urge to action. Those who have the preparation and capabilities will guide the others; there will be disputes, dissensions, con-

flicts, strife, over what should be done; affirmations and negations will succeed each other as partial visions of the welfare
sought. The future, as that which holds within it the desired
weal, may be symbolized either as the coming of the hero,
the saviour, or as the advent to power of a class to avenge
the injustices of others, or as the rebellion of an oppressed
people — a chain of aspirations and fulfilments stretching out
unendingly, shaping the consciousness of the generations and
imprinting themselves within the soul of each individual.

Partial ends with a view to more general ends, willed or
imposed as occasion arises, orient collective activity. Just as
with individuals, for whom life day by day is an accumulation
of energies for the moments of resolution looking to the attainment of the end, and the prospect of such attainment is an
urge to overcome the obstacles in its way, so is it with groups
and their organized activity. The finalistic impulse through
the strengthening of inner forces, arouses the spirit of achievement. This, inherent in man, develops in order to satisfy
needs and feelings, from the most primitive to the loftiest,
and informs the life of the group. If this were not so, a great
part of associated activity would disappear. The harshnesses
and inclemencies of nature, the friction between neighboring
groups, the pride of the rich, the discontent of the poor, the
thirst for dominion or for knowledge, are what feed the spirit
of achievement, but at bottom what brings the urge to achievement is the desire for greater welfare, seen each time as a
necessity or an enhancement of life.

This is a sociological law which informs the course of all
history, in large or in little. But in large or in little, in every
field and sphere, collective activity must either be directed
towards achievement or fail. Conquering achievement, as finalism of action, gives vitality and unification to the collective personality; the renunciation of all conquest, insofar as it denotes

pure acquiescence in the present state, petrifies and dissolves
that personality. Thus the notion of conquest, from both the
sociological and the historical viewpoint, must be extended to
all possible gains in moral, intellectual, religious, political,
economic and social welfare, alike in the internal life of the
group and in its relations with other groups. Any creation of
welfare insofar as it implies activity, efforts, failures, crises,
the overcoming of difficulties, cannot but be called a conquest.
And as any form of welfare won (freedom, for instance) must
be guaranteed, defended and re-lived, so its conquest is always
a becoming, in the continuity of action. The good things
achieved, being insufficient in themselves, call for others to
be achieved in their turn. The achievement of welfare is always
partial, never entire. It is precarious, never conclusive. To be
defended, it must be renewed, augmented, restored. In a
word, the good won must be continually reëxperienced so as
to ensure its existence, continuity and development.

Here, then, is the thread of history — the activity of the
group, directed to its own welfare, stretches into the future;
a finalism then comes into being which, concerning all, presents
itself as a conquest to be achieved. This, when it is achieved,
appears for what it is, partial and precarious, and imposes further activities to preserve what has been gained and to effect
new gains. The activity, or better, the action is the present,
the instant lived, but this is conditioned by the past, which is
what has already been achieved, and is commanded by the
future, which is what can be achieved.

The synthesis of past and future in the present is accomplished, before any action, in the consciousness of the group-
personality. The writer does not attribute to the group a consciousness of its own distinct from that of its single members;
it is our own individual consciousness in reciprocal interpretation of the mind and will that throws the value of the group-

personality into relief. Thus, only of those who have developed the sense of belonging to a group and of its *raison d'être* and action, can it be said that they live its life and represent its personality, and that they truly act in history and make history. But they are not isolated, as we often imagine heroes and saints to be; they are heroes and saints precisely because their consciousness and life is in touch with all the others belonging to their group, and thus they share most intensely in its historical life.

*   *   *   *   *

What is a historical life? The beginning, the development through crises, the flowering, the decline, the extinction of a group's consciousness-personality. We must follow its path, note its passages, discover its laws. Otherwise history remains a closed book, as it is, alas, for many.

The first natural nucleus is the family. The family, as such, does not create a historical consciousness but only a consciousness of affections, of moral and material interests, of perpetuity of life. Where a certain historical consciousness, still in its infancy, begins to take shape, is in the consistency of several families bound together by a bond that unites, organizes and transcends them. We thus find a widening of the nucleus, which is a transition to a new sphere of relationships coexisting with the first and, under another aspect, reaching beyond them. This for the writer is the first sign of an important sociological law, which may be defined at once as the *transcendence of a given social nucleus through the formation of a wider collective consciousness*. In those families that through the widening of the primitive nucleus assume a directing and organizing function, while granting that their activity may be directed to the enrichment and aggrandizement of their own house — all the petty chiefs of clans or lords of castles who would later become princes and kings of peoples passed first, through this stage — the consciousness of a collectivity other than the family develops and ends by superimposing itself on the first. The transcendence is achieved when the collective personality is felt simultaneously by its diverse components, in their common activities and in their conflicts of interests and dominion.

In the same way, the interests of families are transferred into those of economic, professional, civic groups in conflict with the interests of antagonistic groups, giving rise to the formation of a new group consciousness. But if this remains on the lower plane of material interests, it has not yet become historical. It provides the material for history, it creates a certain variety of successive events, but it has not in itself a virtue of transcendence properly so-called until it becomes impregnated, or better, fertilized, by loftier and life-giving ideas, which we may provisionally classify (as is usual in history books) as civil, political or religious.

The history, written or oral, which we know as such is made up of events that concern not this or that family or economic craft or trade group or class or tribe, as groups living their own particular life, but that part of the population, however it may be grouped and organized, which has gained consciousness of its personality over and above domestic and economic contingencies, in a higher affirmation of collective life. It is the transcendent and unifying personality that history alone reveals to us. What has been already noted as collective purpose, as spirit of achievement, as welfare to be won, is here presented from another angle, as the transcendence of the social nuclei through the development of the collective consciousness. When this transcendence begins, history begins, but it becomes concrete in the realm of ideas, which we see as civil, political and religious. The domestic or economic group, too, comes back into the historical field, but transformed into civil, political or religious values. Then do we understand the historical importance of the strife of families and of social classes, because they assume a character of general interest, of moral value, of justice, heroism, loyalty, liberty, or of the opposite, of cowardice, treachery, injustice, tyranny.

A *polis,* a *respublica,* a nation, takes shape; it has its political personality, its civic consciousness, its history. It is then that, turning back to its past, it discovers or reëxperiences the myths of its origin, the prophecies of its greatness, the mission awaiting it in the future. It is then that it feels the urge to transcend its temporal reality: God or the gods have willed and protected it; its story will know no end. There is no people that, having once formed a personality of its own, does not see it as stretching forward indefinitely, in a conception at once human and religious. I have said that we might provisionally accept the classification of history as civil, political and religious. The mythic origins of every people, the sense of continuity of existence which it gains in its activity, a sense as it were of immortality of the collective personality, the religious worship that revives its moral ideals and civil virtues, all show the inseparability of historical values, since these at bottom are nothing else than values of the collective consciousness.

But will the collective personality, once it is formed, know no end? Indeed it will end, but not as many believe. It is not always the fall of a kingdom or an empire, fixed at a given historical date by some event (which may not be thrown into relief till many years after), that is the sign of the dissolution of the collective personality. It may live on and survive the gravest cataclysms, so long as the people concerned maintains the consciousness of its own continuity. Outward events help to in-

crease or diminish the sense of personality, but it is the consciousness that is the sign of it. Catholic Ireland never lost its
consciousness as a nation, in spite of losing for centuries its
political personality together with its own language and the
large part of its property which was confiscated by the victors;
Poland the same, even though divided and subject to three
foreign States for a century and a half. Even if neither had
been reëstablished as a political State after the last war, they
would still have kept their consciousness of collective personality, unified in the constant aim of regaining independence
and freedom.

This is the case with all oppressed peoples and subject
minorities which have their own culture and religion and have
had in the past their own history to differentiate them from
others, giving them their individuality and bringing to birth
a consciousness of their own. It should be noted that for all
oppressed populations, political history, language, culture and
religion are as it were fused in the maintenance of personality.
Where religion and culture are akin and tend to become unified, the collective consciousness is widened through transcendence of the social nuclei and the consequent transfer of personality. This can be noted in the great unitary formations which
were religious and cultural before becoming political. France,
Provence, Toulouse, Gascony, Burgundy, Savoy, were united
through their culture before they came to form a single political unity. And in Italy historical unities of the first order such
as Venice, Florence, Rome, Naples, formed a religious and
cultural Italy before they were joined in political unity.

The most significant historical instance is that of Greece
and Rome. When their political grandeur had been lost, their
cultural legacy remained alive in the consciousness of the peoples forming the great Christian and imperial agglomeration
of East and West. Philosophy, history, law, art — everything

passed into Christian culture and helped to shape its humanistic and religious consciousness. A part was opposed by the
Christians as error, a part was lost, but when what was lost
was rediscovered, it led to a new deepening of consciousness,
renewed by a past that had once more become present. This
occurred in all the various renaissances of the ninth, twelfth
and thirteenth, fifteenth and sixteenth, and nineteenth centuries. Such contact with the past is not a repetition or a copy-
ing; it is a rebirth, a creation of the spirit reintegrating what
others produced under different circumstances — a rebirth
which at a given historical moment responds to the need of
the collective consciousness.

The sphere of human personality may thus widen out into
immense cycles which we call civilizations, transcending single
peoples, particular languages, geographical and political barriers and even oceans. The civil and political history of every
people, with all its particularities, becomes an aspect of wider
and deeper histories, which throw into greater relief the intellectual and moral values of journeying humanity. Kingdoms
and peoples pass away, but their gifts to civilization remain
as a ferment in the human consciousness for the forming of
new collective personalities. The law of the transcendence of
the social nuclei is plain in the development of historic
civilizations.

In no age and in no civilization can the forming of the
collective consciousness be accomplished save under the ægis
of truth, as it may be apprehended and felt at a given time and
place. For this reason we seek for the truths experienced by
the ancient peoples, under the husk of myths, legends and
traditions, and even in the perversions of morals and religion.
This means, not that truth is relative, or merely historical, but
that the collective consciousness, oriented towards truth, appre-
hends and actuates it from the aspect that corresponds to the

cultural state of each people and to the cycle of civilization to which it belongs. And thus is perpetuated the human endeavor to reach the unifying truth, the fulfilling morality, from the highest to the lowest centers of collective life, and even to the most isolated zones and the most primitive and elementary civil and religious forms.

* * * * *

The central point of unification of consciousness is its religious orientation. There knowledge, philosophy and art, civil and political organization, moral elevation, the quest for truth, juridical constructions and forms of civilization, all converge. There the inner justification of our own existence, the moral appraisement of our own acts and all finalism of human activity coincide. Religion is at once philosophy, ethics and history. These three aspects of human thought and activity cannot be separated. Thought seeks truth. The will, illuminated by truth, seeks the good. The good to be achieved urges to action. In history, which is the convergent activity of associated efforts, neither the quest of thought for truth nor the quest of will for good is ever absent. The transcendent expression of the truth thought and of the good willed is religion. Thus there is no history that does not actuate religious values; no people, no civilization without religion.

The formation of the group consciousness receives value and stability from a religious idea. The family, if it has truly a profound sense of its reality, cannot but reach to the root of religion. In antiquity men deified their ancestors. When the life of the group passed to the *polis* or to the *respublica*, the symbols of collective existence took on the figures of protective deities, and the group was unified by religion. This is not to admit polytheism or to recognize as true the myths and fables by which it was symbolized; it is merely to note historically the unification of the group consciousness by religion.

The universalism of humanity could not be conceived of and affirmed save through a universalizing religion. In Hebrew monotheism the God of Abraham, of Isaac and of Jacob is the one and universal God, but the Hebrew people is His chosen people. Thus the universal idea contracts to a national particularism. With the coming of Christ, religious universalism is extended to all mankind, which becomes potentially the people of God. The universalist consciousness cannot be other than religious and Christian. To deny it is to fall into the particularism of a religion of peoples, States, races. Even Christianity, in its various historical deviations, has become particularistic when it has been confounded with the political power, with the nation, with a culture or with a special rite, in a word, when it has been bound to earth instead of transcending it in time and space.

Even though mankind is not yet unified in Christianity, we may seek in it a common trend of unification. We find in the consciousness of peoples a natural law as the expression of rationality applied to action, and at the same time an underlying tradition of a primal divine revelation bound up with a mysterious human decadence. The first, the law of nature, takes concrete shape in the customs of each single people in every age; for all its deviations and perversions, it maintains an underlying element of morality and justice. The second, the tradition of a primal revelation, maintains belief in a Supreme God, Author of things and of the law, and even in the manifold mythological and magical formations the idea emerges of a creation, of a fall and redemption, and of a final justice. At bottom, the elements that may draw the peoples together in mutual understanding and fruitful contact are only the ethico-religious; and on these, through practical collaboration, a historical consciousness and a wider civilization may be created.

It has been and is still believed in various fields that this ethico-religious foundation can be supplanted by a secular consciousness. The most noteworthy general trends in this sense have been those of a humanitarianism founded on science (positivism); that of an idealistic monism founded on the philosophy of the "spirit" or "Idea" (Hegelian idealism); that of a socialism founded on historical materialism, better known as Marxism.

That positivist humanitarianism has not succeeded in creating a consciousness is now plain, both through the failure of that faith in progress which scientism had aroused in the last century, and through the practical effect of the sciences which, while giving men remarkable means of welfare, do not suffice in themselves to regulate the use of those means. It is not the fault of the sciences if life today is harder and wars more tragic; it is the fault of modern man, who has not always thought that the practical use of scientific data should be given a moral direction and imbued with a sense of human solidarity.

The monistic and immanentistic conception of the "spirit" or "Idea" has not in its turn given us a loftier conception of our personality and responsibility, nor an idea of society as human fellowship. Admitting the dialectic of the "spirit" as an end in itself, the sole conscious reality, it led to the conceiving of the State as the supreme realization of the Idea. The Hegelian State gave the theoretic basis for the totalitarian State, as sole will, auto-liberty, auto-formation, auto-consciousness. It is a fearful monster that has been born of idealism. And if certain idealists do not recognize it as their own, it is

because they are not able to draw all the consequences of
their theory.

Historical materialism has been a substitution and counter-
feit of idealism. From the dialectic of the Idea it comes to the
dialectic of economy; instead of the Hegelian State, the economic State — another totalitarianism, the Communist, of
which Russian sovietism has shown the first application.

These conceptions of associated life — the scientistic, the
idealistic, the economic — have not given mankind an orientation of consciousness that could become a permanent value of
life. Their antithesis to any religious conception has resulted
in the negation of transcendence; it has thus rendered almost
inoperative the earthly truths that each of these theories contains and has largely prevented their dialectical function from
influencing historical activity for good. Thus scientism (not
science) sought to exclude all metaphysics from culture. Idealism (not philosophy) sought to absorb all spiritualism into itself. Historical materialism (not the social question) canalized
the moral forces of the worker into the narrowest economic
conception of life. As a consequence, the whole collective effort
concentrated itself in politics, as its supreme actuation in which
science, philosophy and economy should find their real synthesis. The human person vanished from the scene, and with
it man's loftiest destinies, since for such conceptions the human
person was nothing but the pure phenomenon of a process,
either blind as matter or auto-conscious as spirit, but in either
theory without any other purpose than the process of auto-
realization itself.

The logical and practical consequence of such attempts
could be nothing else than the immanentistic conception of
history, stripped of any idea of transcendence, personal or collective, spiritual or historical. There would have been no room

for true history — no autonomous initiative or freedom of action or even of thought, nothing that could make history the real plane of ideas and activities, to which each may contribute through his operative personality; in which the living and life-giving syntheses are provided by the aims of single individuals and of their groups in conquering aspiration, and transcendence comes about in the depths of the individual consciousness mutually reflected as collective consciousness, so that the groups themselves come to be transcended in a continuous widening of contingent purposes towards a higher and religious purpose.

This is why in spite of the wide diffusion of modern areligious conceptions (which have been grouped under the sign of positivism, Hegelianism and Marxism), in the domain of culture and in that of politics and economics, religious feeling is always reborn, far more vigorous than in the past, not only as the inmost need of each one of us, but as a collective aspiration, as the firm basis of social life, orientation of thought, escape from earthly ills, need of the infinite, answering to an obscure but real sense in the collective consciousness which seems never to have lost or to be able to lose its touch with the divine.

* * * * *

To one who is accustomed to read and think of any history only from the standpoint of curiosity about facts, without seeking further, it may seem strange to be told that any particular history is as it were engulfed in universal history and that all secular happenings disclose a religious relationship. The truth is that history, whatever history it be, at whatever point of the ages it be taken, in antiquity or in modern times, no matter

in what place, in Europe or Africa, carries us to the fundamental problem of living and journeying humanity in relation
to its unifying finalism. History prevents us from looking on
man as a single individual in the solitude of his soul, and from
looking on God as the single goal of each, outside the all-
embracing communion of men with one another and with
God. History is the lot of the community living through the
centuries, which presents itself to us through the big or little
window opened upon it in the consciousness of each. This
presence is not of something transient that is lost or has been
lost in nothingness, but of something permanent that we feel
alive in each one of us.

If we wish to find a point of analogy with this "something
permanent" and this "universality" felt in history, we have
only to reflect on our mode of knowledge itself. By common
experience the object known is apprehended as other than
ourselves who know it. All philosophers seek to explain the
duality of subject and object and their conjunction in the act
of cognition. Such an analysis often overlooks the constant fact
that in knowing an object, whatever it may be, real or ideal,
material or spiritual, even while we isolate it we never know
it outside a whole that embraces both us and the object and
at the same time transcends us. Is this whole the space in which
we live? Is it the time into which we project ourselves in
living, thinking, acting? Beyond space and time there is still
a comprehensive and transcendental totality that calls us, making us feel the finite place we occupy and the infinite towards
which we ascend. In any act of our thought, in any knowledge,
inward or outward, the relationship with the whole cannot be
wanting, and indeed is present. Nor should it be said that we
have no consciousness of such a relation as emergent with
every act of knowing, because it is implicit in us and may be-

come explicit whenever we attempt to search more deeply into the object known and the value of knowing.[1]

The complexus of subject and object, of reality and of all-embracing totality, binds us to a collective existence, human and ultra-human. History is a revelation of it, penetrating thought and consciousness. The past resolves itself into the present, and becomes present to us through that of which we are conscious. The present projects itself into the future, and the future too becomes present to us through that which we aspire to be. But the present, that of our living experience, is not at all an "ourselves," it is not our knowledge of it, but it is a totality that absorbs us and transcends us in a striving towards the infinite.

A certain idealist school (the Hegelian) identifies history with philosophy in a dialectic immanence from which there is no way out, no escape, no transcendence. Even without abolishing the various moments of the "spirit" or reducing the historical process to a pure actuality, such identification contracts the reality of the object into the subject and of the real totality into its auto-consciousness. But the identification here of history with thought and the consciousness of thought, is on the threefold plane of the individual (subjective consciousness), of the collectivity (objective consciousness), of the totality (transcendental consciousness). That is why philosophy and history are two facets of the same reality of thought and consciousness. Philosophy extracts the laws of human reality from history; history expresses the concreteness of the laws of human reality in its existential process.

This process, which identifies itself with the journeying reality of humanity, is the life itself of each one of us and of

---

1. See Luigi Sturzo, "The Problem of Knowledge and the Intuition of God" (*Thought,* XVI, 61, June, 1941, pp. 312-324).

the social groups to which we belong and by which we live, in a complexity that is hard to know but which at bottom reveals always our rational nature and our supra-rational aspirations. History goes a step further than philosophy, for it is history and history alone that testifies to us, in the reality of events, that mankind has undergone an insertion of the divine, has received a higher call. Thus the natural unification in rationality, as the term of consciousness, is no longer totalizing and conclusive, for there is a new ordering towards the supra-rational mystery.

The assertion that history testifies to the supernatural, or better, that the human process has been supernaturalized, meets with difficulties on two distinct planes — that of the *immanence* of history and that of its *worldliness*. Are these real difficulties? History is immanent because it is human and remains on the human plane of process which we call the process of rationality (better, the process towards rationality through the winning of rational good), as such responding to the essential nature of man. What at first sight may seem strange is the assertion that the divine is historicized, that is, that it too becomes immanent in history, enters into the process, accepts the laws of human reality.

In the *Essai de Sociologie*[2] I set forth my theory in regard to this problem. Here it suffices to say that the primal revelation, like the Mosaic and prophetic and at last the Christian revelations, inserted itself into history in a human fashion and has become a living and permanent factor of the historical process. The scholar who is no believer will seek to give such facts a human origin, with recourse to naturalistic, positivist or idealist hypotheses. If he does not go so far as to deny God, he will deny any action on His part in history, confining Him

---

2. Introduction, pp. 19-28.

to an inaccessible heaven, separating Him from man who can
have no communication with Him. Thus little by little God
is deprived of all attributes of intellect and will, and the outcome tends to be a naturalistic pantheism, or an unconscious
pantheism, or a meaningless pragmatism.

These would be the consequences of denying to history its
testimony to the insertion of the divine into the human process.
But once this insertion is granted, at least as a hypothesis to be
verified, the doubt may arise whether the historical process can
be said to be truly free, accomplished by man with his faculties and his orientations towards the rational good — in substance, whether a truly immanent process is then conceivable.
Here is the hub of the problem. My answer is founded on the
principle that God reveals Himself by adapting Himself to
our capacities — *per modum recipientis,* as the Schoolmen
would say. His revealing word becomes in us free human activity. Man can refuse acceptance of it, and, once it is given,
he will continue to work as a man. Granted that grace transforms us and makes us partakers in the divine nature, we do
not for that cease to act in a human fashion and to strive together with our fellows to realize the good that corresponds
to our rational nature and which is at the same time, mysteriously, a supra-rational good.

The historicist theory of the writer is defined in these terms
in the work quoted: "The consciousness of history as a human
process realized through immanent forces unified by rationality, a process which, starting from an absolute, transcendental
principle, directs itself to this principle as its goal."[3] Indeed
human activity always seeks the rational even when it is led
astray; it is the mind-consciousness (rationality) that unifies

------

3. Page 23.

it. Even the supernatural inserted in us undergoes this transformation. It is perceived as truth, albeit a mysterious truth;
it is accepted as good, albeit only dimly perceived. Man turns
to it, seeks it, acting in a human fashion, while within him
those transformations come to pass of which we know by
revelation but of which we are not conscious otherwise than
by indirect experiences — save in exceptional cases in which
the experiences may be said to be direct, though as such they
are not communicable.

In every case, this activity if it is immanent in us does not
start from us; we partake in it through an act that transcends
us, whether that of creation or that of revelation. The natural
order and the supernatural order meet in us and give a quickening impulse to the human process. Both the individual and
the collectivity move towards a goal which in its turn transcends us in the two orders, natural and supernatural. It is
plain then that history is not pure immanence, it is not an
internal dialectic that evolves and exhausts itself in itself; it
is immanence-transcendence, it is the immanent human process
from a beginning to a goal, both absolute but both communicated to man, and we may rightly say, *historicized*.

The other difficulty touched on is the question of how the
divine can participate in what is worldly. The answer is implicit in what has been said of how the divine is historicized.
That of the supernatural which is given to us, though becoming the life of man and one of the essential factors of the historical process, remains by its nature supernatural, divine. In
this it resembles reason, which though espoused to the senses
remains reason, and though realized in historic facts remains
reason; if it is ill used by man, through ignorance or malice,
it does not for this lose its value as the light of truth, nor its
function as the faculty to know the true. Man turns from his

path; instead of seeking the rational unification he seeks an irrational or pseudo-rational unification; it is evil that presents itself to him under the aspect of immediate good, inducing him to seek its realization in the tumult of passions and malevolence. As evil is opposed to reason, so it is opposed to supernatural grace, and he who has received such grace and then hurtles into evil bears with him the stigma of apostasy — *corruptio optimi pessima.*

That the divine enters into what is worldly does not mean that it becomes mingled with evil, but only that it communicates itself to man. Man is in the world and bears with him all worldly wretchedness and weakness, but insofar as he detaches himself from the world he partakes in the divine. The ladder of perfection has no limit. Inasmuch as we remain imperfect, we, society, historical reality, form the world, and seek to reduce the supernatural to a mundane element, useful or harmful on this low plane, to be accepted as pure rationality or rejected as irrational, and to be mingled with earthly and selfish interests.

The dialectic of good and evil, such is history. From evil, even if concrete and objectivized in the world, good always develops. This beneficent activity is a continuous purification of the pestiferous substratum of historical reality; and it comes to be also a collective *catharsis,* as the longing for justice and love in the midst of injustices and hatreds; as the need for a mystical life in order to escape from material reality and from the social constraints that oppose the noblest ideals; as a vision of the contingent that perishes seen against the transcendant that survives. The supernatural, grafted into history, becomes a perennial and immanent force for the overcoming of worldliness and the setting of man on the way towards the loftiest destinies.

*   *   *   *   *

If history is the consciousness of collective and processive existence, and this consciousness seeks a unification in rationality and in religion, then to have the historical sense is to reflect on this consciousness, to bring it out, to make use of it in all its bearings and all its complexity. Not in all peoples nor at all stages of culture is the historical sense developed, or given the importance and the place that it deserves. Today there is more of it than there was yesterday. The Christian civilization has made it more fruitful than any other civilization. In modern times its value, at one time ignored, is appreciated.

The historical sense is a result of culture, for the uncultured peoples do not possess it. It is not found in a people that has no history, but if a people has no history it is not because it has not had important events in its past, but because it has not felt the fundamental unity between the present and the past, and has not arrived at creating a course for the future. Thus we find the historical sense more highly developed in prophetic Hebraism, which lived by the thought and expectation of the Messias, than among other peoples of the time. We find it in Rome at the height of her grandeur, and therefore conscious of the roads traversed and of her mission in the world. In both peoples the past was linked to the future, and the historical sense reflected the motives of expectation and of action.

Yet it was Christianity that revealed to Jews and Romans, to Greeks and barbarians, the mysterious sense of the history of each people, and that gave value to prophets, sybils, poets, philosophers, statesmen — the divine revealing itself to man, not by becoming animal, as in polytheism, but by sublimating man in his life and in his destiny. The significance of history was through Christianity raised to that of philosophy and theology in one — Humanism and Christianity, nature and supernature. This new way of looking upon history gave us the first fundamental work, an attempt of genius, even if sometimes naïve and involved, St. Augustine's *City of God*. This work was epoch-making in historical culture down to modern times and is still worthy of more study than it receives.

Bossuet's *Discours* was a renewed effort in this direction, under the influence of a reasoned theology, but along the lines of a history still in its infancy, at a period ill-fitted to a deep understanding of historical values in their full objectivity, while the history then was often occasion for apologetic discussions and moral teachings. Apart from the great or petty church historians, who were rather chroniclers or philologists, the ancients looked upon history from the moral standpoint, as a mine of good examples to be followed or bad ones to be avoided, explaining in their way the intervention of Providence, which was often reduced to a work of justice on this earth. Their aim was didactic and their conception of history rather childish. Outside the didactic office and the chronicles of kings or bishops, the history that was most useful to those monks and abbots was that of their diplomas and privileges, of notarial deeds, of delimitations of land, at a time when the prevailing form of associated life was founded on feudal law.

The historical sense of that period was confused with the Christian-ascetic interpretation of life: that men are on earth as a trial, pilgrims who must suffer much on their travels, who may reach their goal through the grace of God, and by doing penance and good works. Contingent reality lost its meaning in the face of man's destiny in another life. It must not be thought that the men of those days no longer cared for pleasures or riches or honors, that they did not seek to dominate one another, did not make war and peace. All this and worse coexisted with the good. But the culture of the time had other orientations — the world of the universals, juridical values, astrology, speculative theology. The meaning of collective life resolved itself into individual life.

The sense of history crept in with Humanism, with Ecclesiology, with the classical Renaissance. But already from age to age the great contacts of ancient thought with Christian theologism had come to lead men beyond a unilateral vision of reality — the neo-Platonism of the fourth and fifth centuries, the Romanism of the ninth, the legal and Aristotelian renascence of the twelfth and thirteenth centuries. In the same way would come Humanism, the Renaissance, modern Mysticism, "Jusnaturalism," Romanticism. Thus gradually history has been assuming ever more complex and deeper aspects, now abounding in the human and rationalistic sense, now in the mystical and theological sense, till it should present itself as it is, the concrete of life in which all values are transcribed in human consciousness.

The great modern philosopher of history is not Hegel but Vico, he who best saw the intimate relationship between doing and knowing, who threw into relief the value of thought as lived in events, the involucre of the reality in legend and poetry, and who divined the inner law of historical process. The two modern trends of the theory of history, that of pure immanence and that of immanence-transcendence, cannot but find their starting point in Vico. The first, after Hegel's prophetism and statism, found its true interpreter in Croce. But notwithstanding his great contribution to a deeper awareness of the value of history, he cannot find his way out of the closed circle of pure immanence, lessening the value, by this very fact, of the historical process and its continual novelty and creativeness. Whenever Croce does not implicitly deny his own theory — as happens when lightnings of truth flash across his grey skies — he is forced to reduce individual personality to an appearance without origin and without destiny, and to cancel in the "spirit" the true human-divine dialectic of history.

The immanent-transcendent theory of history has not received a complete scientific expression. In the struggle against positivism and idealism, the traditional values of historical finalism and of Providence have been maintained, but there has not been a thorough exploration either of the concept of historical consciousness, or of that of process, or of the immanent side of historical activity. Of all this there are traces in the studies of particular branches of knowledge as historically considered, and that is consoling. Maurice Blondel's philosophy together with that of Vico may serve as the basis for a theoretical construction responding to the present development of thought in regard to the immanence-transcendence of history and its humanistic and Christian character.[4]

---

4. The writings of Jacques Maritain on *Integral Humanism,* the work of the Jesuit C. Boyer (*Il Concetto della Storia,* the Thomistic theory of history), and *Il Valore della Storia* of Nicola Petruzzellis, "the value of history as the life of mankind in the whole of its manifestations," mark very important progress in the modern and Christian conception of history.

CHAPTER X

THE INCARNATION
IN HISTORY

HUMAN history, as we see it at any moment of the twenty centuries of Christianity, is the story of the Incarnation of the Word. I say "at any moment," because the moment in time is the present. Neither the past nor the future exists as a moment in time. Only the present exists, that in which the consciousness of each may feel the throb of the life accumulated through the ages and may divine the throb that will continue in the future. There is nothing else, as living consciousness, than the temporal present.

If making abstraction of our faith and the light that it throws upon history, we seek to understand in what the present consists, we must have recourse to a philosophy that will explain its immanent value. Shall we look upon the present as the divine breath that breathes in us and in the whole? Shall we reduce it to a nihilistic phenomenalism, a succession of sensations that leave nothing behind and of evanescent thoughts? But we have the most sublime passage that ever has been or ever will be written, bringing together the eternal act and the temporal act, the Godhead, creation, mankind, and showing us their significance:

"In the beginning was the Word, and the Word was with God; and the Word was God.... All things were made through Him.... In Him was life, and the life was the Light of men.... And the Word was made flesh, and dwelt among us. And we saw His glory — glory as of the Only-begotten of the Father — full of grace and of truth" (John 1:1-14).

The moment in time is "the Word was made flesh," the Word who manifests "the glory of the Only-begotten of the Father. . . . " The repetition of that day is in every day; that moment is every moment. The moment in time has not and cannot have any other significance, any other value than that of mirroring the eternal moment when "in the beginning was the Word, and the Word was God," and "was made flesh."

We have seen how the divine grafts itself into history and how it becomes a factor of human process without diminishing man's freedom to choose between good and evil, between heaven and earth. Nor is this all. Although God respects our human liberty — for without that, of course, there could be no voluntary participation in the divine — in the spiritual and historical life of man, God cannot be other than unfolding truth, compelling, winning love.

This twofold aspect of a freedom that seeks and of a truth-and-love that attracts gives us the inner significance of the union of nature with the supernatural, in their continuous and mysterious contact which began in Eden and was sublimated on Calvary. It has been said that at any moment of the twenty centuries of Christianity we see history hinging on the Incarnation; now we must extend our vision to the whole of human history, for even before Christianity we shall find the Incarnation, in its preparation. Man could not see this preparation save in the light of the tidings brought to Mary. He was wandering by the flickering gleam of a primal tradition that passed into the subconscious among the pagan peoples, or else in the expectation of a Messias popularly conceived of among the Hebrews as a national hero.

Even since the coming of Christ, the development of His religion and the growth of a Christian civilization, there have been many peoples who, like those before Christ, have had only a glimmer of the divine idea in the world; not to speak of those who, though living in a Christian environment, no longer believe in God. Yet insofar as they sincerely aspire to reform and redemption, they too enter into the orbit of the history of the Incarnation, not only as potentially redeemed but as bearing witness to the necessity for a divine intervention that will realize in mankind the truth that was "made flesh," so that men may see the "glory of the Only-begotten of the Father."

Indeed it is a spiritual necessity to find a historical center that will give an orientation towards truth. A subjective idea is not enough, the voice of conscience is not enough; we need in addition something that has found realization in life — that has been embodied, "incarnated," as some say in the widest sense of the word. In science and culture men rally round the leader of a school; the more they are attacked by criticism and tormented by doubt, the more firmly do they cling to their masters. The *ipse dixit* has its psychological value. But if for the constructions of the mind the authority of a genius might suffice, a Plato or an Aristotle for example (to seek no further than non-Christian humanism), for social constructions some higher authority than that of genius is required. They call for divine inspiration. The legend shows Numa in contact with a Nymph, Solon with the gods; the Scripture, Moses ascending Mount Sinai, Solomon obtaining from God the gift of wisdom. The law as divine emanation — here is a fundamental concept in the history of all peoples; justice, the work of God; social institutions mirroring divine values; authority only from God. God in communication with men, awaited by men, and in their midst.

When the Word was made flesh the divine light manifested itself to men who were in darkness, and the angelical song was heard: "Glory to God in the highest, and on earth peace among men of good will." That message implied the double idea of truth revealed (which is glory) and of goodness realized (and that is peace). History cannot but move between these two poles, or it would be devoid of meaning.

A history based solely on the succession of kings as data showing the passage of the years, would have no other value and would get no further. The peasant buried in the mountains, with no other contact with the world than the sale of his produce, is interested in his king as figuring on the coins that buy what he needs and pay his debts and taxes. The succession of kings might interest him if it meant a new coinage; the memory of the various dead sovereigns would have significance in helping him to count his age or to date his domestic and economic vicissitudes. That is what history would be for him, merely a rudimentary consciousness of time. And even for that purpose, the changing aspects of the trees or the sale of his donkeys and foals at the different fairs would be a more practical aid than the succession of rulers.

It is not here that we shall find history. The changes that have been mentioned will become history when they come to reveal fresh aspects of life, to create new spiritual exigencies, to arouse the feelings of social groups and stir them to action, to feed revolution, first in the mind, then in events. There is no history without the manifestation of a truth to be actuated, and without the impulse of a love to be communicated — without raising man from the sphere of the rational to the divine mystery and bringing back the divine word into human life and historicizing it. It is thus with all history, at whatever point we take it, whether the first yearnings of mankind or modern civilization.

The Incarnation is its culminating point — a mysterious sign of the infinite in the circumscribed, polarizing the transient towards the absolute; a historical revelation that makes the past and the future converge towards itself, and remains ever present in the human process. All the aspirations worthy of man are here fulfilled and all of the divine communicable to man becomes history. We Christians believe by faith in the dwelling of the Word in our midst as true man, the revelation to men of the glory of the Son of God.

*   *   *   *   *

The meaning of history is very hard to understand, for little of its transcendental character appears from any single event; it cannot be grasped in the particular data of the process, and only from afar does it become a revelation to the few who meditate on it with sufficient knowledge.

What can our small personal labors give to society and what will be their worth for history? Hardly anything. That is the case in regard to millions and millions of men who live and disappear into the shadows. It would seem that the makers of history are very few; and if we analyze even their contribution we shall see it vanish as soon as we touch it. What has a Louis XIV given to mankind? Or a Napoleon? Did they really make the greatness of a nation? Have they left a beneficent legacy of lasting value? Of many who were once believed great, nothing remains. If we limit our investigation to those who have left immortal works in science, in art, in philosophy and theology, we know that only a few profit by them till others take their place, so that their contribution is the memory only of the specialists and initiates.

Everything seems to vanish into a useless labor of making and unmaking, of creating and destroying, of heaping up and scattering. A flood, a cataclysm, a general war, and the past is reduced to mere remains and documents which will then be preserved with pious care only to be dispersed again by fire or flood or the senseless frenzy of man himself.

Such a vision of history as the progressive destroying or undoing or vanishing of human activity makes us understand that it is not from this standpoint that we can evaluate the past. The material aspect of human labors is composed and decomposed like our bodies, which when alive assume alluring aspects and with the failure of life fall into decay, food for the worms, dust that the wind blows away. Only the soul, which gives life to corporeal matter — historical matter like any other — is able to reveal itself, and to show within itself the eternal beauty; it alone represents the living embodiment of a higher principle, and through it alone can the past regain in our consciousness (the act of our soul) its revealing virtue and continue in the present the function that its fleeting worldly existence had in temporal reality.

To attain this spiritual continuity we ourselves need to be initiated into a sure grasp of the present in which we live and in which the whole of the historical past is reconcentrated and exists as in its fruit (for nothing of good that has once been is lost in its essence), so that we can ask of the present the title-deeds of its reality, the meaning of its existence, and bid it unveil to us its mysterious face. The answer, if it is entire, cannot but illuminate the whole of history, which in its fashion speaks to us of the Everlasting Word. In saying this I do not confuse a mystery of faith with natural reality, but I simply aim to bring into the light the human-divine synthesis which is the history of man on earth.

It is not speculative reason that can arrive at the knowledge of such a synthesis; it is history that shows it to us, because into history has been grafted revelation, as original tradition, as the Mosaic Law, as the Good News of the Gospel. And Christ is the center of this revelation and His Church is its continuance through the ages. It is the function of history to give us the factual elements grafted into the human process which shows us the existence of the mystery of God's communication to man.

One of the historical facts that will always remain dark for unaided human reason is that of the personality of Jesus. It is inexplicable without the faith that it is God who speaks in Him and that He is God. The Jews saw the miracles of Jesus and heard His words, but many of them were closed to the truth because they were expecting a national Messias who would overcome their enemies and restore the kingdom of Israel, and because they shrank from accepting a man as the Son of God: this to them was blasphemy. St. John tells that on the Feast of the Dedication: *"Jesus was walking in the temple, in Solomon's porch. The Jews therefore gathered round Him and said to Him, 'How long dost thou keep us in suspense? If thou art the Christ, tell us openly.' Jesus answered them, 'I tell you, and you do not believe. The works that I do in the name of My Father, these bear witness concerning Me. But you do not believe because you are not of My sheep'"* (John 10: 23-26).

The doubt in those Jews might have been legitimate. They were witnesses to the extraordinary fact of the preaching of Jesus. They found a radical conflict between their Messianic conception and that which was being realized under their eyes. They wanted to resolve this doubt, but they were not docile enough to understand the facts. Thus, when Jesus declared categorically: "I and the Father are one," the Jews took up stones to stone Him. And when He rebuked them, referring them to His works, *"The Jews answered him, 'Not for a good work do we stone thee, but for blasphemy, and because thou, being a man, makest thyself God.'"* And Jesus then replied in one of those luminous passages that recall us to the mystery of our participation in the divine: *"Is it not written in your Law, 'I said, you are gods'? If he called them gods to whom the word of God was addressed (and the Scripture cannot be broken), do you say of Him whom the Father has made holy and sent into the world, 'Thou blasphemest,' because I said, 'I am the Son of God'? If I do not perform the works of My Father, do not believe Me. But if I do perform them and if you are not willing to believe Me, believe the works, that you may know and believe that the Father is in Me and I in the Father"* (ibid. 30-38).

This clear teaching is directed also to all those who doubt the Divinity of Jesus or deny it. The historical fact of Jesus, His preaching, His miracles, cannot be separated from His affirmation that He is the Son of God, that He and the Father "are one." They must either be accepted together or denied together. But to deny them is not to solve the historical problem of Jesus, of His influence, of the realization of His word through the centuries. It would have an unforeseen yet logical result: that of depriving history of any intrinsic meaning, reducing it to an interplay of facts without outcome, to a continuous immanent repetition of human activity without resolution. To deny the communication of God to us through Jesus Christ is to deny any other historical communication of God, so interconnected are the primal, the Mosaic and the Christian revelations. And if we may find in other religions traces of the primal revelation, or derivations from the Mosaic and even the Christian, no sensible man and no serious historian could take Brahmanism and Mahommedanism, as divine revelations in place of Christianity. That is why to deny the revelation of Jesus is to deny every true and real revelation and to deprive history of any supernatural significance.

*   *   *   *   *

It may be objected that neither before our era — whether for forty or four hundred centuries does not matter — nor since, down to the present day, have the greater part of men known the truth of the Incarnation of the Word in the Person of Jesus, nor its historical function.

The objection seems a grave one, but it runs counter to the human-divine fashion of historical realization. Such realization is founded on God's freedom to present His gifts to men in the twofold order, inward and spiritual, outward and historical, and upon human freedom to accept and realize in deeds the divine gifts. The contact between man and God is a contact of freedom. Without freedom there would be neither the quest for truth nor the union through love, there would not be life. A deterministic, compelling force exercised upon us would not be a contact of spirit between us and the Godhead. That is why the inner life of grace of each one of us, though the result of divine initiative and intervention, is free, is in our hands, and we can cleave to it in love or reject it in hatred. On the same principle, history is our free activity, it is human realization, though it is the result of the initiative and intervention of God. It represents the alternatives of acceptance or rejection of the divine which come to us and which dwell within us.

To grapple more closely with the objection to which reference has been made, and to expose the sophism that it contains, let us try to review some of the more important facts of our inner life. The achievement of an idea, of a principle that synthesizes many others and throws light on the ways of our heart, is such an event for each one of us as to remain unforgettable; all later deviations through weakness or malice cry out upon us, repeating that unifying idea that gave us light and warmed our hearts.

Something of the same sort happens in history for those who arrive at a knowledge of the facts, or at a contact with the geniuses or saints, that give the sense of a higher force manifest in them. The ancient figures of Socrates and Plato, of Fabricius and Regulus, the Hebrew prophets Moses or Isaias; in the Middle Ages, Hildebrand, Dominic, Francis, Thomas Aquinas, Louis IX of France, Dante, Catherine of Siena; or among the moderns, Teresa of Jesus, Francis Xavier, Galileo, Vincent de Paul (I take the first names that come to mind) — such figures remain in the treasure-house of historical truth, they are signs of heights reached in the epic of mankind, because in a certain fashion they reveal the divine, either through their ideas or through their virtues and their heroism.

Everyone does not know about Socrates or Regulus or Isaias; they may know of others who come closer to their own experience and the common knowledge of the environment in which they live. Some will be historical figures and others only believed to be such. Men may come to be glorified in the general estimation who had not the virtues attributed to them or had some and not the rest — a Constantine, a Charlemagne, will have a whole panegyrical literature, reaching the imagination of the people but not their heart. There will be chaff in the immense patrimony of historical greatness — it is the human side that cannot be eliminated so long as we have passions urging us and an imagination that colors reality, and the worse for us if we had them not! Actually, we should never be able to understand our own reality if we could not relate it to the spiritual greatness which mankind has achieved in the course of history.

The figure, the life of Jesus infinitely overtops all the heroes, geniuses and saints of which history tells us. His name not only is adored by Christians, who today comprise over a third of mankind, but is known by Jews and Mussulmans and by the cultured sections of the other non-Christian populations. The missionary spirit in Christianity has never failed; the Good News is being spread increasingly among native peoples. Our civilization, in its roots and in whatever of good exists in the domain of morals, law, manners and culture, is substantially Christian. Among Christians, it is true, many have neither faith nor religious interests, but these too live unconsciously by Christian thought, environment, history. The Incarnation for many may not be a belief, but no one can escape the influence of the Jesus of the Gospels, and historical knowledge will oblige them to date from Jesus the changed course in moral and social life that has created our civilization, and to brand as anti-Christian all the graver collective deviations.

All this is fact, but only those who believe in the Incarnation and study its significance can grasp its true historical value. How else? Could the historical values of the sciences be known to those who have not learned them? Could the development of painting and sculpture or the other arts be fully understood by those without either technical or historical knowledge on the subject? And yet historical notions of the sciences, of the arts, of philosophies, form a patrimony of thought which no one can evade, even if he has no clear idea of it, through that part of it that radiates from the life of his environment. But still more than science, art and philosophy, it is religion — which indeed embraces and makes fruitful all other human activity — that spreads through the world by the twofold spiritual and historical contact. Those who at one time may be refractory to it, at a given moment will feel its efficacy. Those who have never felt within themselves even remote reflections of it, may come to feel its revelation as a light making plain what was earlier hidden in

the shadows of their consciousness, kindling in their hearts
affections that were unknown or stifled.

And not only in respect of its psychological reflections but
indeed in respect of objective values can we affirm that the
Incarnation is at the center of history. If the fact is not understood by all, and many still do not know it or appreciate it,
this does not mean that it is not a fact. Those who strive towards the values that the Incarnation represents, will draw
near, it may be unconsciously, to this center, and will assimilate
what they are capable of receiving. History, the whole of history, leads to this term by a path at once clear and mysterious,
with natural and supernatural laws, with movements alternating between attraction and repulsion, with free proffers and
also by compelling ways; it is the whole historical complexus
that speaks to us at once of the human and the divine.

* * * * *

One people alone in antiquity had the consciousness of
the divine pure of naturalistic and magical taint, in doctrine
and in worship, although they too fell several times into
idolatry — the Hebrew people. Abraham is their forefather not
so much genealogically as spiritually. Moses is their liberator,
lawgiver and organizer. Judges, kings, prophets, scribes, priests
and leaders voice their consciousness as a chosen people.
Israel had a history and a historical consciousness because in
that people earthly happenings and religious meaning were
fused together, unified in Messianic finalism.

One of the exceptions that are historically inexplicable
is precisely the rigidity of the spiritual, monotheistic conception of the Hebrews, set as they were in the midst of the
peoples of Asia and the Mediterranean who had filled every

corner with gods and goddesses and whose ideas and images
were entirely anthropomorphic and mixed with magic. Such
an achievement as spiritual monotheism remained the sacred
trust of a people enclosed within itself, yet in contact with
the world — Asia, Egypt, Greece and Rome.

We do not know of any other ancient peoples that may
have been able to preserve and augment their faith in the one
personal God, their own God and the God of all, as did the
Hebrews. We know of primitive peoples like the Pygmies
who have kept the monotheistic idea, and of others that admit
a supreme god, together with particular and subordinate deities, but there is nothing to suggest that they have made of
monotheism a religious and cultural mission. It must be granted
that, both for single individuals and for groups, every conquest
of truth, when it becomes conscious, gives birth to the feeling
that it must be guarded, defended and propagated. Whether
there were in Africa, in Asia, in America or in Oceania peoples who, before the Gospel was preached to them, felt such
a monotheistic mission, we do not know, but we cannot exclude the hypothesis as absurd.

It is not intended, however, to draw hypothetical compari-
sons with the history and documents of the Hebrew people.
The formation of the Sacred Books, the purity of the religious
conception which they reveal, the Messianic tradition that
grows out of it, give the exceptional line to their history. Although we may find among other peoples spiritual canticles,
loftiness of thought, purity of affection towards the Godhead,
we do not find a complexus of beliefs like that of the Hebrews,
without superstitious obscuration, without the taint of naturalistic fables attributing licentious adventures to their gods. It is
here that the sense of collective sin and of individual sin, the
idea of justice and of justification, of the Law, of the need for

redemption, of God's mercy, of His indwelling in us, of His love and of our duty to love Him, gradually come to light.

One of the surprises of history is the maturity of religious and moral thought that we find about the sixth and fifth centuries before Christ, not only in the Hebrew people but, almost contemporaneously, among the other Mediterranean peoples that have left us writings and documents. Yet it is from this period that the Hebrew people, in the extremity of trial, through the voice of its prophets, the sayings and visions of scribes and priests, renews its own religious life and gives it its definitive stamp; whereas the other peoples have only philosophies of the elite, esoteric cults, and do not succeed in refashioning a collective religious consciousness in communion with God.

Here is the central point that differentiates the Hebrew from all the other peoples of antiquity. Although the conception of God is rigidly uni-personal (the few Trinitarian references in the Old Testament could not suffice to make the existence of such a mystery known), the whole life of that people is felt as a continuous communication with God. The other peoples conceived of their deities either as protectors to be invoked or placated or as malign genii to be kept at a distance; but only in regard to their outward life, collective and personal. Their gods did not enter into the soul, they did not fecundate the spirit, they did not lift men up to them in the joy of communication or the terror of chastisement. It is not denied that there were in paganism elect spirits who arrived at the conception of the Godhead in communion with man, but this did not become a common consciousness and did not mould the historical activity of other peoples, as happened with Hebrewism.

If we say today that the whole long history of the children of Abraham was ordained in preparation for the Redeemer who was to be born of their people, to accomplish His life and sacrifice in their midst, we cannot be accused of arguing *post hoc ergo propter hoc*. The whole of the Scriptures and the orientation of that people looked towards the Messias. After Jesus Christ, neither the Hebrew scriptures nor the history of the Jewish people has any longer consistency or meaning. Without declaring the whole of Hebrewism a historical falsification, it is impossible to escape the evidence of the function of that people in preserving and fecundating the revealed word and in preparing for its historical fulfilment — the Incarnation of the Word.

If the Hebrew had such an exceptional mission — God, in willing to become incarnate, had to choose a people and prepare it — the other peoples too shared, insofar as it was possible for them, in the affirmation of the truth and in the spiritual and historical preparation for the Incarnation. On this I have touched more than once in the present book, but from other aspects; what concerns us here is the historical value of such an affirmation.

St. Paul sets Jews and Gentiles on the same plane in the face of the justification given by Jesus Christ, not as though he ignored the merits and privileges of the Mosaic Law, but to celebrate the gratuity of the Redemption for all men and to underline the spirituality of the response to the divine gift which, setting aside all historical considerations, sank into the depths of the soul: *"Tribulation and anguish . . . upon the soul of every man who works evil; of Jew first and then of Greek. But glory and honor and peace . . . to everyone who does good, to Jew first and then to Greek. Because with God there is no respect of persons. For whoever have sinned without the Law, will perish without the Law; and whoever have sinned under the Law, will be judged by the Law"* (Rom. 2:9-12). And pursuing this thought, he declares further on: *"Is*

God the God of the Jews only, and not of the Gentiles also?
Indeed of the Gentiles also. For there is but one God who
will justify the circumcised by faith, and the uncircumcised
through the same faith. Do we therefore through faith destroy
the Law? By no means! Rather, we establish the Law" (ibid.
3:29-31).

St. Paul is here anxious to make it clear that justification
is by faith, through the sacrifice of Christ, the same for all,
and hence not a privilege of the Jews. But in establishing the
ethical function of the Law he presupposes its historical function, and in the same way for the Jews as for the Gentiles;
to the first he gives the responsibility coming to them from the
Law, to the second that from the light of reason. Apart from
the tradition of the original revelation scattered through the
ages, the Gentiles should have been able, on the moral plane,
to give worship and adoration to God and to keep the precepts
of the natural law, so they too are worthy of reward or punishment.

From the historical standpoint, there is founded on this
Pauline principle the criterion of the attainment of truths
which little by little come to form real collective conquests,
remaining in the consciousness and in the life of the peoples
as guiding stars either for a return to such truths or for the
conquest of others. When at last these peoples (and similarly
each individual) arrive at a knowledge of the substantial truth,
the Word of God in His Incarnation, then all their past conquests are lit by a new life, the glimmerings of truth grow
bright, everything is reoriented and coördinated, and their history reveals itself as a hesitant journey in the dark towards
this term, a secret symbol which is now unveiled, a secret voice
that now speaks plainly *"to shine on those who sit in darkness*
and in the shadow of death, to guide our feet into the way of
peace" (Luke 1:79).

*   *   *   *   *

Few are the immortal books that speak to the mind and
heart of all peoples and generations, all classes and ages, and
that remain as milestones of history. Among these few, the
New Testament is unique, with its Gospels, Acts of the Apostles, Epistles and Apocalypse. Here is a wealth of life, a constant humanity, a moral sureness, a revealing and life-giving
word, a real and deep contact with God. And it is history:
the history, not only of those years from the beginning of
our era to John's vision on Patmos, but of that Christian seed
that was to have so abundant an increase, and never fail.

The Gospel presents itself at first sight as the historical,
moral and mystical accomplishment of the Law and the Prophets — the fulfilment of the promises. Thus it is closely bound
up with the whole of Hebrew history. The God of the Christians is *"the God of Abraham and the God of Isaac and the
God of Jacob, the God of our fathers"* (Acts 3:13). It is
Jesus who tells the Jews: *"Abraham your father rejoiced that
he was to see My day. He saw it and was glad"* (John 8:56).
The whole of Stephen's discourse to the men of Jerusalem,
all the discourses of Peter and Paul reported in Acts, stress
the historical bond of the Old Testament with the New. The
new Christian consciousness is created on the historical continuity that goes back to Abraham through the vocation and
the promise. St. Matthew's Gospel opens with the historic
words: "The book of the generation of Jesus Christ, the Son
of David, the Son of Abraham." The promise that God made
to Abraham is fulfilled in Jesus. Of this promise St. Paul
speaks, relating it to the natural descendance of those Israelites who did not believe in Christ, where he speaks of his great
grief for his brethren who yet had had *"the adoption as sons,
and the glory and the covenants and the legislation and the*

*worship and the promises; who have the fathers, and from
whom is the Christ according to the flesh . . . "* (Rom. 9:4-5).
And he goes on to affirm that the word of God is not lost:
*"For they are not all Israelites who are sprung from Israel;
nor because they are the descendants of Abraham, are they all
his children";* but *"qui filii sunt promissionis, æstimantur in
semine"* (ibid. 8).[1]

It might be objected that the Trinitarian God of the Christians is not the unitarian God of the Hebrews; that the religious continuation had been altered at the roots rendering
impossible the historical unification. But this objection, which
might appear insuperable to the Hebrews of the time of St.
Paul, is not so for Christians, who understand the gradual
revelation of God, mysteriously three and one, His Trinity
neither lessening nor changing His unity. Nor is it so even
for non-Christian students who are in a position to acquaint
themselves fully with the link between the Old Testament
and the New and the passage from one to the other without
discontinuity either theological or historical. Jesus in His
preaching little by little insinuates and then clearly proclaims
His divine nature and His unity with the Father, and in diverse
ways gives the understanding of the Personality of the Holy
Ghost in the very unity of God, and precisely of the God of
Abraham, of Isaac and of Jacob.

One of the evident intentions of the Gospel teaching
is that of banishing the current idea of a national, worldly
Messias, who would have restored the kingdom to Israel and
thus fulfilled the promise to Abraham by the triumph of the
chosen people and of its Law. Jesus escapes from the crowd
who, stirred by His miracles, would have proclaimed Him
king. He dwells on His imminent betrayal and abandonment

---

1. " . . . *it is the children of promise who are reckoned as a
posterity."*

and death. He suffers persecution without retaliating. He declares that His kingdom is not of this world. He consents to be judged, condemned and crucified. When after the Resurrection, the disciples, still not wholly detached from the ideas of their environment, ask Him: *"Lord, wilt Thou at this time restore the kingdom to Israel?"* He replies: *"It is not for you to know the times or dates which the Father has fixed by His own authority; but you shall receive power when the Holy Spirit comes upon you, and you shall be witnesses for Me in Jerusalem and in all Judea and Samaria and even to the very ends of the earth"* (Acts 1:6-8).

Here is the new sense of the history that is about to unfold. The Hebrews awaited the Messias; they had the promises of a chosen people aided by God or chastised by Him according to their faithfulness or unfaithfulness to the Covenant given through Moses. It was on these lines that their marvelous history developed, through manifold experiences of the divine mingling with human happenings, individual or collective, in a process of spiritual enrichment that was consolidated in the Holy Books. Not even the Hebrews could know "the times or dates." They lived by memories and hopes, a life in which they now sought God with ardor and now forsook Him to seek aid of Moloch or Baal. They experienced the fire of Elias and the deportation to Babylon. Thus they prepared a consciousness that would be ripe for the advent of the true Messias, whom they for the most part failed to recognize because He presented Himself as God and died as a condemned man.

From the apostles and disciples before the Ascension, Jesus took all that might remain of the illusions of their subconscious national Messianism, and assigned to them their true historic task to "be witnesses" of Him, among the Jews and among the

Gentiles and "even to the very ends of the earth." And that the witness they bore might be true, vigorous, constant and organized, He would send the Holy Ghost, the Spirit of truth and of love, to dwell in them.

This witness to Christ would continue through the ages. There would be His Church — His apostles and disciples, the women, the multitude as at Jerusalem — disseminated throughout the world. The history of the many peoples evangelized would become the history of a new chosen people, not confined to one place or one nation. The Christian name would be spread throughout the world, even among peoples that would retain in by far the greater part and for long ages their ancestral beliefs. With reason did Paul and Barnabas, to justify their preaching to the Gentiles, quote the passage of Isaias on the servant of the Lord: *"I have set thee for a light to the Gentiles, to be a means of salvation to the very ends of the earth"* (Acts 13:47).

To know "the times or the dates" of the history to come is never given to men, not even to those who may think that our activity is tied to a merely earthly cycle, matured and developed by immanent forces, with no transcendence at all. "The times or the dates" of the historical process, looked upon as human events, will have their unforeseen happening. Men will believe that they have arrived at peace and it is war that meets them. They will believe that they can buy tranquillity with concessions and be faced by revolts. They will strive to consolidate kingdoms and empires and these will collapse. They will have confidence in economic and political laws only to see them annulled or overruled. "The times or dates" are kept in the "power of the Father." They depend on a Providence that is not and cannot be human. Man's duty is to collaborate with Providence, freely indeed, but to collaborate.

And the substance of such collaboration is to be "witness to the truth," each man to that truth at which he has arrived or may arrive; for we are all called to the light, but for Christians that witness is centered in Christ, the Incarnate Word, the realization of the divine promises and of the hopes of mankind, placed at the center of the whole of creation and at the center of human history.

CHAPTER XI

CHRISTIANITY IN HISTORY

THE place taken by Christianity in history is such that no polemical arts can belittle it. It has become so integral a part of history that any attempt to ignore it must make history incomprehensible. Those who divide history into the civil and the religious may write didactic books or chronicles, special studies and works of erudition (apart from the polemists and panegyrists who do not concern us), but they will never create a constructive history, true history. For when we wish to reach to the deeper meaning of events, their repercussions on thought, culture, art, manners, and vice-versa, we have to go down to the religious substratum, giving its full value to Christianity and bringing together all that goes to form historical reality, every form of human activity in its twofold characteristic, civil and religious, natural and supernatural. In substance, true history cannot be written if what has here been called the insertion of the divine into history is ignored.

Christianity gives us the key to this insertion; indeed it continues it, teaching and propagating the doctrine of Christ, continuing and extending the Church and the institutions willed by Christ and entrusted to the apostles, in whose midst, in their succession, He has promised to remain "even unto the consummation of the world."[1] The Church is the Christian organization in society; the Church as a spiritual, permanent, universal institution is the positive actuation of Christianity

---

1. Matt. 28:20.

through the ages. This fact in itself has brought into human life and society a fundamental and indestructible dualism, a dualism of forces, of organisms, of spiritual values, which is salutary and fruitful. It has given the history of mankind another mould, a character, a significance, to be found in no other period and in no other civilization.

Christianity introduced and made fruitful an idea of universality. This was not to be found among either the Greeks or the Romans, who strove for no more than the primacy of culture or that of arms. But apart from rays of light in philosophy, in art, in law, they never reached the conception of the brotherhood of all men. Who, then, could have thought of a Church divinely invested with the function of affirming itself by itself alone throughout the whole world, propagating a unique and saving message to all, creating an organism fitted to this mission and therefore superior in dignity, purpose, extent and powers (albeit spiritual powers, indeed, because they were spiritual powers) to those of all earthly authorities? It is true that this fact brought onto the social-organic plane the dualism between the kingdom of this world and the Kingdom of God, which is not of this world yet is in the world; for the Church is a social organism, standing by itself, speaking in the name of God and as the visible embodiment of Christianity through the ages. This dualism releases a historical dialectic that tends to surmount all duality by a higher unification, that of universal brotherhood.

Such ideas did not easily penetrate society, nor can they be said to have completely penetrated it even now, or in such a way as not to lose something, for they have often been set aside and rejected by social life. But they are always in ferment and are the active elements of a transformation, both inwardly in the individual and in the life of society, which could not possibly come about without them. Mankind received through

Christianity an orientation towards universalism and solidarity above classes, nations and races. So long as each people (indeed, each city, each family) had its own god or gods, unification came as the act of a central power at once political and religious, and man could not acquire the sense of universality. This is possible only when, in the name of one God, the true God, particular deities are supplanted. It could never have been achieved save through a Church divinely instituted for all, the Christian Church.

The Church is not universal through having fulfilled the prophecy of the "one fold and one shepherd," nor will it become universal upon that fulfilment. The Church is universal in act, even today, because it has the mission and the means to become so; because the faith and truth that the Church believes and propagates is universal. This universality forms a bond of brotherhood above that of blood, for it is a spiritual bond of love uniting men to God because God Himself is united with them. *"For where two or three are gathered together for My sake, there am I in the midst of them"* (Matt. 18:20).[2] This bond is operative insofar as faith in God through love is operative. Universality and brotherhood have meaning only through a life lived in communication with God, and this is proclaimed, promoted, nourished by the Church. The sociologico-mystical value of the Church in society thus assumes a capital importance.

I have several times in the course of the present work touched on the character of society as the product of associated activity, not apart from or above individuals, but consisting of individuals united together. The social institutions that objectivate human action and render it lasting have value and are real just insofar as they are animated by the consciousness

---

2. In the Vulgate: *"in nomine meo."*

of the associated individuals themselves and by their processive continuity. Society may therefore be regarded either as a
plurality, in the multiplicity of social nuclei conscious of their
individuality and purpose, or as a duality, in the affirmative
and negative positions taken up in the contest of action, or as
one, in its unifying and transcendental orientation.[3]

These aspects of sociology may be applied to the Church
in respect of all that is human in it, all that it comprises of
social activities, ways and orientations. But we must at once
affirm, so as not to fall into error, that the Church has a mystical social nature all its own, giving it a real and permanent
consistency that only believers can fully know, by faith and not
through human experience. For the Church is the mystical
body of Christ, and as such, can come under no human sociological theory. That which for society is unity of consciousness (a dynamic, variable unity, a tendency towards unification) in the Church is the union with Christ through grace,
in the indwelling of the Holy Ghost. Hence the social reality
of the Church comprehends the associated individual and
reaches beyond him, not through a conceptual or symbolical
value, but through an effectual participation in the divine nature of Christ and His eternal Sonship.

The non-believer sees nothing of all this. He sees only an
institutional organization of Christian worship, with all its
practical ramifications in law, culture and custom. He sees, too,
a body of doctrines which he is unable fully to understand and
which he interprets in a human sense. Assuredly the Church
can be regarded, sociologically, also from its visible aspect,
with all its interplay with the world, influencing and influenced
by the human society in which it lives, in a reciprocal flux

---

3. See L. Sturzo, *Essai de Sociologie,* chap. I, p. 42; chap. II,
pp. 49-50.

and reflux of energies and a duality of moral and also of material forces, which affect the whole historical process. But if, in thus regarding the Church, we were to preclude its mystical and supernatural character, we should fall into the error — no new one, and yet under certain aspects ever new — of wishing to make of the Church either an organism subordinated to the power of society (today the State), or else its antagonist. And since every attempt at subordination fails, there is often a quest for compromises entailing the coexistence of two laws and two organisms and two authorities, conceived as outside the social body itself. These compromises are not always resistant, just as attempts at subordination do not always succeed. It is then that the most violent persecutions are unloosed, in order to eliminate the Church and blot out even the name of Christianity.

* * * * *

In the historical process, from the appearance of Christianity down to the present time, one of the most interesting phenomena to study is precisely that of the renewed attempts to eliminate the Church, to exterminate it, or where this is not possible, to enslave it; and in any case, to contest its development and increase. To this end men have put forth a twofold effort — the use of the activity of the mind, through education, culture, propaganda, controversy; or else the use of legal, political, judicial or military force on the part of heads of States, cities, peoples, tribes, or, finally, the anarchic violence of excited and fanatical mobs.

Jesus foretold that there would be this hatred on the part of the world against Himself, His name, His disciples, His Church. And for this He promised His aid so that "the gates of hell shall not prevail against it."[4] But what for us is theological certainty does not alter the course of events as these arise from human causes and conditioning factors. History shows us now the long centuries of persecution and Christian life in the catacombs under the Roman Empire, now the heretical agitations supported by Christian emperors, now Islam, which for many centuries stifled all Christian ideas in the Arabic, Persian and Berber world and in various European countries. Vast and far-reaching are the crises of the Reformation, of Jansenism, of the Enlightenment. The Christianity introduced into Japan in the sixteenth century was repressed there for nearly three hundred years; a like parenthesis is to be found in China and elsewhere. Half of Europe has today lost all Christian faith, through Positivism, Hegelianism, Marxism, Bolshevism, Nazism. And yet, not only is the invisible Church, the mystical body of Christ, alive, and often through the very persecutions greatly on the increase, but the visible, institutional Church too resists, reorganizes itself, expands, reconquers the ground lost, enduring through twenty centuries with an unbroken succession of Popes who maintain the center of unification on the solid rock on which the Church was built by Christ.

In the attempt to destroy the Church or to transform it to worldly uses, it has never been possible to find anything that could either rival it or supplant it in its two characteristic features of universality and brotherhood among men. Human means for attempting a universal unification cannot be other than either power and force, or reason. But these do not provide us with even a trend towards universality. The first is by nature friable, through diversity of tongues, of customs, of interests, of geographic zones, of political aspirations to world

---

4. Matt. 16:18.

power. The great empires fall to fragments by their own weight. The Middle Ages sought to realize the universal Christian idea also in a political power set side by side with the Church, the Holy Roman Empire. But western Christendom was never politically unified, while that of the East was dissident, and the imperial institution little by little contracted to Germany, revealing itself as merely a historical phase of feudal organization.

The other means, that of reason, was also used by medieval Scholasticism in the quest for a Christian universalism in philosophy. But all human philosophies, those of the Schools included, failed to find an issue from the particularism of their systems, contradicting one another in a continual making and unmaking, so that unaided reason found itself a prey to the most discordant doctrines; without the light of revelation Scholasticism itself would not have remained immune against the grave errors that nominalists, conceptualists, ultra-realists, upheld in the name of their dialectic. In any case, the domain of Scholasticism became increasingly assimilated to that of the Church, while the whole anti-Christian world followed and still follows the most widely different philosophies, which lead to scepticism or to pantheism with no possibility of unifying mankind under the guidance of reason. The idea of natural law and that of philosophical humanitarianism in the seventeenth and eighteenth centuries were soon submerged by the particularistic conceptions that sprang from them at the same time as their laicism. If they had grafted themselves into the Christian conception (from which they originally came), the law of nature and humanitarianism would have rendered a great service to civilization. Set against it, through historical circumstances and intellectual libertinage, they soon ran dry and were superseded by the immanentistic and positivist conceptions of law and of society.

Pure human brotherhood? It is but a vague philosophical idea, which has never been able to avail against the egoistic passions of *homo homini lupus*. Only in Christianity can such an idea become concrete in life as lived, in a continuous struggle against ourselves, slowly, painfully and yet unfalteringly finding realization. This is not to deny that many charitable institutions were established by States and by private individuals in the nineteenth century with humanitarian and secular inspiration. It would be foolish to seek a comparison between what constitutes the organization of public assistance from the nineteenth century onwards (starting with accident and unemployment insurance, maternity clinics, the Red Cross and the like) and what existed in earlier centuries. Anyone going thoroughly into the study of this phenomenon will find it the product of three factors — the wider distribution of wealth due to the capitalistic transformation, state intervention in social matters, the lessening of class differences. All three are organic factors and are interesting, but since by their nature they do not pass from the material to the spiritual (they call for an impulse of love to transform their value), they are impotent to prevent the immense hatred that capitalism has produced both between classes and between nations.

What may be called secular charity is at bottom Christian, inasmuch as it means help to fellow-men as fellow-men, though perceiving in man not the likeness of God, but only a being who has equal rights with others. The fact is that human egoism can be mortified only by a religion of sacrifice like Christianity. Universal brotherhood, or better, the love of our neighbor widened to include all, cannot be achieved save insofar as there is mortification (and not exaltation) of the egoism of persons, classes and peoples. It is not at all strange that together with laicism and under its ægis we have seen the unbounded glorification of powerful men, precisely at a time when they were compassing the most monstrous form of particularism and egoism through the combination of political and spiritual tryanny.

It seemed possible in the last century that — once society had thrown off the yoke of the *ancien régime* and the ecclesiastical temporalism associated with it — natural morality and religious toleration, guaranteed by the secularized State, would provide a conception for all civilized peoples that would lead to an ethico-juridical universality wider than Christianity. In such a system reason and force were to have worked together. But it must be recognized that all endeavors made or yet to be made with the aim, open or disguised, of eliminating the Christian influence and substituting for it the laic conception of life, must meet with the same difficulties as we have already noted in regard to force and reason taken separately. The ethico-juridical organization of States, whether internal or in their international relationships, becomes particularized as soon as local interests prevail over laws, over agreements and over the principles that have inspired them. Has not slavery reappeared under new forms, even in civilized countries, since it was formally abolished? And after equality among all citizens was proclaimed, were not acute inequalities produced by capitalism? Soon after the League of Nations had been founded, was not international understanding shattered in the name of such conceptions as nazism and fascism, based on an exclusivist morality? And are the democracies inspired by uncontested ethico-juridical principles, or are they not riddled by such a variety of policies and conceptions as at bottom to deny the very law of nature on which they should be founded?

I do not mean to condemn all the efforts made, even on the purely political and economic plane, for understanding between peoples and between classes, for the unification of systems of law, for the improvement of human relationships.

I mean merely to affirm that even in the ethico-juridical field, and even in non-Christian countries, universality cannot be attained save through Christianity and in actuation of the Christian spirit and ethics. Christianity alone can present a universal morality for all ages and for all peoples in its principles and in its general applications, both because it interprets the natural law in its most accurate formulation, and still more because it bases all true morality on the precept of combined love of God and love of our neighbor.

Apart from particular norms according to peoples and periods, Christianity penetrates the moral life of peoples, even if these are not converted or do not practice the Christian religion, insofar as the spirit of love penetrates, and informs their institutions, culture and life. But Christianity would not bring transformation and moral unification if it were not above all a religion, and as such preached to men for their free and voluntary acceptance. In this inner freedom the moral act and the religious act coincide and complete each other. Any external and imposed morality and any purely formalistic religion would never be able to reach man's inner life and bring the sense of universality.

It is often said that the Christian morality too is a particular morality, enjoined upon the faithful by their Church. This is a grave error. I have said that Christian morality is founded upon natural morality (as formulated in the Ten Commandments), that it would be universal if men were of themselves capable of carrying it into practice and bringing out its full value, and that it is centered in the love that Jesus confirmed and extended even to enemies. Who can remain outside this precept, be he Christian or no? Only he who denies human universality and the principle of brotherhood. But on the other hand, who can speak truly of human brotherhood save in the name of that religion that makes us all creatures of God, like to Him, and through grace sons of adoption, all called to His divine fellowship? And who can achieve this spirit of brotherhood in earthly life save one able to bridle his selfish passions? Who can succeed in this without the spiritual help given by a religion that is not human but divine? This is the reason for affirming the true universality of the Church for all ages and places; a universality reaching beyond all social particularisms, and ever renewing its mission of establishing the brotherhood of men in the name of God.

* * * * *

Christianity is not only an ideal conception, an ethical praxis and a form of worship. It is, as we have seen, a positive organization of the faithful, within and not outside human society. It is the Church of Christ. As a spiritual, supernatural society, it is indefectible in its purity and divine wealth, and may well be called the Kingdom of God, the bride of Christ, the temple of the Holy Ghost, the faithful guardian of revealed truths, the teacher of men. But as a historical organism, the Church cannot but make use of earthly facts, present itself clothed with flesh, made up of saints and sinners, of martyrs and traitors, of worthy ministers and of others who are unworthy, of fervent faithful and of others who are but lukewarm. The organization of the Church will make use of riches and powers both for good purposes, for the benefit of divine worship, and for personal and selfish ones, as simony and oppression.

The Church is therefore, under this twofold divine and human aspect, in contact with all the other social forms, the family, the class, the city, the State, the society of States, influencing and being influenced according to the phases of the historical process and the diverse confluent and divergent activities that it implies. Never does the Church become wholly worldly without profound revivals of spirituality. Never does the world allow itself to become ecclesiasticized without reacting to regain its independence. In these movements, alternating or simultaneous, two broad currents develop in the social complexus — the mystical current and the organizational current. The mystical current tends towards an ideal which, though particularized in the concrete of history, is universal in spirit. It arouses feelings, encourages sacrifices, stirs whole generations with a sense of the need to renew, reform, revolutionize the world. And this current is a dynamic force in every society dissatisfied with present reality and impelled towards a future that will supply its deficiency and bring a new well-being.

The other current, the organizational, is also necessary in all society. Through it the social body becomes articulate; with diversity of organisms, institutions grow up, laws take shape and step by step the benefits achieved by every social nucleus are consolidated, together with its defects. All concrete reality is limited. The very fact of this limit makes what has been achieved unsatisfying. With use, the ideal values expressed by organic social forms when they first came into being grow feeble and fade. The letter is dead when there is no longer the spirit that gives life to human constructions. Thus the work of organization should be continuous, synchronizing with that of renewal. But conservation too is necessary. Those responsible for it fear rapid and convulsive renovations, whereas the mystics, taken up with the ideal to be pursued, come to set too little store by what has been constructed in the past.

This alternation is to be found first in our own mind (and we must fully appreciate it for our inner development) ; it is to be found in all social groups that are really alive; and it is in human society as a whole, in the continual movement of groups and development of activities. In the Church this alternation is not lacking. Here it is carried on at a higher level, for what must be conserved and what must be renewed and regained has always a spiritual value and is founded on an unfailing supernatural virtue. It is this that brings the great crises, stirring the whole of society to the roots, like the persecutions, the schisms, the heresies, the Reformation and Counter-Reformation, and so forth down to our own time, filling history in every century. What wonder if these spiritual movements have their repercussions in earthly life as such, in the immediate interests of classes and peoples, in cultural and artistic configurations, in political and economic orders?

It might indeed be objected that, since the Encyclopedists, the mysticizing movements in society no longer start from the Church; that the world has known ideal impulses of renewal which the Church itself has either merely endured or opposed. Liberty, democracy, socialism and even today nationalism, bolshevism, fascism and nazism, however they may be judged, enter into the category of human ideals. We need a clear insight into history to recognize that every age expresses its ideals with the means it finds to hand. In the Middle Ages, for instance, the social question expressed itself in theological terms, not because it was of a different nature from the social question of modern times, but because in the thought, culture and organization of the time religious motives prevailed. Thus the Franciscan Spirituals maintained that the Church should not have possessions, basing themselves on their interpretation of the Gospels. The Wyclifites went deeper into theology, declaring that only the righteous, and not the sinful, should have wealth and power. The formulas were erroneous, but their aim was to restrict or abolish ecclesiastical riches and to purify power from the abuses of wealth. In modern times the wealth is held, not by the clergy, but by anonymous capitalism or the socialized State. The problem of the sharing of wealth (an everlasting social problem) has to be set in other terms than theological or Scriptural, but in both cases, Christian morality has its word to say and its rules to lay down.

What makes a difference between the past and the present is that the secular mysticizing movements present an ideal complexus that is purely earthly, whereas the Christian movements, even when they were heretical, presented the same human problems as having their spiritual and supernatural aspects — things to be achieved in this life, but in order to reach a higher aim in the other. This diversity is due to the naturalistic orientation of thought, which has progressively detached itself not so much from Christianity as from any idea of the supernatural. But it must not be thought that these naturalistic movements can win the heart if they lack a finalistic content that is at bottom religious. They deny the supernatural, but as a result they conceive of or feel nature pantheistically. Divine worship is suppressed, but God's place is taken by humanity, the race, the class, the nation, or any other symbol of human reality. The men who incarnate these ideas become quasi-deities, beyond all criticism. Such phenomena, which may reach the pitch of collective fanaticism, are historically fleeting. There was the cult of the Goddess of Reason in the French Revolution. Napoleon knew the intoxication of being quasi-deified. Liberty had its trees, tyranny always has its thurifers. Anti-Christian philosophers do not content themselves with these ephemeral and living divinities. Under the guidance of Hegel they have deified the State, setting it at the summit of the manifestations of the "spirit" or "Idea." For them the Church of today, after the splendors and power of the Middle Ages (when, in substance, it functioned as State), is nothing but a phenomenon of survival due to mental inertia and atavistic habit, which cultured persons and advanced peoples must little by little cast off as culture makes its way among them and supplants all myths. These thinkers do not see that on those who have thrown overboard any Christian conception of life, naturalistic myths — which from the Goddess of Reason to the Nazis have overshadowed a hundred and fifty years of secular experiments — have a far greater hold than their intellectualistic theories, which would have reduced mankind to an academy.

Men always divide into two currents, the mystical and the organizational, which according to times and places assume different names and aspects, and often interchange or alternate their influence and bearings. Christianity is never extraneous, as some might believe, to any of the movements in either sense, even when they assume a secular or worldly character, because there is nothing in human life that is not influenced by the loftiest and noblest ideals, nothing that is untouched by the influx of truth and the hold of love. Every epoch has its own characteristics. The Church as an organism founded by Christ for supernatural ends is always the same, but in its human past it differs today from what it was in early or medieval times or under the *ancien régime*. In the modern struggles the human and variable part was often confounded with the institutional and permanent part. Not all wished or were able to make the distinction. Popular fury and the cold attacks of governments against the Church were often directed against its doctrines, its mission, its hierarchy and Sacraments, transforming political feelings into religious persecutions.

Today the Catholic Church is no longer a co-partner in political power; it has lost almost all its patrimony, as well as the organized influence of the clergy in the social forms — a human defence suited to a particular age. But it is morally stronger, more widespread in the world; its head gains a wider and more respectful hearing, its discipline is more effectual, its mystical and spiritual religious orientation more evident, its social influence deeper; while the politico-social order from which it has detached itself (notwithstanding the contacts provided for by concordats) has now become almost completely secularized, showing a continual unsureness in ethical and juridical principles, political and social conceptions, discipline and understanding. And in view of this, the more responsible and clear-sighted men feel the need for a return to Christian values, to traditional civilization, stressing the appeals of Popes, bishops and heads of churches, urging the Christian education of the young, looking to Christianity as the lighthouse of salvation.

On the other hand, the Church is not of this world but in this world. It cannot and must not deny the world its contribution even in the realm of earthly interests, raised to embrace spiritual values and subordinated to the higher ends of man. Such a denial would estrange it from men, make it less efficient in its spiritual ministry; or else, which is still graver, and has happened in moments of uncertainty in the orientation of social life, it might itself fall under worldly influence and suffer a particularistic deviation.

*   *   *   *

The historical fact that defines and clarifies the permanent function of Christianity in society, where the Church has been able to organize itself, is that of its diarchic sharing in the governing power. The diarchy of State-Church or of Church-State (according to the period) is one of those historical facts which up till today have received too little attention from the point of view of the structure of society. The writer himself has sought to call attention to it in various studies.[5] Here it will be sufficient for the purpose to touch briefly upon it. By

5. *Kirche und Staat*, 1932; *Essai de Sociologie*, 1935; *L'Eglise et L'Etat*, 1937; *Church and State*, 1939.

diarchy is meant an autonomous participation in social power. Although it is not the end of the Church to take over any portion of the civil dominion, by the fact of the exercise of its religious function it so influences society as to be morally a sharer in its power. The Church cannot remain indifferent to the construction of civil society, its laws, its culture and education, its repercussions on ecclesiastical life, to the defence of right, to the assistance of the poor. Above all, it cannot but claim for its religious ministry the freedom that will keep it spiritually independent.

Many theoretical formulas have been worked out in the course of the centuries for the relations between Church and State. The most famous and fundamental one is that of Pope Gelasius I, in the fifth century. He sought to separate the functions and to guarantee the autonomy of the two powers. But it is history that realizes, composes, creates; the happiest formulas are subject to the proof of facts. The delimitation of fields of action and influence in periods of confusion and spontaneous overlapping can provide nothing more than a vague direction. When it is the same men who make up society and form part of the Church, they cannot maintain such a duality, but tend towards the unification of the two powers. And unable to suppress either Church or State, they tend to pass the powers of the Church over to the State or those of the State over to the Church, creating either an oppressive subordination or an intolerable confusion. Since these phases cannot be lasting, there comes to be more or less tacit diarchy between State and Church.

The historic types of this diarchy are various — the Cæsaro-Papism of Byzantium, the Romano-papal organization, the medieval *sacerdotium* and *imperium,* concordatory "jurisdictionalism," the recognition of the king as head of the Church in the Reformed Churches, and separation, or *indirect* diarchy.[5] No one questions that from Constantine to the end of the *ancien régime,* the Church had in practice a share in the power of the State, and that in modern times with the Napoleonic Concordat and other concordats drawn up with many States, this sharing in power though restricted has continued to exist. It is usual to deny to the Church any real, autonomous power, as did the "legists" and "jurisdictionalists," presenting the various historical institutions of the past either as ecclesiastical usurpations or as royal concessions. In face of the impossibility of hindering such power, in the past as well as in the present, it has been usual to make the effort to subordinate the Church to temporal ends. Those who think thus do not reflect on either the sociological values or the historical values which the Church represents, guarantees and renders fruitful.

Looking upon the problem from the sociological standpoint, the writer takes his stand on the theory of the fundamental forms of society which are by nature distinct, each tending to its own autonomy — the domestic, the political and the religious form.[7] If in actual fact we find them interwoven or confused, in every epoch, even the pre-Christian, we see that each has its own features and reality and power. Woe to mankind if society were wholly, nothing other than, political power, as the modern totalitarian would have it! If this were possible it would be the end of the organico-social reality. But it is such excesses that create the great reactions. Now, if even in non-Christian society, where positive religion may identify itself with the family, the clan, the dynasty, and where religion

---

6. In the works mentioned I spoke of *individualistic* diarchy (not of *indirect* diarchy) as founded on the individualistic conception of the Reformation (free inquiry) or on the liberal-democratic form of the nineteenth-century State.

7. *Essai de Sociologie,* chap. I, p. 9.

is particularistic and split up, the religious form none the less maintains an existence of its own often above the temporal rulers, how is it thinkable that this could disappear in the Christian epoch, when revealed religion has constituted itself into a universal Church, with its codes, its structure and hierarchy, its power exercised in the name of a one and universal God? There is no choice possible for the State other than understanding, toleration or persecution: that is, organized diarchy, *de facto* diarchy or diarchic strife.

Against those who dream of the extermination of Christianity, we proclaim its indestructible nature, even in the name of historical experience. We may be told that we are mortgaging the future, since we cannot know or foretell what mankind will be two or three thousand years hence. This is true, yet there are certain fundamental factors in society that no one can ignore, and the first of these is religion. As long as mankind is unable to root out of itself the religious form of society, positive religions too will persist. Among these Christianity stands out incomparably. To dream of forms of statal or civil or racial religions is to fall into state totalitarianism. The past bears witness: neither schisms nor heresies nor persecutions have supplanted Christianity.

It is said that Christianity today has no longer a real influence on modern thought and culture; that the State has taken the place of the Church in regard to education, the family, public assistance; that the rôle of the Church in the world decreases more and more and with time all its influence will vanish. Now we have seen that in this attempt to devaluate the action of the Church in the world there is a misreading of history. The intervention of the Church in civil, political and cultural life varies according to the epoch, the peoples concerned, their needs, their stage of development. When no one thought of public education or public assistance, the

Church was creating its parish schools and hospices and *monts de piété*. When the State and great public bodies see to social insurance, the Church concentrates on moral and religious assistance. When the Church had wealth and property, it had to fulfil the social function consequent on this position, even in the organism of the State (which was then feudal or aristocratic). Now where the citizens have organized themselves in democracies, the Church confines itself to contributing to their moral and civil education. But when, as in the last century, the proletariat is placed in economic and moral conditions of absolute inferiority and is a prey to Marxism, while the wealthy classes neglect it and the State fails to intervene, then the Church creates the Christian social movement and Leo XIII intervenes with his famous Encyclical, *Rerum Novarum*.

The action of the Church is in substance religious, directed to religious ends. Hence its great battles in modern times, in the field of state politics, have been those for the Christian education of the young, against the atheist or neutral school, and for the integrity of the family against attempts to laicize and dissolve it, which go as far as compulsory divorce, birth control and state sterilization. That is why the struggle has been carried even into the organization of the State, by the formation of great parties, openly Christian, though confessional or non-confessional according to the country and period, and of which the Christian democrats have acted as mystical currents among the masses. But while these movements, though inspired by Christian teaching, have been at bottom autonomous and lay, a movement increasingly dependent on the Church till it could be described by Pius XI as a lay apostolate has been that of Catholic Action, which has been spreading in every country as a spiritual movement of renewal. Apart from mistakes and defects, which are never absent from human activity, in these — as in like movements among the dissident

Churches — there is a reassertion of the character of Christianity as responding to all situations and all needs, influencing by its teaching and its spirit every society, even those as refractory to it as ours of today. Nor should we pass over the great contribution made by the Church to the sciences, to letters and the arts, the modern growth of universities all over the world, the ever-expanding number of missions, the continuous increase of institutions, especially among women, for education, relief, charity, of which the most outstanding as examples of sacrifice are the leper settlements in Asia, Africa and America.

It is curious to have to note that while on the one hand there is the desire to reduce the Church to impotency and to blot out even the Christian idea from the hearts of the young by a naturalistic and secularized education, on the other the Church or the Papacy are accused of not intervening or of not intervening with enough efficacy in favor of just causes, to prevent the evils afflicting mankind, to make their influence felt on the governments of Catholic countries. The charge was made repeatedly during the First World War, over the Vatican's attitude to Austria-Hungary, and since then, in the Abyssinian and Spanish wars. But many forget the work of Benedict XV and his appeal on August 1, 1917, for a just and lasting peace, and the continuous concern of the Papacy for peace.[8] It is too early to speak of Pius XII's action during the Second World War; but even now, no one can forget his five points for durable peace, his Christmas addresses of 1939 and 1941, or his intervention in favor of invaded and oppressed peoples and prisoners of war.

This is not an apologetic work. It must be admitted that not all Catholics nor all the clergy have fully appreciated or

---

8. See Luigi Sturzo, *Les guerres modernes et la pensée catholique,* l'Arbre, Montreal, 1942.

supported what the Popes have said and written in the cause
of peace, from Leo XIII till today; and that in particular cases
after the First World War there was uncertainty, weakness,
failure to set sufficient store by collective security and the solidarity of all peoples, forgetfulness of the inviolability of
treaties, of the duty to defend the weak, of the fundamental
injustice of recourse to arms when other human means would
sooner or later have been able to remedy present evils. But
admitted all this, with whatever attenuating circumstances
may justly be claimed, what does it mean? Does not history
present us with far more troubled periods, in which either
the voice of the heads was feeble, or the practical paths appeared confused, or the general lines of guidance were not
applied? And then? A moment is enough, and a man rises
up to interpret fully the deepest thought of Christianity in
its eternal values.

Let us not attribute to the Church the responsibility that
accrues to the whole of Europe for the present war. It is the
consequence of the previous wars and aggressions, in China, in
Abyssinia, in Spain, in Austria, in Albania, in Czechoslovakia.
It is the consequence of the totalitarian, anti-Christian conceptions dominant over half Europe, but also of the lack of faith
in moral principles and those of international law, which is a
product of Christian principles. Those who have forsaken it
have all sinned, by unfaithfulness, weakness and short-sighted-
ness. And if churchmen also have a responsibility, this will
unfailingly be ascribed to them.[9]

What must today be stressed for all men of good faith,
whether Christians or no, is that the great battles to be fought
in the present period are three, and that they can neither be

---

9. See Luigi Sturzo, "Modern Wars and Catholic Thought," in
the *Review of Politics,* Notre Dame, Ind., April, 1941.

joined nor won save through a deeply Christian spirit. The first is against the pantheistic totalitarian State, which seeks to absorb all human activity, even that of the spirit, into the political power and system. The second is against the exploiting capitalism that perverts the function of money to the detriment of the community at large and of the poorer classes. The third is for an international construction of justice and peace strong enough to avert any war. In all three cases it is a battle against the naturalism that has entered into the fiber of modern society. In all three cases it is the spirit of love, of brotherhood, of solidarity that must prevail.

Neither culture alone, nor earthly power, nor the discoveries of science, nor a wealth accessible to all, nor human ability, will be able to face and master these three grave tasks of the modern epoch. Christianity as principles and teachings, the Church as the positive organization of Christianity — and also the dissident Churches and even the other religions, by whatever they contain of truth and love — will be able to make fruitful and effectual the strivings of man towards a better future.

This will not mean that history has exhausted its good and its evil, or that the Church has exhausted its activity and achieved its end of establishing the Kingdom of God on earth. New goods, new evils, will face those who come after us. *"For nation will rise again nation, and kingdom against kingdom; and there will be pestilences and famines and earthquakes in various places. But all these things are the beginnings of sorrows. Then they will deliver you up to tribulation, and will put you to death; and you will be hated by all nations for My name's sake. And then many will fall away, and will betray one another and will hate one another. And many false prophets will arise and will lead many astray. And because iniquity will abound, the charity of many will grow cold.... And this*

Gospel of the Kingdom shall be preached in the whole world, for a witness to all nations" (Matt. 24:7-14). Thus in wide outline did Jesus prophecy, not only the fall of Jerusalem, but the history of the whole world, the vicissitudes of persecutions, of heroisms, of fallings away, and the function of His Church to bear witness to Him among all peoples and in all ages to the end.

CHAPTER XII

NEW HEAVENS AND A NEW EARTH

IT would seem that the idea of the end of life and of the cosmos, like that of the beginning of life and of the cosmos, lies in the depths of human consciousness. It is natural that our personal life, which has a beginning and a term, should thus project its shadow and figure onto the universe, attributing to it also a beginning and an end. In any case, man is not only just a part of creation, but its epitome and interpreter.

Ovid sang in his *Metamorphoses:*

"He [Jupiter] remembered that it was in the fates that a
time would come
When the sea and the earth and the royal reaches of
heaven
Should burn, and the heavy mass of the world be in
travail."[1]

Lucan adopted this idea as a poetic simile, which must therefore have been comprehensible to his readers:

". . . Thus, when the structure of the world
Is dissolved, and closing many centuries the ultimate hour
Reverts to ancient chaos, then the constellations
All mingled shall clash together, the fiery stars

---

1. "Esse quoque in fatis reminiscitur adfore tempus,
   Quo mare, quo tellus correptaque regia cæli
   Ardeat, et mundi moles onerosa laboret."
   — Book I, 256-258.

269

Shall seek the sea . . . the fabric of the cosmos
Thus torn asunder will subvert its laws."[2]

The scientists who study the physical phenomena of the
cosmos cannot exclude the hypothesis that the earth, which
passed through a long period before the life of plants, animals
and men became possible, may pass through other periods in
which there will be no more life. The same might be said of
the millions of stars of which we know nothing, but cannot
therefore bar the idea that they may become, first habitable,
then unhabitable or vice versa. We do not know enough of the
resources of the globe and of the workings of its hidden forces
to give us a clue as to how the earth may cease to be our
nourishing mother. Will it be by loss of heat, compelling all
men little by little to live like Eskimos, till life even among
the glaciers becomes impossible and ends in deathly cold?
Or will flames burst forth from within the earth's core? Or
will a clash of stars shatter the terrestrial crust?

We may allow ourselves the strangest hypotheses, or seek
the aid of the most up-to-date physical and astronomical
knowledge, or decide that all this is hundreds of thousands
of centuries ahead of us and not worth troubling about. Yet
at bottom there is an instinctive craving that induces us to
speculate on this problem, as though to discover a secret which
will guide our course. Assuredly there is something inherent
in us that makes us think that if all things change and all
forces fail, if we ourselves quit this earthly life, if we are
journeying towards the infinite, then the cosmos too is jour-

---

2. " . . . Sic, cum compage soluta
     Sæcula tot mundi suprema coëgerit hora,
     Antiquum repetens iterum chaos, omnia mixtis
     Sidera sideribus concurrent, ignea pontum
     Astra petent, . . . totaque discors
     Machina divolsi turbabit fœdera mundi."
                              — *Pharsalia,* Book I, 72-80.

neying; that when its course is run it will no longer have any reason to be, and it too will be transformed, or else blotted from the register of existence.

In creation God manifested His glory to creatures, and each in its place and for the period of its existence serves Him and His design. We may ask ourselves why in course of time all that exists should be reduced to nothingness. The idea of a passage from being to not-being repels us, even though the death of living things is our daily experience. Thus, to reconcile our aspirations and our hopes, we who have consciousness of a transforming survival find it easier to think of the complexus of creation as indestructible, even while single beings cease to be and are continuously transformed. Everything becomes transformed, either in cycles or in unending series. Living things themselves, subject as they are to germination and corruption, in returning to earth or to the waters give rise to innumerable germs of fresh life as long as life is possible. And if life ceases in one star, like the earth, no one can exclude the possibility that it may develop or may have already developed in other myriads of stars, when the matter of which they are made and the atmosphere that surrounds them have reached the condition necessary to give beings to us unknown life, sense, intelligence.

There are thus two hypotheses — that of a cosmos in perpetual dynamism, so that an end is only individual and partial, whereas the energies of creation evolve in a temporal continuity that does not call for any term; and the other, that of a cosmic exhaustion through the crisis of its forces. And the two can either be so conceived that one excludes the other, or else reconciled in a transforming synthesis. The writer himself inclines to believe in a cosmic persistence culminating by stages and cycles in living and intelligent creatures such as

man. And he thinks that such creatures will have in their turn
their beginning and their end, their historical path, their own
crises and solutions, in which God will not fail to manifest
Himself according to His providence and their needs; for all
things work together for the glory of God.

Blondel's theory of cosmic thought is close to the view
of the cosmos, not as the mere servant of earth and of
man who inhabits it for a given period, but as an ever
wider and continuous manifestation of creative thought. According to Blondel, in all beings there is the realization of a
thought that manifests itself by stages as an inherent reality.
And this, at every stage, postulates and at the same time conditions a higher development, so that the further stage on the
one hand is a pacification and on the other a stimulus to ascent,
up to the flowering of "thinking mind" — that which attains consciousness of its being and of the reality of the
thought that is to be found in the whole cosmos. In this culmination all created beings share, each according to its own
reality and capacity, not as individuals complete in themselves
and isolated or capable of being isolated, but as part of a
whole and premise of a development that can find significance
only in the intelligent consciousness.

But we may ask ourselves, will this consciousness be that
of man only? Or may it not be sown through the universe
in indefinable cycles of cosmic life, ever in transformation and
ever in being?

*   *   *   *   *

There will be some readers to whom the idea of such
perennial continuance will seem to conflict with our belief on
the end of the world, or who may fear that time indefinitely

prolonged might, in the human mind, take the place of eternity. But in these and other more or less instinctive objections is there not a certain confusion regarding time and eternity? It is worth while dwelling a little on this theme so as to gain a clearer understanding of it.

Time in the concrete is not an entity distinct from the cosmos, as though there could be an extra-cosmic time, or a time prior to creation, which would be nothing else than a time outside time. Time is nothing other than the cosmos itself viewed in the succession of its phenomena, or we might say, its rhythm. The idea of time can be defined as the mental expression of the cosmic rhythm. In order to form this idea, man must derive it from the rhythm of his sensible existence, which binds most closely the pattern of his own life with that of the things surrounding him, the days and nights, the phases of the moon, the yearly circle of the sun. There is no age or people that, however methods and measures may vary, has not regulated itself by the rhythm of sun and moon and has not felt the flowing process that is called time.

It is possible to pick out other rhythms, from that of our own personal life to that of light. The first, subjective and variable, is what gives to each the sense of time, now swift, now slow, according to his mood of the moment. The second, which is scientific and has only recently been established, has opened vast and unexplored horizons, enabling us to appreciate the coexistence, harmony and indefinable immensity of the universe. The rhythmic basis is essential to existence, to motion, to life. It is a measure of extension that is transformed in duration, so that duration becomes conceivable inasmuch as there is coexistence, and the whole is thinkable as a harmony of all rhythms. Time shows one aspect of this immense structure, that of duration, which could not be achieved without the intrinsic potentiality of one universal rhythm with which all others are coördinated. Hence there is a twofold manner of envisaging time, as a succession in reference to particular events the line of which we follow — each of us being able to trace his own trajectory — or as a simultaneous, comprehensive rhythm which gathers up all the particular rhythms and resolves them into a single higher process.

It is under this aspect that time, the human conception of the solar rhythm, is comprehensive of our historical process, the rhythm of which, unique because intellectual, is conditioned by both the succession and the extension of things. This notwithstanding — and this is its higher aspect — the ideas and moral values released by the historical process are not affected by the temporal rhythm, surviving men or returning to life when they have long been forgotten. From another standpoint, they too are subject to time, if they are to be established, realized and renewed in outward works, in laws, institutions, works of art. Thus they too in a certain fashion take on the rhythm of time and express it in their manner, sharing in the reality of the cosmic process.

Thus ideas and moral values, transcending the rhythm of time in which they share, give us an initial conception of the timeless, of a duration imaginable without succession. We might say that they mark the passage between two planes, the temporal and the timeless. Through them we may after a fashion have an inkling of what eternity is or may be.

When we say that God is eternal, we mean not only that God has had no beginning and will have no end, but also, implicitly, that in Him there is neither succession nor change. And this excludes any idea of incompleteness, limitation, potentiality, that is, of the finite, which under diverse aspects must be subject to rhythm, to time, to integration and disintegration. God everlasting is the same as God in act, pure act, infinite act. The idea of eternity is implicit in the idea of God. And in the same way the idea of time is implicit in the idea of a cosmos. It is the cosmos that makes time by its rhythm. It is God who makes eternity by His act. Every other eternity would be nothing but a participation in that eternity which is divine, the truer and more real the closer it cleaves to this latter and is filled with it. Angels and the souls of the blessed partake in His eternity insofar as is possible for created beings to whom is given the beatific vision, and according to their degree of vision. And since in seeing God their partaking of the divine increases, we may say that while God is eternal act, the blessed are made eternal in the divine act.

It is quite clear why God's eternity is not to be confused with the unending continuity of a temporal process, even that of the whole of creation. When we think of a world that will have no end, we imagine a temporal rhythm of continuative successions, which, at each of its present instants, is limited, whereas in the vision of its future process it appears unlimited, though susceptible of limitation. It is the same optical illusion as with space. Space in its actual existence cannot be conceived save as limited to really extended matter; space is nothing else than cosmic reality in the extension of matter, just as time is the same cosmic reality in its rhythm and succession. Such reality in act, or in the present, which is the same thing, cannot be other than limited, but its potentiality is illimitable. For the series of worlds can always increase in number without our ever being able to say that space is filled, since every new world is space to itself. And as

no one can say that God must stop creating, or that He is
unable to give continuative impulsion to His creation, thus
no one can set limits to creation either in space or in time.

When it is said that the world is eternal *a posteriori*, it
means that the world will not come to an end; but here the
word eternal is taken in an analogical sense, and means only
interminable — that temporal duration will have no end. The
same significance is to be given to the hypothesis discussed by
St. Thomas, that of the possibility of the creation of the
world *ab aeterno*. Just as we may think hypothetically of an
indefinite temporal prolongation into the future, in the same
way we may think hypothetically of a temporal prolongation
into the past without reaching a fixed point at which to say
that here is the date of creation.[3] In both cases, whether the
temporal process is prolonged into the past or into the future,
it is always time that is prolonged, it is the processive rhythm
of the creation that is realized; it is not the eternal act. And
we cannot do other than think of a beginning or an end,
that is, think of it as limited. And if we prolong it in time
or space, we can no longer discern its outlines. If we find
it easier to think of a world prolonged indefinitely into the
future than into the past, that comes more from our imaginative forms of thought than from the possibility of the philosophical hypothesis.

What concerns the author in studying the problem of
time and eternity is how to bring the coexistence of the two
planes into relationship and establish the points where, so to
speak, they coincide, since two of them are of import for our

---

3. Needless to say, this hypothesis has nothing to do with the
theory that the world, matter or spirit, is uncreated, which leads to
either pantheism or atheism. For such theories the concept of a
beginning *ab æterno* is confused with the auto-existence of the cosmos.

whole life, natural and supernatural — Creation and the Incarnation. Given that God is pure act and that in Him there
is no succession but the single fruition of Himself, in whom
everything exists and everything has its pacification, we must
exclude the idea that there could ever have been "a time," a
period, that could be described as the solitude of God with no
works *ad extra*. Everything was present in God even when,
according to our way of expressing ourselves, the world was
not. The Scriptures use the same term to indicate the begetting of the Word and the creation of the world: *"In the
beginning was the Word"* (John 1:1) ; *"In the beginning God
created heaven and earth"* (Gen. 1:1). These two beginnings
are not of the same value, but they show that everything has
its origin in God. The difference is that the begetting of
the Word in God is necessary, like the procession of the
Spirit, whereas what are called His operations *ad extra* are
simply free acts of His goodness; for no created thing could
impose necessity on God. Thus the two planes are established,
the one the eternal, pure and perpetual act, the other the
temporal, the rhythm of the succession of the cosmic forces
that have their beginning in the divine *"Fiat."* Creation as
the beginning of the rhythm of time may be thought of as
having happened a hundred millions or a thousand millions
or a hundred thousand millions of years ago, but before God
it is the same moment of His infinite present.

We may say the same of the Incarnation. It does not
matter that we know the date of the birth of Jesus and can
count the years as before or after Christ; in God's eternal
act there is no counting of years and no before or after Christ,
as though something could have changed in the Godhead.
Did God in creating the world add anything to His essence?
In the same way, the Word in putting on human nature added

nothing to His essence. In both cases it is the temporal that has manifested the eternal. Let us seek the aid of a comparison. Dante wrote the *Divine Comedy,* Michelangelo painted the *Last Judgment;* without these works neither would be for us what they are, in our esteem and thought. Yet creating these works of genius did not make them other than they were before; their personality was always such as to be able to produce the works, and having produced them, their personality was not enhanced intrinsically — only in the opinion of others. The analogy is plain. God, in creating, made manifest His infinite power to beings that can understand Him. God is infinite love; the Word in becoming incarnate has manifested this love to those who follow Him. The infinite power and infinite love of God, which are His very act, one and threefold, has suffered no change in becoming manifest to creatures, with the entrance of the eternal into the temporal, just as it suffers no change because the temporality of His creatures put on eternity in Him. When it is God who comes down to us, we may even say that He puts on time with us; when it is we who come to God, we may say that we put on eternity with Him.

That God should put on time and that we should put on eternity, are expressions that must be clearly understood, to avoid error. I need not repeat what has already been said more than once of the entrance of the divine into history. Of the blessed who put on eternity it is clear that their eternity cannot be measured with that of God, since the one is essential, the other a partaking, and among the blessed themselves there are as many degrees of eternity as there are degrees in their partaking of the fount of life. What we do well to repeat, so that it may become a habit of thought, is that duration is not something added to being, but is being itself

in its proper mode of existing; existence is in its degree a
fruition. Thus we may well say that the time of a plant or
of an animal is not the same as man's time; and each man has
his own mode of existing and of enjoying his existence. Who
has not noticed that for the young time passes slowly and
for the old it flies? that for the busy man time is short and for
the idler very long? Thus, God's eternity is pure act, it is
God Himself who understands and loves Himself. Our eternity in God is the act of the beatific vision, proportionate to
our own receptive capacity.

We may also think that we shall carry with us something
of time into heaven when we shall once more be clothed with
our bodies. Sensitive life will not be suppressed for us but
will be changed; as such it will call for succession and spatial-
ity, though as in the risen Christ it will transcend the spatial
and temporal laws of this present life. Granted that the condition of glory will bring in us a continuous increase of comprehension and hence of love, we may think of a continuous
passage from light to light, from brightness to brightness,
from glory to glory, in which even the senses will partake,
in an intimate process that we cannot describe as one from
potentiality to act, but rather of act indefinitely increasing.

To gain a picture of what the eternal present may be, the
act that has neither contingency nor succession, while the
cosmos continues in a temporal rhythm from which we shall
not wholly be estranged, we may seek it from those mystics
who, like St. Paul, while still in life were in a certain fashion
rapt into the divine vision. Was it an instant, a day, a week?
There is no counting. It was an actful present while the
earthly present running its rhythmic course towards the future
was being engulfed in its past. What here is a fleeting moment
there is a present without varying or change.

Let us see if our own experience cannot give us some sort of image of this eternal present. A joy, even earthly, which lays hold on our senses, makes us lose consciousness of time. We say that time has flown and we did not notice it. The contemplation of the stars for an astronomer, of a work of art for an artist, of a metaphysical truth for a philosopher, makes them lose the sense of time; they are rapt away from it in their enjoyment. And we say that they have an image of eternity, just as a painted fire is an image of real fire. One of the arts that is entirely temporal in its manifestation is music, and it is the one that can so take us out of ourselves as to abolish the sense of duration, when the whole of duration becomes music. The synthesis represented by a piece of music, which we could not have outside time, becomes for us timeless, as though it were a simultaneous coexistence, a real construction imagined in space rather than in time. The true listener abstracts from time and is transported into a rhythm which might be called absolute. It is not absolute, but he has of it as it were a single impression. After the musical performance, memory seeks to refresh itself, reducing it to pieces and replacing the various rhythmical phases into before and after, but the music has fled. There remains its imprint on time, the memory of the evening, of the place, of the company, joy, excitement, fleeting impressions; the music has fled. It may come back, but perhaps then we will be bored, weary, critical, comparing the present performance with the other; then it is time that prevails over artistic enjoyment, and we look at the clock to see how many minutes have passed. We may have some similar impression in the theater, in church, in a hall, listening to dramatists, orators or poets, as long as there is nothing to bring us back to time. These are remote images, pale analogies of the immense reality which is our participation in the eternal present.

Although eternity is attributed also to hell — and the word is in the Gospel — yet, according to the positive sense which has here been given to it, the writer prefers to speak of perpetuity to indicate a negative condition like that of hell, where there is no fruition of any good, nor hope of attaining it, nor possibility of issue or of ceasing to exist. This is more an endless timelessness than an eternity. When the word eternity is taken to indicate together the duration of paradise and of hell, it is by a mental abstraction from everything else, and serves us as an image of a time without end. For us the eternal is the act in which there is participation, and everlasting participation inasmuch as it is the eternal act that is God Himself.

*   *   *   *   *

Let us return to the subject that suggested this long but not irrelevant digression. In order to be able to speak with other than hypothetical arguments of the end of the world and of its perpetuity, we must refresh ourselves at the founts of Scripture and Christian thought. In the Old Testament the prophets put together the advent of the Messias and the renewal of earth and the heavens. Thus in Isaias (65 and 66) and in Daniel (7). The two advents are foreseen in a logical and historical continuity.

The New Testament gives us elements still more closely connected with the Messianic idea, so as to make a single whole of the first and second comings of Christ. The time separating them, however long it be, matters nothing. What counts is the basic reason of this connection, the Saviour and the Judge. Here we are no longer on the plane simply of the physical end of the world or of its transformation, but on the spiritual plane — the final recognition of the elect who have followed the voice of the Son of God, and that of the reprobate who have refused salvation. But the two planes are not cut off from each other. Man is the term of the creation of the world and the term of the coming of the Son of God into the world. If mankind on earth is to have an end, it is because this world as it is, the natural condition of human life, will have an end.

Both in the Gospels and in the Epistles there is the prophecy that the world must pass away: *"Heaven and earth will pass away . . ."* (Matt. 24:35). This agrees with Psalm 101: *"The heaven shall perish but Thou remainest. And all of them shall grow old like a garment: and as a vesture Thou shalt change them, and they shall be changed."* St. Peter in his Second Epistle says still more clearly: *"But the heavens that now are, and the earth, by that same word have been stored up, being reserved for fire against the day of judgment and destruction of ungodly men"* (3:7). In Christ's prophecy on the destruction of the temple and the fall of Jerusalem, as it appears in the Synoptic Gospels, the passage is plain from the end of Judaism and the evangelization of all peoples, to the second coming and the end of the world. Apart from exegetic details that result from the study of the texts,[4] what is interesting to draw from the whole context is two points that might seem contradictory. The first is that the return of Christ will be like the coming of a thief, when least expected: *"But the day of the Lord will come as a thief . . ."* (2 Pet. 3:10); *"For you yourselves know well that the day of the Lord is to come as a thief in the night . . ."* (1 Thess. 5:2); indeed, like a lightning flash: *"As the lightning comes*

4. See M. J. Lagrange, O. P., *Evangile selon Saint Marc,* 1920; *Evangile selon Saint Luc,* 1921; *Evangile selon Saint Matthieu,* 1923; Gabalda, Paris.

forth from the east and shines even to the west, so also will the coming of the Son of Man be" (Matt. 24:27) ; like the master who arrives at night when the servants are drunk and quarreling (ibid. 48-50) ; or like the bridegroom who comes when the foolish virgins have hurried to buy oil for their lamps (ibid. 25:10) ; and so on. But in these same prophecies and in other places of the New Testament it is said that the end of the world shall be preceded by signs in the heavens and on earth, by persecutions against the faithful, by the seduction of many on the part of the Antichrist; and that the Last Judgment will coincide with devouring fire, and with a transformation into new heavens and a new earth.

In this final vision the natural and the supernatural, the historical and the eschatological, are mingled together. What wonder? Is not our whole life, as this book has tried to show, a mixture of all this which, however it be presented, always reveals itself as tending towards unification in God? To the scholar as to the believer it is interesting above all to seek the truth that shines out in its real beauty.

Jesus urges us to be watchful for His coming. This should be taken as a personal reminder to each one of us. His coming is the vocation to grace, the first grace and the graces regained after sin. If we are not attentive, He is as the lover in the Song of Songs, who knocks at the door, and if it is not opened goes his way. His coming is also at death, when He will judge each soul as worthy of punishment or reward. No one knows when death will come. Even when we are near to it we never believe that its hour has really struck. When it comes it is a surprise for which we are not prepared. But the secret encounter between the soul and its Judge is not enough; there is need for a general and manifest judgment, not of the separated soul but of the whole man with his risen body "in the resurrection of life or in the resurrection of judgment," as St. Paul says.[5]

The first Christians believed the second coming of Christ, "the day of the Lord," to be near at hand. But St. Paul warned the Thessalonians *"not to be hastily shaken from your right mind, nor terrified, whether by spirit, or by utterance, or by letter attributed to us, as though the day of the Lord were near at hand"* (2 Thess. 2:2). And St. Peter, to those who declared the end of the world a false prophecy, as though it should have come at once, replied with the magnificent sentence, that *"one day with the Lord is as a thousand years, and a thousand years as one day"* (2 Pet. 3:8). The time which the prophecies seemed to telescope towards an end believed imminent had to be spaced out. St. John wrote: *"Dear children, it is the last hour; and as you have heard that Antichrist is coming, so now many antichrists have arisen; whence we know that it is the last hour"* (1 John 2:18). In St. John the word Antichrist is applied both to the chief enemy of Christ and to the heretics who forsook the Christian camp. But the true Christians, he says, must stand fast in the truth, in the Father, in the Son and in His Unction (the Holy Ghost). The "last hour" is the whole period of the preaching of the Gospel in the world; there will always be "antichrists," "false christs" and "false prophets," "deceivers" who will rise up in the midst of the Christians, as in the apostolic age, and denying the truth will seek to seduce the elect.

---

5. St. Paul, though he uses the same word for the resurrection of life and that of judgment — because of the identical act of reunion of the soul with the body — notes clearly the difference. The veritable resurrection is that of life, of second life, as St. John says, for the elect are sons of God being sons of the resurrection. Jesus Himself said to the Sadducees: *"For neither shall they be able to die anymore, for they are equal to angels, and are sons of God being sons of the resurrection"* (Luke 20:36).

Seen in historical perspective, centuries would have to pass before the formation of "one fold and one shepherd," the total conversion of the Jews foreseen towards the end of the world, and the coming of the Antichrist with apostasy and the final persecution. St. Paul is here categorical: *"Let no one deceive you in any way, for the day of the Lord will not come unless the apostasy comes first, and the man of sin is revealed, the son of perdition, who opposes and is exalted above all that is called God, or that is worshiped, so that he sits in the temple of God and gives himself out as if he were God . . ."* (2 Thess. 2:3-4). And a little further on: *"Then the wicked one will be revealed, whom the Lord Jesus will slay with the breath of His mouth and will destroy with the brightness of His coming. And his coming is according to the working of Satan with all power and signs and lying wonders, and with all wicked deception of those who are perishing. For they have not received the love of the truth that they might be saved"* (ibid. 8-10).

It may be asked how it will be possible, once the world has become one sheepfold with one shepherd, the Jews too having been converted, for a satanic man to take up such a position and launch an unprecedented persecution, luring the world into apostasy. But is it so strange? How often have not Christian countries and nations fallen into apostasy! Did not the Hebrew people, only just freed from the Egyptian slavery, when Moses was speaking with God and receiving the Law from Him, make the golden calf? Did not the Christianity of the fourth century, when it had just emerged from over two centuries of persecution, become in large part Arian? And in modern times, did not France, the eldest daughter of the Church, fall into public apostasy during the Terror? Today we have Bolshevist Russia and Nazi Germany which have openly repudiated Christianity, while the totalitarian State that has spread through Europe under various guises has become a sign of idolatry.

Dom Delatte, in his treatise on the Epistles of St. Paul, asserts that worldly apostasy has come about as a process of diminution of the public powers of the Church; he marks its stages — the opposition of the legists to the Church in the fourteenth century, the Reformation, the French Revolution. To the present writer this interpretation of history seems ill-founded; it is mentioned here because Dom Delatte is by no means alone in believing in an integral Christianity that culminated in the Middle Ages (or rather, in one or two centuries of the Middle Ages), and subsequently has waned down to our own time, so that the present situation may be envisaged as preparatory to the coming of Antichrist. To justify this thesis, it would be necessary to assert that in the Middle Ages the Catholics of the West (limited though their numbers were in comparison with those of the dissident Christians of the East, of Russia, of Asia and of Africa), formed indeed "one fold and one shepherd," while there were vast regions where the Gospel had not yet been preached. Here it seems that Dom Delatte confuses Christianity with Christendom, the politico-ecclesiastical unity that then confronted the Mussulman peril. Moreover, it would be necessary to think of such a nucleus in the Catholic West as an example of Christian virtues, forgetting the heresies, the simony and concubinage among churchmen, the schisms great and small, the struggles between Popes and emperors, between Popes and anti-popes; not to speak of the customs of the time, serfdom, feudal strife, family vendettas, the tyranny of the cities and the licentiousness of the courts. But what is strangest is that such an interpretation conflicts with the religious reality of

seven other centuries of Christianity in the world, filled with
the virtues of so many saints, and with new religious orders,
missionary fervor, purification of the Church and improvement in civil and religious customs.

The true historical vision, as it may be formed from experience and right interpretation of the Scriptures, is that the
last days, which will follow the preaching of the Gospel in
the whole world, will always have heroic Christians and
saints, and false christs and false prophets; that the struggle
between good and evil is inherent in the world and must
take its course as Providence permits and men (as free secondary causes) take part in it with their forces, on this side
and on that. Thus the struggle may appear, according to the
point of view, as always at its beginning or always at its conclusion. Thus it may be said that "the day of the Lord" is
at hand, for the Lord is present and strengthens His own in
their warfare, and gives them vigor to resist seductions and
does not allow them to be tempted beyond their strength; and
that "the day of the Lord" is not yet come, for "all these
are the beginnings of sorrows."

The time will come when Christianity, preached to all men,
will be able to number all in the fold of Christ. And then?
It is not on this earth that we are to look for a happy eternity.
Even if the fold is one, apostasies will not be lacking, as
they have not been lacking in the past. Times succeed one
another, generations pass away, the unity that was formed
becomes disintegrated. Russia before 1917 was all Christian
by faith, while today in Russia Christianity is reduced to a
few churches or to scattered secret sects, and the young are
growing up without religious ideas and in anti-Christian
hatred! Thus it may come to pass with the world if it be-

comes unified materially and spiritually by an anti-Christian power that has seized its reins. On the other hand, how could the prophecy of an unprecedented persecution be fulfilled unless there are to be faithful who will resist the power of the Antichrist? He will prevail for a season, till Christ shall slay him with His word. Whether this means a real slaying or a spiritual fall (and St. Paul's text lends itself to both interpretations), the sense is clear: the final triumph will be with Christ, who will come to accomplish His mandate at the end of the world.

* * * * *

We can now in a manner understand this passage in St. Matthew: *"And as it was in the days of Noe, even so will the coming of the Son of Man be. For as in the days before the flood, they were eating and drinking, marrying and giving in marriage, until the day when Noe entered the ark, and they did not understand until the flood came and swept them all away; even so will the coming of the Son of Man be"* (Matt. 24:37-39). How could it be otherwise? Men will be led astray by the Antichrist, the faithful will be persecuted and put to death or will flee into the woods and hide themselves in the catacombs; and life will go on as it does today, as it did in the troublous times of war and persecution. There will be buying and selling, and men and women will marry and have children, and no one will understand that it is the end — save those who feel it in their hearts and prepare for it as the personal end of each. The end will come, but no one shall know it: *"of that day and hour no one knows, not even the angels of heaven, but the Father only"* (Matt. 24:36) ; *"at that time the heavens will pass away with great violence, and the elements*

*will be dissolved with heat, and the earth, and the works that
are in it, will be burned up"* (2 Pet. 3:10).

Does this mean that the end of the cosmos will coincide
with the end of mankind, with the slaying of the Antichrist
and the Last Judgment? St. Peter himself, after having bidden
us reflect *"what manner of men ought you to be in holy and
pious behavior, you who await and hasten towards the coming
of the day of God, by which the heavens, being on fire, will be
dissolved and the elements will melt away by reason of the heat
of the fire"* — adds, full of confidence: *"But we look for new
heavens and a new earth, according to His promises, wherein
dwells justice"* (ibid. 11-13). And in the Apocalypse this renewal is seen as a final reality: *"And I saw a new heaven and
a new earth. For the first heaven and the first earth passed
away, and the sea is no more"* (Apoc. 21:1). (The sea for
the ancients was a dreadful element, a remnant of chaos, which
was to have no place in the new world.) The theme of the
new heavens and the new earth is to be found in Isaias, where
it is written: *"For behold, I create new heavens and a new
earth: and the former things shall not be in remembrance, and
they shall not come upon the heart. But you shall be glad
and rejoice forever in these things which I create . . .* (Is.
65:17-18).

It is easy to give to the "new heavens and new earth" —
the environment of life for men — a spiritual sense, as the
fulfilment of the promises, the reward, the Kingdom, the
possession of God. In the passages quoted, such a sense is
brought out by the inspired writers themselves. None the less
the tradition was formed that the words apply also to the
cosmos, which will not end in nothingness but will be transformed, after fire has destroyed the works of human pride
which for so many centuries have tainted air and earth.

It is the judgment against the ungodly which will be extended to things, to the "world," as sharing their condemnation, but creation will remain. This tradition not only is not at variance with the prophecies on the end of man and the Universal Judgment, but is so grafted into them as to harmonize the cosmic continuity with the justice which, according to St. Peter, shall dwell in the new heavens and new earth.

In every age scholars and exegetes apply such scientific data as are available to the hypothesis of the physical continuity of the cosmos, if only to prove that it is not at variance with the contingent and transmutable nature of matter. St. Thomas in his *Summa contra Gentiles* treats of the "state of the world after the judgment." He declares: "After the last judgment has taken place, human nature will have reached its term. But since all corporeal things were made in a certain manner for man, . . . it will be fitting that the state of all corporeal natures should be changed, so as to be in conformity with the state of the men, as they will be then. And seeing that men will then be uncorruptible, all corporeal creatures will cease to be in the state of generation and corruption."[6]

St. Thomas' argument of congruousness can subsist with another nearer to our own thought. Whether this cessation of life in our planet will be a natural happening through the exhaustion or evolution of physical forces, or else the result of God's miraculous intervention, will make no difference, for God can use for His ends either secondary causes in their normal workings (their origin and strength is from Him),

---

6. "Peracto igitur finali judicio, natura humana totaliter in suo termine constituitur. Qui vero omnia corporalia facta sunt quodam modo propter hominem, ut in libro tertio est ostensum, tunc etiam totius creaturæ corporeæ conveniens est ut status immutetur, ut congruat statui hominum qui tunc erunt; et quia tunc homines incorruptibiles erunt, a tota creatura corporali tollentur generationis et corruptionis status" (*C. Gen.*, Lib. IV, Caput XCVII).

or, in an exceptional manner, manifest more strikingly His power and His will. Thus all the Apocalyptic prophecies on the signs before the end of the world and on the fire that will burn up the heavens and the earth, may be interpreted in the sense of a supreme manifestation of power, however this may come about and whether in natural or preternatural form.

The cosmos as we envisage it today is not limited to the earth or to the solar system. It extends to such countless systems and groups of systems that our imagination cannot set any bounds to it at all. It would surely be a forcing of the Scriptural text to extend the end of our world to all the millions and millions of worlds and to bind up their fate with that of the life of man on earth. I have already touched on the hypothesis — which is my own theory — that life is and will continue to be sown through the whole cosmos, including the life of intelligent beings as little by little the separate stars become suitable for its conditioning and development. In the same way, life would cease there whenever the forces rendering it possible ceased to exist. There would thus be a kind of circulating life through the whole cosmos, in modes and forms unknown to us, but imaginable in ways analogical to our own. And this circulation of life, as such, would have no term, because the cosmos has no term in the perpetuity of its creaturely fulness, whereas each single life-group would have its end at the time appointed by the development of the natural conditions of each star.

The hypothesis of the existence of intelligent and conscious beings in a countless number of stars best fits the theory that conscious thought is the crown and completion of cosmic thought, as Maurice Blondel calls it; it is in a way, as St. Thomas says, the proximate end of the creation of the visible world, for the intelligent being is the only organ of creation that can after a fashion understand and adore the glory of God. Just as it is with man on earth, so is it, or will it be, with the other intelligent beings on the other habitable stars; and throughout the ages, the ladder of corporeal beings rises in an ascension of life and thought, till, living and conscious, it can give voice to the hymn glorifying God the Creator — millions of millions of creatures journeying towards God, amid the circling of the innumerable stars, in the whirlpool of an immense and everlasting cosmic life.

What prevents us from thinking that all these are reached by the Redemption, that in all the habitable stars the Incarnation of the Word and the Divine Trinity have been or will be revealed, and that all are called to supernatural life and to the beatific vision? And if the sight and thought of so many stars leads us to glorify the power of God, what of the idea — even if it be only hypothetical — that the name of Jesus (thus or otherwise known, but always indicating the Son of God made Man) is or may be known and praised in other myriads of starry heavens, for ages upon ages? What of the idea that the name of Jesus circulates through the whole of creation, as an interweaving chorus not only from generation to generation of man on earth, but from star to star, through solar universes which no mind can number — certainly not the mind of tiny beings like ourselves — exalting more and more the goodness, liberality and wisdom of God? Instead of thinking of the heavens as mute, praising God only by a motion without intelligence and consciousness, following the physical laws He has appointed to them, it is heartening to think of them as enriched by milliards of beings; so that, in continuous alternation of birth and death, as long as the cosmos endures, there will be journeying spirits lifting up mind and heart to God and singing His goodness, panting and yearning for the time when they will be joined to Him in eternal union.

* * * * *

It is thus that every being is recapitulated in God as its proper term. All lower creatures are disposed towards the intelligent creatures, and by them interpreted and expressed in their being and degree, as a long preparation and a rich conditioning of existence, and above all as a means of spontaneous manifestation of the divine power and providence. The intelligent beings are called to God by their spiritual nature itself, but God has willed them to be still closer to Him and has raised them to the supernatural life.

This is how the new human and divine fellowship is founded. God is the center, as He is the origin and the end; for nature and for grace, He is the way and the goal. Purely spiritual beings like the angelical orders, and all men whether before or after Christ, are called to share in this fellowship; and the intelligent beings scattered through the cosmos are, in hypothesis, called to knowledge and love of God. Among all these, past, present and to come, there is at once a real and an ideal fellowship. This fellowship is between the soul and God — God the Father and all the intelligent beings His children, called to an intimate sharing in His goodness and life. This sharing cannot remain enclosed in each separate soul, but overflows in charity towards the rest, like a river of goodness watering the banks through which it passes and making fruitful the lands that it washes. Our fellowship is with God and with our brethren, and is a real fellowship productive of good. Natural society contains at the same time supernatural society, natural knowledge and love are ennobled, receiving a new and supernatural value. In one and the same love we embrace all, even the angels of heaven, the men who have been or will be, the other intelligent beings whom we do not know or have reason to know, but who we think exist in the celestial worlds.

We all have been, are or shall be journeying from the created world towards the Uncreated Infinite, towards God who will give Himself to us as He is. All of us are moving, as surely as the heavens, towards our goal. For each personally, it is death that bears us from this to another world. We know nothing experimentally of what death may be. Those who have gone before us through this personal gateway of mankind can tell us nothing of their experience. God has made death mysterious so that each of us may feel a holy fear together with a boundless trust in Him. Death seen from life reveals the inner mystery of our soul. Those who do not believe in the survival of the spirit after bodily death are unhappy in knowing nothing of the trepidation of such a passage and the hope of celestial revelations. But even the unbeliever is not so sure that everything perishes as not to hear an inner voice insisting that something in man resists death, and that even if no one sees again on earth the dear ones who have gone before him and whom he still loves, he yet feels them as if they were alive and near to him.

We have faith in eternal life, and we know that the first whom we shall meet after death is our Lord and Brother, Jesus, who will judge us according to our works — a faith full of trust and love realized in deeds. There will be much to be said about our life, and if this were the title of our hope, that hope would already have faded without the possibility of laying hold on it. The true and sole title is the sign of the Redemption, quickened by grace and made everlasting by the mercy of God, who gives us confidence in our going, and hope of forgiveness. And if even after death there should be need for purification of the effects of our forgiven sins, purgatory will be a necessary crucible, where we know that through the communion of saints and the prayers of friends and kinsmen, we may draw upon the merits stored up in the treasury of the Church. Thus purgatory too is a mystical fellowship, giving a foretaste, in suffering, of the love and union of the fellowship of heaven.

When God shall manifest Himself to us, then shall we know what we shall be, as St. John says. *"Beloved, now we are the children of God, and it has not yet appeared what we shall be. We know that, when He appears, we shall be like to Him, for we shall see Him just as He is"* (1 John 3:2). In God fellowship will be perfect and will extend to all the blessed, in mutual communication of bliss, in simultaneous fruition of the love of God and of the vision of Him, and will be poured back upon all creatures as the everlasting and glorifying expression of God's goodness.

This will be given to each soul singly after bodily death, when each has become worthy of it, but its complete and public confirmation will be in the Last Judgment, when all souls shall be clothed again in their risen bodies. Even today there are many who, like the Athenians of St. Paul's time, scoff at the idea of a final resurrection, which we repeat in the Creed as one of the foundations of our faith; or at most they may say, like the Athenian sceptics: *"We will hear thee again on this matter"* (Acts 17:32). But St. Paul is clear: *"For the Lord Himself with cry of command, with voice of archangel, and with trumpet of God will descend from heaven; and the dead in Christ will rise up first"* (1 Thess. 4:16). What does "rise up" mean? St. Paul tells us when he declares that Christ *"will refashion the body of our lowliness, conforming it to the body of His glory by exerting the power by which He is able also to subject all things to Himself"* (Phil. 3:21). How could it be otherwise? It is Christ's Resurrection that is the reason and measure of our resurrection. *"Christ has risen from the dead, the first-fruits of those who have fallen asleep,"* wrote St. Paul triumphantly to the Corinthians, after having confuted those who denied the Resurrection (1 Cor. 15:20). He himself, a little later, seeks to banish the doubts of those who ask: *"How do the dead rise? Or with what kind of body do they come?"* (ibid. 35). He answers: *"Senseless man, what thou thyself sowest is not brought to life, unless it dies. And when thou sowest, thou dost not sow the body that shall be, but a bare grain, perhaps of wheat or something else. But God gives it a body even as He has willed, and to each of the seeds a body of its own. . . . So also with the resurrection of the dead. What is sown in corruption rises in incorruption; what is sown in dishonor rises in glory; what is sown in weakness rises in power; what is sown a natural body rises a spiritual body . . ."* (ibid. 35-44).

A little after this magnificent prospect of the resurrection of the body, St. Paul rises to the heights of the mystery of the divine judgment: *"Behold, I tell you a mystery: we shall all indeed rise, but we shall not all be changed — in a moment, in the twinkling of an eye, at the last trumpet. For the trumpet shall sound, and the dead shall rise incorruptible and we shall be changed"* (ibid. 51-52). St. Paul's words do not explain to us the mystery, which surpasses human understanding, but they give us the terms of what will be the resurrection of the dead and their distinction as incorruptible and changed or incorruptible but not changed, the former destined to glory, the latter to woe.

Of the Last Judgment Jesus spoke often during His three years of teaching, either in the form of parables or openly, as we read in the Gospels. It is Jesus who stresses the solemn and collective character of that Judgment. The state of conscience of each as it was found at the end of the test, whether worthy of grace or of condemnation, will be revealed before all.

Two pages of the Gospels in particular call our attention
to it, and may be said to epitomize the whole meaning of our
life and of the sovereign judgment to be passed on it. The
first is Jesus' reproof to the cities wherein He has worked so
many miracles, for their lack of faith, their failure to hear
Him and do penance: *"Woe to thee, Corozain! Woe to thee,
Bethsaida! For if in Tyre and Sidon had been worked the
miracles that have been worked in you, they would have repented long ago, sitting in sackcloth and ashes. But it will be
more tolerable for Tyre and Sidon at the Judgment than for
you. And thou, Capharnaum, shalt thou be exalted to heaven?
Thou shalt be thrust down to hell."* And Jesus adds to His
disciples: *"He who hears you, hears Me; and he who rejects
you, rejects Me; and he who rejects Me, rejects Him who sent
Me"* (Luke 10:13-16). Jesus turns to the cities as to a social
complexus bound together in solidarity, to give the idea of
mutual influence for a common end. To believe in His miracles,
to hear His preaching and that of the apostles (in whom is
figured the Church), to do penance, is the beginning of salvation. Those that have received less have less to answer for,
like Tyre and Sidon; and those that have received more have
more to answer for, like Bethsaida and Capharnaum.

Another page of the Gospels completes this one, showing
how the practical response or lack of response to Christ's
teachings will be judged — a page in St. Matthew incompara-
ble in its beauty and light: *"But when the Son of Man shall
come in His majesty, and all the angels with Him, then He will
sit on the throne of His glory; and before Him will be gathered all the nations, and He will separate them one from another, as the shepherd separates the sheep from the goats;
and He will set the sheep on His right hand, but the goats on
the left. Then the King will say to those on His right hand,
'Come, blessed of My Father, take possession of the Kingdom*

prepared for you from the foundation of the world; for I was hungry and you gave Me to eat; I was thirsty and you gave me to drink; I was a stranger and you took Me in; naked and you covered Me; sick and you visited Me; I was in prison and you came to Me.' Then the just will answer Him, saying, 'Lord, when did we see Thee hungry, and feed Thee; or thirsty, and give Thee drink? And when did we see Thee a stranger, and take Thee in; or naked, and clothe Thee? Or when did we see Thee sick, or in prison, and come to Thee?' And answering, the King will say to them, 'Amen I say to you, as long as you did it for one of these, the least of My brethren, you did it to Me'" (Matt. 25:31-40). Condemnation, on the other hand, is for those who have performed no act of mercy. To their question the King will answer: *"Amen I say to you, as long as you did not do it for one of these least ones, you did not do it for Me."* And thus the Judgment is concluded, in Jesus' own words: *"And these will go into everlasting punishment, but the just into everlasting life."*

What wonder that Jesus stressed that to works of mercy for our humble, suffering, disinherited brethren shall be accorded the merit of love towards Himself? The path to heaven starts with love and ends in love; love makes us know reality, and knowledge of love increases love. To give loving help to those who suffer leads us to know and love our brethren more, and to see in them the image of God, and all this leads us to God. Human brotherhood is a stair to brotherhood with Jesus Christ, Man and God, and by Him and in Him to the state of adoptive children which God has granted us by His grace. There is no other way. "He who loves not remains in death," says St. John. Love and love only is life, and the want of love is pride, envy, anger, sloth, avarice, greed, lechery — it is the egoism that separates us from others and from God, and condemns us to remoteness from any fellowship with good.

The True Life is love — natural and supernatural, human and divine, on earth and in heaven, in an ineffable fusion in which, though we are absorbed in God, our own personality will not be lost, but changed. God will make us partakers of His Godhead, so that without our losing the consciousness of being men He will make us feel that we are His children, sharers in His nature, beatified by His vision. Then *"God will wipe away every tear from their eyes. And death shall be no more; neither shall there be mourning, nor crying, nor pain any more, for the former things have passed away"* (Apoc. 21: 4). There will be neither before nor after. The past with its sins, tears of repentance, heaviness of heart, all will be changed into love, taken away from our consciousness, in a "renewal of youth." And the future will not be unknown to us nor distress us by its shadow. All will be present, in an infinite act in which we shall partake, the divine act itself; while time will flow on at our feet in the new heavens and new earth which, with their countless rhythms, will join in the song of the blessed: "Glory to God in the highest."

" 'I am the Alpha and the Omega, the first and the last, the beginning and the end. . . . I, Jesus, have sent My angel to testify to you. . . . I am the Root and Offspring of David, the bright Morning Star. And the Spirit and the bride say "Come!" And let him who hears say "Come!" And let him who thirsts come; and he who wishes, let him receive the water of life freely. . . . It is true, I come quickly!' Amen! Come, Lord Jesus! The grace of our Lord Jesus Christ be with all. Amen" (Apoc. 22:13-21).

INDEX

Aaron: 45, 152.

Abandonment, spiritual: 120-123, 124-127, 130.

Abel: 145, 152, 182.

Abraham: 30, 57, 81, 88, 152, 210, 235, 237, 240, 241.

Abstractionism, or intellectual separatism: 1, 2, 7, 9-10, 17, 25, 39, 46, 71, 74.

Abyssinia: 266.

Action, Catholic: 57, 264-265.

Activity, or active spiritual life: 43, 60, 122, 124, 125-126.

Activity, personal or collective: 1-2, 4, 5, 9, 10, 13, 40, 41, 42-43, 55, 66, 72, 114, 122, 132, 163, 171-172, 176, 178, 183, 186, 189, 190, 198, 213, 219-228, 232, 234, 247, 249, 256, 257.

Acts of Apostles: 53, 76, 87, 120, 135, 187, 240, 242, 243, 295.

Adam and Eve: 70, 145, 149, 154, 157.

their fall: 27, 68, 139, 145, 181, 182-184, 193, 195-197.

Agatha, St.: 121.

Albania: 266.

Antichrist: 283, 284, 285, 287, 288.

Apocalypse: 137, 240, 289, 299.

Aristotle: 226.

Art: 187, 191, 245.

Ascension of Jesus Christ: 148.

Askesis, or asceticism: 40, 68-69, 103-105, 121, 124-125, 164.

Augustine, St.: IX, 62, 183, 221.

Austria: 266.

Authority: 118-120, 141-143, 179, 188-189, 226.

Baptism: 31, 36-37, 39, 50, 59, 81, 91, 151, 186.

Beethoven: 168.

Benedict XV: 265.

Benedictine Rule: 60.

Beneficence: 96.

Bible, or Scriptures, Sacred Books: 52, 70, 184, 193, 194, 226, 231, 236, 237, 238, 241, 242, 277, 281, 291.

Blondel, Maurice: 19, 223, 272, 291.

Body, mystical: 82, 119, 153, 156-157, 194-195, 248, 250.

Bolshevism: 250, 257, 285.

Bossuet: 221.

Boyer, C., S. J.: 223.

Brotherhood: 94-96, 117, 119, 148, 180, 246, 247, 250, 252-255, 267, 298.

Capitalism: 252, 257, 267.

Catherine of Siena, St.: 233.

Charity, a theological virtue: 81, 85, 88, 91, 94, 95, 96, 99, 100, 102, 103, 104, 118, 119, 122, 131, 136, 138, 141, 195, 293.

Charlemagne: 233.

Christendom: 54, 286.

Christianity: 12, 15, 16, 18, 29, 52, 54, 57, 122, 133, 146, 201, 210, 221, 224, 225, 231, 234, 285, 286, 287.

in history: 243-268.

Church, in general: 18, 31-32, 33, 34, 48-51, 56, 59, 82, 124, 136, 153, 154, 158, 184-185, 194-195, 229, 243, 245-246, 285, 287, 295, 297.

Catholic Church: 18, 49, 259-260.

dissident Churches: 50-51, 262.

universality of the Church: 247-249.

mystical body and Church, see: Body, mystical.

State and Church: 13-14, 54, 249-255, 260-268.

diarchy of State and Church: Caesaro-Papism: 261-262; Roman-papal organization: 261-262; concordatory jurisdictionalism: 261-262; *sacerdotium et imperium:* 261-263; ecclesiastic temporalism: 253.

sociology and the Church: 246-249, 255-260.

Civilization: 12, 208-209, 225, 227, 246, 251.

Columbus, Christopher: 165.

Communion: 2, 28, 81-99, 127, 145, 146, 154, 226, 231, 237, 247.

communion of saints: 156, 295.

Eucharistic Communion, see: Eucharist.

Conditioning, in general: 10, 57, 66, 108, 163-164, 166, 171, 172, 174, 180, 198-199, 250.

See also: Sociological laws.

Confession, Sacrament of: 81.

Confirmation, Sacrament of: 81.

Conformity to the will of God: 110-111, 113-118, 141.

Conscience: 33-35, 73, 114, 143, 145, 178, 226.

Consciousness, individual: 1, 33, 144, 179, 198, 224, 229, 235, 263-264.

historical or collective: 28, 29, 30, 87-88, 200-201, 203, 204-208, 209-213, 215, 216, 227, 235, 237, 239, 247-250, 269, 272.
objective: 215
subjective: 215
transcendental: 215
Constantine: 233, 262.
Contemplation, in general: 60, 65, 106, 110, 125, 127-130, 145.
infused: 100-101, 130-136.
contemplation and mystical union, see: Mystical union.
Creation: 35, 79, 137, 138-139, 141, 154, 170-173, 174-176, 180, 181, 196, 224, 244, 269, 271, 273, 275, 277, 290.
creation *ab aeterno:* 276.
creative Idea: 139, 174-176.
Croce, Benedetto: 222-223.
Czechoslovakia, and Czechs: 15, 266.

Daniel: 138, 281.
Dante: 168, 233, 278.
David: 152, 185.
Death: 36-37, 39, 40, 97, 105, 110, 123, 149, 150, 151, 157, 163, 166, 181, 184, 199, 294, 299.
De Caussade, Père J. P.: 121.
Delatte, Dom Paul: 286.

Democracy: 253, 257, 264.
Christian Democrats: 264.
Determinism: 5, 8, 9, 10, 17, 19, 66, 67, 161, 198, 232.
Devil, Satan or Lucifer: 88, 91, 109, 139, 182, 184, 185, 186, 189, 192.
Dominic, St.: 233.
Durkheim's sociologism: 8.

Ecclesiasticus: 107.
Elias: 56, 57, 122, 133.
Epictetus: 139.
Eternity: 149, 272-281.
Eucharist, Sacrament and Mass: 81, 82, 133, 147, 151, 152.
Evil: 33-34, 42, 50, 62, 64, 67, 68, 69, 71, 72, 73, 109, 116, 156, 158, 161-181, 182, 198, 200, 219, 267.
physical: 162-168, 186.
metaphysical: 162, 168-173.
moral: 162, 176-181.
society and evil, see: Society.
Evolutionism, or evolution: 6, 15, 198.
Exodus: 55.
Ezechiel: 107-108.

Faith, a theological virtue: 10, 33, 35, 40, 48, 51, 72, 81, 85, 88, 89, 91, 92, 100, 106, 122, 123,

131, 135, 141, 224, 228,
229, 230, 238-239, 248,
250, 287.

Family: 12, 16, 40, 42, 53-
54, 97, 98, 178, 183,
187, 204-205.

Fascism: 253, 257.

Finalism, and finality: 4, 8,
26, 28, 38, 44, 47, 62,
83, 86, 165, 170, 173-
176, 177-181, 196, 201-
204, 235, 258.

finalism and history, see:
History.

France: 207, 285.

Francis de Sales, St.: 132.

Francis of Assisi, St.: 132,
233.

Francis Xavier, St.: 233.

Freedom, or free will, inner
liberty: 4, 6, 8, 10, 19,
28, 38, 62, 63, 65-71,
74-77, 85, 116, 158,
176, 186, 198-199, 203,
206, 207, 213, 225, 232,
254.

freedom and predestination,
see: Predestination.

Galileo: 233.

Garrigou-Lagrange, R., O. P.:
107.

Gelasius I: 261.

Genesis: 3-4, 138, 144, 149,
170, 277.

Germany: 15, 19, 285.

Glory of God: 110-111, 136,

137-158, 161, 197, 225,
226-227, 272, 299.

eternal glory: 76, 77, 79,
85, 154, 194, 197, 272,
299.

human glory: 140, 141-
143.

Gospel, or Gospels: 30, 31-
32, 87, 101, 112, 113,
119, 150, 158, 183, 189,
190, 191, 194, 229, 234,
240-242, 257, 281, 282,
284, 287, 296, 297.

Grace, divine or sanctifying:
26-27, 28, 29, 31, 35,
36, 38, 39, 40, 42, 47,
58, 59, 71-72, 74, 75,
76, 77, 82, 83, 84, 86,
89, 91, 92, 100, 124,
128, 134, 158, 183, 194,
195, 232, 255, 294.

habitual: 71, 102, 104.

actual: 71, 102, 104, 124.

efficacious: 63, 64, 72, 77-
79.

sufficient: 77-79.

grace of perseverance: 63,
64, 79.

distribution of graces, see:
Predestination.

grace and Communion, see:
Communion.

grace and mystical union,
see: Mystical union.

grace and the glory of God,
see: Glory of God.

Greece: 200-201, 236.

Heart, Sacred: 133.

Hegel, or Hegelianism: 19, 45, 211-213, 215, 222, 250, 258.

Hell: 297, 298.

Heresy, or heretic: 33, 34-36, 50, 57, 257.

Hildebrand, Gregory VII: 233.

History, in general: 5, 12, 13, 15, 27, 34-35, 46, 48, 50, 51, 67, 71, 167, 173, 175, 188, 198-223, 225, 227, 228-229, 263.

    history and sociology: 4-8, 13, 20, 216-219.

    history and the supernatural: 12-13, 224-244, 278.

    historical dialectic: 198-201, 215, 223, 225, 230, 246, 249-250, 274, 275.

    historical finalism: 201-204.

    historical life: 204-209.

    historical sense: 220-223.

    historicism, theory of the author: 13-14, 18-22, 218-220.

    history and Christianity, see: Christianity.

    history and the Incarnation, see: Incarnation.

    history and religion, see: Religion.

    history and universalism, see: Universalism.

Hope, a theological virtue: 81, 85, 100, 122, 131.

Humanism: 122, 221-222, 226.

Humility: 68-69, 117-120, 122, 124.

Immortality: 2, 149-151, 206.

Impurity and purification: 31, 114-115, 116, 124, 143-146, 149-150, 156.

Incarnation of the Son of God: 27, 28-29, 32, 39, 75, 82, 117, 133, 134, 136, 140, 147, 148-153, 154-155, 185, 196-197, 277, 292.

    Incarnation in history, the: 224-244.

India: 52.

Infinity: 154, 169.

Intention, right or spiritual: 104, 110, 111-113.

Ireland: 207.

Isaias: 55-56, 133, 139, 233, 281, 289.

Israel, Hebrew or Jew: 29, 30, 31, 51-52, 55-56, 210, 230, 235-243, 285.

Italy: 201-207.

James, St.: 91.

Jansenism: 250.

Jeremias: 86.

Jesuits: 125.

John the Baptist, St.: 32.

John the Evangelist, St.: 11, 30, 36, 38, 57, 58, 59, 73-74, 85-86, 88, 93, 94, 97, 99, 105, 108, 119, 120, 124, 132, 137, 140, 141, 144, 147, 151, 152, 180, 184-186, 191-192, 224, 230-231, 240, 277, 284, 289, 295, 299.

John of the Cross, St.: 134.

Joseph, St.: 32.

Judgment, the last: 95, 157-158, 283-285, 289-290, 295, 296-298.

"Jusnaturalism": 222, 262.

Justice: 76, 83, 89, 95-96, 107, 109, 158, 187, 188, 210, 226, 236.

Kingdom of God, or Kingdom: 30, 36, 51, 52, 53, 54, 56, 61, 79, 109, 184, 193, 194-195, 197, 198, 242, 246, 255, 267, 289.

Knowledge: 16, 39, 40, 48, 49, 82-85, 86-91, 114, 145, 155, 158, 165, 173, 214-215, 228, 229, 232-233, 239, 293.

Labor: 145, 187, 228.

Lagrange, M. J., O. P.: 282.

Laicism: 252-253.

Law, in general: 5, 96, 166, 177-178, 187, 189, 190, 226, 235, 243, 248, 253.
natural or law of nature or

moral law: 28, 29-30, 31, 32, 35, 39, 92, 108, 125, 142, 180, 210, 251, 253.

Mosaic Law: 30, 229, 236, 238-239, 241.

sociological law, see: Sociological laws.

League of Nations: 253, 267.

Leibniz: 168.

Leo XIII: 264, 266.

Liberty, social and political: 187, 206, 257, 258.

liberty as inner freedom, see: Freedom.

Life, in general: 1-2, 18, 25-26, 39-40, 41, 62, 67, 82, 84, 91, 101, 109, 111, 114, 120, 131, 132, 157, 163-164, 169, 171, 172, 174-175, 180, 182-183, 187, 193, 204-227, 232, 252, 254, 259, 260, 271, 273, 279.

eternal: 62, 136, 184, 194, 298-299.

supernatural: 1-2, 4, 11, 16, 21-22, 26-43, 58, 65, 71, 72, 74, 84-85, 86-91, 97, 100, 109-110, 116, 154, 161, 183, 224, 225, 293, 299.

life as one: 8, 25, 37, 38-39, 42-43, 289.

life and mystical union, see: Mystical union.

circulation and end of life, see: "New heavens and a new earth."

Liturgy: 37, 152.

Louis IX, St.: 233.

Louis XIV: 228.

Love, in general: 11-12, 39, 40, 58, 67, 69, 71, 82-83, 86-91, 93, 97, 98-99, 105, 109, 115, 123, 141, 151, 155, 157, 165, 177, 180, 184, 185, 193, 225, 227, 232, 243, 247, 254, 259, 267, 279, 293, 298-299.

love as a commandment: 92-99, 237.

love and mystical union, see: Mystical union.

Lucan: 269-270.

Luke, St.: 50, 101, 102, 113, 118, 120, 125-126, 239, 284, 297.

Maritain, Jacques: 223.

Mark, St.: 113.

Marxism, or historical materialism: 211-213, 250, 264.

Mary, the Mother of God: 32, 75, 128, 144, 225.

Mary of the Incarnation, Sister: 131.

Matrimony, Sacrament of: 42, 82.

Matthew, St.: 50, 58, 72, 80, 95, 99, 101, 112-113, 114, 119, 135, 145, 149, 152, 189, 195, 240, 245, 247, 250, 267-268, 282-283, 288, 297-298.

Melchisedech: 152.

Messianism, or Messias: 30, 51-52, 119, 133, 230, 235, 241-242, 281.

Missions, or missionary apostolate: 12, 16, 54.

Michelangelo: 278.

Molinists, or Molinist theory: 64-65, 78.

Moralism: 5, 26.

Morality: 32, 39, 64, 209, 210, 253, 254, 258.

Moses: 45, 52, 133, 142, 226, 233, 242, 285.

Music: 280.

Mystic union, in spiritual life: 100-136, 154, 156, 161.

mystical nights: 128-131.

mysticism: 103, 222.

mystic catharsis: 28, 36, 115, 116, 219.

mystic currents: 50, 256-260; see also: Sociological laws.

Napoleon: 228.

Nationalism: 257.

Naturalism, or conception of a purely natural man: 5, 6, 9-10, 11, 12, 14, 26, 46, 103, 143, 235, 258-259, 267.

Nature, or the natural, or

natural reality: 1-2, 6, 9-11, 12, 17, 28, 29, 34, 39, 41, 46-47, 64, 72, 74, 75, 83-84, 90, 100, 144, 145, 147, 151, 157, 162, 168-176, 177, 181, 188, 199, 203, 215, 277.

nature and history, see: History.

Nazism: 15, 250, 253, 257, 285.

"New heavens and a new earth": 167, 269-299.

"Numinous," the: 144-145.

Obedience: 113, 118-120, 122.

Orders, Holy: 82.

Ovid, *Metamorphoses* of: 269.

Pantheism: 84, 134, 169, 258, 267, 276.

Paul the Apostle, St.: 30, 36-37, 48-49, 50, 53, 54-56, 59, 63, 65, 74-75, 76, 87, 89, 94-96, 99, 101, 106, 111-112, 113-114, 119, 122, 124, 132, 141, 142, 150, 153, 184, 193-194, 197, 238-239, 240, 241, 279, 284, 285, 286, 288, 296.

Paul of the Cross, St.: 131.

Peace: 221, 226-227, 239.

Philanthropy: 96.

Perfection, spiritual: 35, 41, 43, 44, 46, 47, 58, 82, 102-111, 155.

perfection and *askesis,* see: *Askesis.*

perfection and mystical union, see: Mystical union.

Personality: 3, 44, 45, 47, 58, 68, 85, 132, 164, 177, 211, 278.

personality and history, see: History.

Peter, St.: 49, 52, 63, 79, 120, 142-143, 240, 282, 284, 288-289.

Petruzzellis, Nicola: 223.

Pius XI: 264.

Pius XII: 265.

Plato: 226, 233.

Poland, and Poles: 15, 207.

Politics: 205-209, 259-260, 261-267.

politics and history, see: History.

Positivism: 4-6, 211, 250, 251.

Prayer: 108-111, 123, 125, 127, 179.

prayer of the Our Father: 109.

mental and vocal prayer: 127-130.

contemplative prayer, see: Contemplation.

Predestination: 62-80, 81, 154, 158.

Pride: 12, 68-69, 71, 74, 88, 92, 118, 119, 141, 177,

181, 184, 189, 190, 202, 289, 298.

Progress: 198.

Prosper of Aquitaine, St.: 63.

Proverbs, Book of: 147.

Psalms, Book of: 107, 146, 282.

Purgatory, 123, 131, 136, 295.

Pygmies: 236.

Rationality: 33-34, 190-191, 210, 216, 217-219.

rationality as sociological law, see: Sociological laws.

Reformation: 250, 262, 286.

Regulus: 233.

Religion, in general: 4, 13, 29, 49, 179, 187, 191, 205-208, 209-213, 234, 252, 254-255, 262.

Renaissance: 222.

Resurrection, in general: 39, 151, 295.

Resurrection of Christ: 36-37, 148, 149, 242, 295-296.

resurrection of the human body: 149-151, 295-298.

Revelation, in general: 10, 27, 48, 62, 89-90, 92, 123, 124, 154, 227-228, 294.

primal revelation: 29, 49, 87, 145, 210, 216, 229, 231, 239.

Mosaic and prophetic revelation: 29, 49, 87, 210, 216, 229, 231.

Christian revelation: 29, 49, 87, 210, 216, 229, 231.

Revolution: 227, 258, 286.

Rome, Roman Empire, Holy Roman Empire: 52, 201, 236, 250, 251.

Russia: 285, 286, 287.

Sacraments: 31-32, 42, 48, 50, 81-82, 100, 107, 108, 124, 154, 195, 259.

Sacrifice, or expiation: 31, 105, 143, 145-146, 150, 151-152, 252.

sacrifice of Christ, and the Mass: 27, 105, 147-153, 154, 155, 156, 195, 259.

Sanctity, or saints in general: 40, 94, 101, 102, 124, 135-136, 157, 200, 204, 287.

Schisms, or schismatic: 33, 34-36, 50, 57, 119, 257.

Scholasticism: 251.

Sin, in general: 35, 39, 40, 47, 67, 69, 70, 71, 74, 85, 92, 93, 105, 108, 109, 118, 143-144, 161, 179, 182, 188, 192, 193, 195, 236.

original sin: 27, 28, 29, 40, 68, 72, 79, 183-184, 192, 195.

collective or social sin: 28, 182-183, 236.

mortal sin: 32, 38, 107.

sin and the world: 184, 197.

Slavery, and serfdom: 15, 40, 166, 188, 253, 286.

Socialism, in general: 257.

materialistic socialism, see: Marxism.

Society, in general: 2-4, 42-43, 55, 58, 60-61, 67, 83, 120, 177-179, 246-247, 255-260, 261, 263, 293.

society in the concrete: 3, 5, 7, 8, 9, 14, 41-44, 186-192.

society as historical process: 3, 5-6, 13, 14, 198-219.

society and social forms: 7, 13, 58, 255, 259, 262-263.

natural society: 7-8, 13, 14, 58-61, 82-83, 161, 162, 166-167, 178, 179, 182-183.

supernatural society: 11-13, 45, 58-59, 83-91, 255, 293.

society and evil: 186-192.

society and history, see: History.

Sociological laws, in general: 3, 5, 17, 251.

law of achievement or conquest: 202-204, 205.

law of social coercion: 17.

law of group-consciousness and personality: 200-201.

law of mystical and organizational currents: 17, 50, 256-260.

law of "critical cycles": 167.

law of liberating forces, or currents: 190-191.

law of freedom and conditioning: 10, 198-199.

law of "life-knowledge-love": 11, 86-90, 120, 147.

law of cathartic purification: 191.

law of rationality: 33-34, 190-191, 210, 216-219.

law of solidarity, human and cosmic: 174-175, 176-181, 188-189, 247.

law of solidarity of evil: 182-186.

law of transcendence: 204-209.

Sociologists: 4-5, 8, 10-11, 12, 14, 15-16, 201.

Sociology: 2-3, 5, 6-11.

abstractionist sociology: 14-18.

historicist and integral sociology: 13-14, 15-16, 18-21, 216-219.

sociology of the supernat-

ural: 2, 4, 11-18, 21-
22; see also: Supernat-
ural.

Socrates: 233.

Solidarity: 117, 156-157, 167,
174, 176, 177, 179-180,
185, 188, 191, 211, 247,
267.

solidarity and history, see:
History.

solidarity as sociological
law, see: Sociological
laws.

Solomon: 226.

Song of Songs: 283.

Space: 169, 175, 210, 214,
275-276, 291.

Spain: 266.

Spirit, Holy Spirit or Holy
Ghost: 29, 36, 39, 48,
49, 67, 81, 85, 98, 99,
121, 133, 138, 142, 147,
148, 151, 153, 154, 155,
185, 195, 241, 248, 255,
277, 284, 299.

gifts of the Holy Spirit, or
charismata: 81, 85, 100,
106, 124.

"Spirit," or "Idea," in Hegel's
theory: 45, 211, 223,
258, 276.

Spirituals, Franciscan: 257.

State, in general: 53-54, 98,
206, 207, 210, 211, 249,
252, 253, 255, 258.

totalitarian State, or totali-

tarianism: 211-212, 262,
263, 267.

State and Church, see:
Church and State.

Stephen, St.: 135, 240.

Sturzo, Bishop Mario: VII,
107.

Sturzo, Luigi: 7, 13, 18, 19,
21, 54, 215, 216, 248,
260, 265-266.

Subnatural, a state of decadence: 27-29, 33, 35.

Supernatural: 2, 4, 6, 9-11,
12-15, 16, 17, 18, 25-
43, 65, 72, 77, 81, 84,
87, 90, 91, 154, 157,
215-223, 257, 259, 277.

supernatural and mysticism,
see: Mystical union.

Teresa of Jesus, St.: 131, 233.

Theologism: 26.

Theology, and theologians:
6, 8, 9, 11, 17, 18, 19,
26-27, 31, 63, 64, 67,
72, 73, 76, 77, 83, 84,
96, 102, 103, 106, 112,
130, 153, 155, 196, 221,
228, 257.

Thomas Aquinas, St., and
Thomists: 31, 33-34, 38,
64-65, 78, 172, 233,
276, 290-291.

Time: 169, 175, 210, 214,
227.

continuity of time: 271,
272-281, 290.

Tobias, Book of: 51.

Tradition: 29, 30, 51, 57, 143, 150, 210, 229, 236.

Trappists: 125.

Trent, Council of: 74.

Trinity, Holy: 69, 85, 98, 132, 133, 136, 141, 147, 153, 196, 237, 241, 292.

Truth: 5, 16, 34, 48, 49, 51, 57, 67, 70-71, 89, 90, 98, 105, 108, 117, 118, 119, 156, 180, 192, 208-209, 225, 227, 239, 244.

Tyranny: 40, 142, 206, 253, 286.

Unction, Extreme: 81.

Universality, or universalism: 47-48, 61, 97, 210-213, 214, 246-249, 250-255.

Vico, Giambattista: 87, 101, 222, 223.

Vincent de Paul, St.: 233.

Virginity: 59.

Vision, beatific: 82, 101, 136, 155-158, 275, 279, 299.

Vocation, natural and supernatural: 44-61, 62, 79, 81, 100, 108, 154, 161.

War: 166, 188, 221, 228, 265-268.

World, in the physical and human sense: 191-192, 245, 246, 269, 271, 272, 281-290, 292, 299.

world, in the spiritual sense: 105, 114-115, 126, 184-197, 242, 256-259, 290.

end of the world, see: "New heavens and a new earth."

Wyclifites: 257.

1954

◆ Writer Priest, Don Luigi Sturzo, the 83-year-old world-famous Philosopher and Italian Senator, leaves the Italian Parliament after a session devoted to the country's turbulent political situation.   *United Press Photo*

in his remarkable *Essai de Sociologie*. THE TRUE LIFE is the ripened and complete presentation of Don Sturzo's ideas on human society, the culmination of his many years of study and action. It is particularly approachable in that it deals with society in the concrete; it is reassuringly full in that it gives full weight to the importance of society's supernatural elements; it is telling and irrefutable in its analysis of the historical process and finality of human association. Interesting from every angle, it has its message for the philosopher, theologian and professing sociologist, and equally for the representative lay reader. In it are to be found, treated with the author's characteristic originality and with that timelessness which is supremely timely, the answers to the fundamental questions of our harried day.